New to this edition

New case coverage

- *O'Donnell v Shanahan* [2009] illustrating the operation and scope of fiduciary obligations
- *Ridgwell v Ridgwell* [2007] on the variation of trusts

Equity & Trusts
Concentrate

2nd edition

Iain McDonald

Lecturer in Law, University of West England

Anne Street

Visiting Lecturer, The College of Law, London

OXFORD
UNIVERSITY PRESS

OXFORD

UNIVERSITY PRESS

Great Clarendon Street, Oxford OX2 6DP

Oxford University Press is a department of the University of Oxford.
It furthers the University's objective of excellence in research, scholarship,
and education by publishing worldwide in

Oxford New York

Auckland Cape Town Dar es Salaam Hong Kong Karachi
Kuala Lumpur Madrid Melbourne Mexico City Nairobi
New Delhi Shanghai Taipei Toronto

With offices in

Argentina Austria Brazil Chile Czech Republic France Greece
Guatemala Hungary Italy Japan Poland Portugal Singapore
South Korea Switzerland Thailand Turkey Ukraine Vietnam

Oxford is a registered trade mark of Oxford University Press
in the UK and in certain other countries

Published in the United States
by Oxford University Press Inc., New York

British Library Cataloguing in Publication Data

Data available

Library of Congress Cataloging in Publication Data

Data available

Typeset by Newgen Imaging Systems (P) Ltd, Chennai, India
Printed in Great Britain
on acid-free paper by
Ashford Colour Press Ltd, Gosport, Hampshire

ISBN 978–0–19–958775–9

10 9 8 7 6 5 4 3 2

Contents

#1

The history and development of equity

- Equity tackles injustice caused by a strict application of the common law rules or unconscionable behaviour.

- Equity was originally dispensed by the King. However, this role was soon delegated to the Lord Chancellor and the Court of Chancery.

- Equity and the common law were originally administered by separate courts. The two court systems coexisted uneasily until the *Earl of Oxford's Case* (1615), when the King finally held that equity prevailed over the common law in the event of a conflict.

- The administration of equity and the common law was unified by the Judicature Acts 1873–1875 with the result that all judges could apply both equitable and common law rules and responses.

- It is still debated today whether the Judicature Acts 'fused' equity and the common law into a unified body of rules. While the two systems have become closer over time, the distinction still remains of importance in some areas.

- Equity benefits from a number of equitable maxims which can guide the courts in the exercise of their discretion.

The history of equity

> *Revision tip*
>
> It is unlikely that you will be asked simply to discuss the history of equity in an examination. However, it is more common for questions to reference some aspect of the development of equity as a basis for discussing the operation of equity today. Try to think about the themes which characterize equity's development and their significance to modern equity.

The legal system of England and Wales began to emerge in the twelfth century. Common rules and approaches to the resolution of disputes were gathered so that a legal order could be applied consistently throughout the nation. However, as the common law began to emerge, so too did instances of injustice and unfairness. These situations were brought about by both:

- the operation of the legal system itself; and
- the strict application of common law rules.

Problems with the early common law system

The early common law system was complex and expensive. Legal actions were based on writs, which had to be spoken precisely in Latin. Consequently, cases were often lost on a technicality due to mistakes being made in their delivery. The problem of this system was compounded by the **Provisions of Oxford 1258** and the **Statute of Westminster**, which limited the number of writs and sometimes precluded a legal action simply because there was no legal writ which covered it – no remedy without a writ.

The strict application of common law rules could also lead to injustice. An example of this would be where someone built a home on land on the understanding that ownership of the land parcel would be transferred to them on completion. If the landowner refused to carry out this promise, the builder of the home would have no action under the common law as *legally* the land did not belong to him. Moreover, the remedy of damages available at common law was not always appropriate. For example, if someone trespassed upon your property, an award of damages would not prevent the defendant from repeating their actions.

The origins of equity

Alongside the common law system, it was possible for individuals to appeal to the King's conscience to provide them with justice. As the number of these appeals rose, the King delegated this role to the Lord Chancellor. Originally, the position of Lord Chancellor was held by high-ranking religious officials, and the justice dispensed was rooted in the religious morality of the times. As the number of appeals continued to grow, a separate court of equity, the Chancery Court, was established in the fifteenth century and equity as a rival system of law began to take shape. This process was continued during the sixteenth century as the position of Lord Chancellor gradually came to be held by lawyers, rather than religious officials.

Conflict between equity and the common law: the *Earl of Oxford's Case*

The laws of England and Wales therefore became the sum of the common law rules and the equitable decisions of the Court of Chancery. Where the common law courts would apply their legal rules, the Court of Chancery acted as a check upon these rules, ensuring that their application did not lead to a manifest injustice. However, this relationship was not a settled one and judges in the common law courts would frequently reach decisions based on the common law rules, despite knowing that the Court of Chancery would reach a different result. This created confusion and expense for claimants who would have to mount two separate actions to reach a satisfactory conclusion. Moreover, the different approaches of each system led to resentment that equity was interfering with the certainty of the common law. John Selden famously attacked the discretionary nature of equity by comparing it to the length of 'a Chancellor's foot' – insinuating that it was a random standard that would change from Chancellor to Chancellor. This conflict came to a head in the *Earl of Oxford's Case* (1615):

....

Earl of Oxford's Case (1615) 1 Rep Ch 1

A defendant appealed against a judgment in the common law courts on the grounds that the judgement had been obtained through fraud. The Lord Chancellor, Lord Ellesmere, agreed and issued a 'common injunction' restraining the claimant from enforcing the judgment. These 'common injunctions' were seen as a direct challenge to the authority of the common law courts as they effectively deprived the recipient of the ability to pursue a remedy from the common law courts. However, the Lord Chancellor argued that there was no conflict between the two courts, as equity did not interfere with the operation of the common law. Instead, it acted *in personam*, meaning against the conscience of the recipient. Therefore, the common law decision was left undisturbed; equity only acted to compel the recipient to act according to good conscience. This dispute was finally resolved by King James I in 1616, when he declared in favour of the Court of Chancery. This gave birth to the equitable maxim (discussed further below) that where the law and equity conflict, equity prevails.

....

Reform of the administration of common law and equity

With the primacy of equity now confirmed, the number of petitions to the Court of Chancery continued to grow. Delays and corruption grew and as a result three additional judges, Vice-Chancellors, were appointed between 1813 and 1843. However, the existing legal system underwent major reform in the nineteenth century through two Acts, commonly referred to as the **Judicature Acts 1873–1875**:

* The previous dual system, comprising courts of common law and equity, was merged into a single Supreme Court, comprising the High Court and the Court of Appeal.

- The jurisdiction of judges in the new Supreme Court was 'fused' so that all judges were able to use the whole range of common law and equitable rules. This meant that litigants no longer faced the delays and expense of pursuing two separate actions at common law and equity.

- **Section 25 Supreme Court of Judicature Act 1873** gave statutory authority to the principle that where the common law and equity conflicted, equity prevailed. (This was later re-enacted by s **49 Supreme Court Act 1981**.)

The 'fusion' debate

The reforms introduced by the **Judicature Acts of 1873 and 1875** mark the birth of the modern legal system of England and Wales. While it is clear that the **Judicature Acts** fused the *administration* of common law and equity, there is continuing debate over whether the Acts, in fact, created a *unified system of rules*:

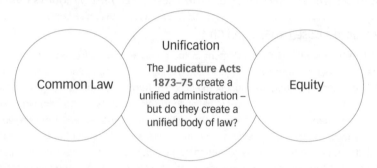

Figure 1.1 The fusion of equity and the common law

There are three main positions regarding the fusion debate:

The Judicature Acts only unified the administration of the law

This position argues that the **Judicature Acts** only created a unified *court system*. Ashburner in *Principles of Equity*, 2nd edn, eloquently expressed this viewpoint when he likened the common law and equity to two streams running alongside one another, but never mingling their waters.

The Judicature Acts effected a more substantive fusion of equity and the common law

In *Walsh v Lonsdale* (1882), Jessel MR argued that 'There are not two estates as there were formerly, one established at common law...and an estate in equity...There is only one Court and the equity rule prevails in it.' More explicitly, in *United Scientific Holdings Ltd v Burnley Borough Council* [1978], Lord Diplock argued that Ashburner's metaphor of the two parallel streams had become 'mischievous and deceptive' and that the 'streams' of equity and the common law had long since mingled together.

It is clear that the rules and remedies of equity and the common law have moved closer together:

Seager v Copydex Ltd [1967] 1 WLR 923

The claimant had been involved in negotiations with Copydex Ltd regarding the marketing of a new type of carpet grip. While these negotiations did not come to anything, the defendants later unwittingly used confidential information received from the claimant on how his idea could be improved to develop their own product. Breach of confidence is only protected in equity and Seager sought an injunction to prevent their use of this information. He also argued that the equitable remedy of account of profits (see chapter 12) would be inadequate. The Court of Appeal agreed and awarded the claimant common law damages which could more readily take into consideration the loss of the claimant's ability to exploit his invention.

The House of Lords have also proven willing to grant equitable remedies more flexibly in respect of the breach of a *legal* right in exceptional circumstances:

Attorney-General v Blake [2001] 1 AC 268

George Blake, an infamous spy who had defected to Russia, entered into a contract to publish a book about his experiences, for which he was to receive £150,000. The memoirs contained sensitive information which he had contracted with the state not to reveal. The usual remedy of damages for breach of contract would be inadequate as the government had an interest in discouraging its servants from breaching their commitments. Therefore, the Attorney-General sought a different *equitable* remedy, account of profits, to ensure that Blake would not be allowed to benefit any further from this breach.

As the information contained in the book was no longer confidential, it was difficult to argue that there was a continuing **fiduciary** obligation towards the state which would enable such a remedy to be granted. However, the court noted that the existence of more commonplace equitable remedies for breach of contract, such as specific performance or injunctions, was based on the idea that normal damages may be inadequate. Therefore, in exceptional circumstances, it was prepared to award an account of profits to protect the state's legitimate interest in discouraging such conduct.

These cases suggest only an incremental and, often, exceptional coming together of equity and the common law. Indeed, there are many more examples of how the law has retained a distinction between common law and equity. For example, the concept of the trust still relies on the distinction between legal and equitable ownership (see chapter 2) and the rules for tracing property into the hands of third parties differ at common law and equity (see chapter 12).

Moreover, equity and the common law also perform different functions:

- Common law – establishes general rules which provide certainty. This allows individuals to plan ahead and promotes commercial efficiency.
- Equity – acts as a check upon the common law. This remedies hardships which may arise from a strict application of the common law. Equity restrains the full exercise of legal rights where this would be unconscionable.

Terminology tip

Unconscionability – describes conduct which goes against good conscience. While the early Lord Chancellors restrained unconscionable behaviour on moral grounds, common examples of 'unconscionable behaviour' gradually hardened into the rules of Equity (see JH Baker, *An Introduction to English Legal History*, 4th edn, p 106). Today, it is no longer correct to assume that equity will restrain all immoral conduct. However, as equity has always attempted to respond to changing social conditions, 'unconscionability' remains a flexible device through which the court may choose to intervene.

While it is difficult to argue that equity and the common law have been fully fused, the **Judicature Acts** have encouraged the development of a more *supportive* relationship between the two systems.

Equity and the common law should be fused

This third position accepts that while equity and the common law have become closer, there is a pressing need to complete the unification of the two systems. Sarah Worthington, in her book, *Equity*, 2nd edn (2006) argues that as equity and the common law continue to develop, they increasingly encroach on the other's usual territory. This creates the risk that like cases will not be treated alike and that the ability of judges to make clear and principled decisions will be clouded.

Worthington convincingly argues that equity and the common law have always borrowed from one another and that neither system now occupies a distinctive conceptual position. A good example of this is the parallel development of **undue influence** in equity and **economic duress** by the common law, both of which look to questions of knowledge and unconscionability, but approach similar factual situations through increasingly difficult factual distinctions.

✅ *Looking for extra marks?*

You will need to do additional reading if you are to do well on a question about the fusion debate. Sarah Worthington's book, *Equity*, 2nd edn (2006), manages to be both detailed and accessible. The main thrust of her argument can be found in the first and last chapters. These chapters also provide useful cross-references to the more detailed discussions which make up the remainder of the book.

The maxims of equity

During the nineteenth century, a number of general rules of thumb began to emerge from the courts' exercise of its equitable jurisdiction. These are known as the maxims of equity.

They do not have their own authoritative value, but operate at the level of broad general principles which can guide the court in the exercise of its equitable discretion.

Revision tip

Trusts and equity cover a diverse range of situations and it can sometimes be very difficult to get a sense of how these areas of law operate. Having a good knowledge of the maxims of equity can provide you with an effective template to discuss both the successes and problems of many different areas of equity and trusts. This type of question is common in examinations and to perform well it is important not just to know what the equitable maxims are, but also to be able to provide illustrations of their application.

The maxims of equity cover a broad range of issues which may be approximately grouped under three headings:

- Maxims concerning the nature of equity and its jurisdiction
- Maxims concerning the conduct expected of claimants
- Maxims concerning the circumstances in which equity will operate

Maxims concerning the nature of equity and its jurisdiction

Equity will not suffer a wrong without a remedy

Equity will not intervene in respect of every wrong – *moral* wrongs will not be remedied by the courts. They will only intervene to prevent an *unconscionable* reliance upon legal rights. Two examples illustrate this principle well:

- The trust – in a trust, the trustees hold the legal title to the trust property. Should they claim the property for themselves the beneficiaries have no *legal* right to enforce. It is equity which recognizes their equitable entitlement to the property. In an express trust, the legal ownership of trust property is only transferred to trustees on the basis that they will hold it for the benefit of the beneficiaries. Therefore, to claim the property for themselves would be unconscionable.

- In *constructive* trusts of the family home, it would be unconscionable for a legal owner to insist upon their full legal rights due to an agreement to share the property combined with detrimental reliance on that agreement (see chapter 9 on implied trusts).

- Search orders – injunctions are typically awarded only after a court has heard arguments from both parties. If the claimant has to inform the suspected person of their action, it is likely that the defendant could hide or destroy the stolen documentation, thus making it impossible for the company to prove their case and depriving it of a remedy. Search orders are a type of interim injunction (ie a temporary injunction which is awarded without notice to the defendant) allowing the defendant's premises to be searched, thus preventing normal court procedures from frustrating the claimant's action (see chapter 13 on equitable remedies).

Equity acts in personam

This maxim describes how equity acts against an individual to prevent them from acting unconscionably. There are a number of consequences which flow from this:

- Failure to comply with an order is punishable by **contempt of court**.
- As equity acts against the individual *personally*, it does not matter if the property in dispute is outside the jurisdiction of the court; *Penn v Lord Baltimore* (1750).
- By acting personally against a defendant, equity does not interfere with common law decisions.
- This aspect of equity's operation is also sometimes expressed as the maxim, 'where equity and the law conflict, equity prevails'. Equity prevails over the common law not because it destroys the common law right but because it imposes limits on the extent to which those rights can be enjoyed.

Equity follows the law

This maxim reflects the relationship between equity and the common law. Equity supplements common law rules to ensure fairness; it does not replace them. Equity may prevail over the common law in the event of a conflict but the maxim 'equity follows the law' reminds us that the relationship between the two bodies of rules is respectful. Equity will only intervene when there are exceptional reasons for doing so – typically, the prevention of unconscionable behaviour. However, the general common law rule will still remain as the starting point for any future disputes.

Maxims concerning the conduct expected of claimants

He who comes to equity must come with clean hands

Equitable remedies are discretionary in nature and are granted following a full consideration of the particular circumstances of a case. The court will consider the *past* conduct of a claimant to decide if it is appropriate for equity to intervene.

- If a claimant has himself breached an obligation or otherwise acted inequitably, an equitable remedy will not be granted; *Cross v Cross* (1983). This is because equity cannot be seen to favour one party if both are in breach of their obligations.
- It is not for the court to judge the morality or character of a claimant: only conduct related to the equitable relief sought will be taken into account.

. . . .

Tinsley v Milligan [1994] 1 AC 340

Stella Tinsley and Kathleen Milligan jointly purchased a property. However, the property was solely registered in Tinsley's name so that Milligan could fraudulently claim social security benefits. This was done with the full knowledge of Tinsley. When the couple's relationship ended, Milligan sought a declaration that Tinsley held the house for them both equally on resulting trust. Tinsley argued that, as Milligan had defrauded the Department of Social Security she did not come to equity with 'clean hands' and that no equitable relief should be granted. The House of Lords held in favour of Milligan: as the resulting trust was created by her contributions to the purchase price, she did not have to rely on the fraud to establish her claim. In fact, ironically, it was Tinsley who had to rely on the fraud (of which she was a part) to found her argument that Milligan was entitled to nothing!

He who seeks equity must do equity

Equity looks to do justice *between* the parties. Equity scrutinizes not just the claimant's prior conduct, but also their *future* behaviour in respect of the claim. Therefore, if a claimant is unwilling or unable to fulfil their own future obligations to the defendant, equitable relief will not be granted.

In *Chappell v Times Newspapers Ltd* [1975] following selective industrial action, the defendant threatened to terminate the employment contracts of *all* union members unless they returned to work and agreed not to take further action. Several members of the trade union who had not been involved in the strike sought an interim injunction to prevent their employer from taking this action. While the threat to dismiss all trade union members, regardless of their involvement in the industrial action, might have supported their application, the claim failed as they would not agree not to take part in any future action.

Delay defeats equity

This maxim expresses the doctrine of *laches* which prevents a claimant who has delayed from obtaining equitable relief. This principle again confirms the way that equity tries to do justice between the parties. It would be inequitable to allow a claim for equitable relief on an issue or contract which the defendant has long since considered settled. In *Leaf v International Galleries* [1950], an attempt to rescind a contract for a painting which the vendor had innocently misrepresented to be the work of Constable failed for delay as the action took place five years after the purchase.

Note: as equity follows the law, statutory limitations such as those in the **Limitation Act 1980**, will displace any equitable jurisdiction to decide whether or not a claim is too late.

Maxims concerning the circumstances in which equity will operate

Equity looks to intent not form

This maxim provides another example of how equity tends to assess the whole circumstances of a case, rather than applying broad and generalized rules. For example:

- Certainty of intention – in considering whether a settlor intended to create a trust, the use of the word 'trust' is not essential and the court will consider the whole circumstances of the case (*Comiskey v Bowring-Hanbury* [1905]). (See chapter 3 for more detail.)

- Constructive trusts – this maxim explains the recognition of implied trusts whereby the court may find that the circumstances of the case, including discussions between the parties or certain types of contribution, demonstrate the intention to create a resulting or constructive trust. (See chapter 9 for more detail.)

Equity will not permit a statute to be used as an instrument of fraud

Equity follows the law and will not interfere with situations governed by statute. However, equity can also act as a guardian to ensure that statutory provisions are not abused. Therefore, equity will intervene if a claimant seeks to rely unconscionably on a lack of statutory formalities.

This maxim explains the enforceability of fully secret trusts (considered in chapter 8). In a fully secret trust, the testator leaves property to a legatee without mentioning their intention that she should hold the property as trustee for someone else. Property disposed of by a will must satisfy the requirements of the **Wills Act 1837**. However, secret trusts do not comply with these requirements and therefore, on a strict reading of statute, cannot be valid. This would mean the trustee could claim the property for herself. However, as the property was only left to the trustee on the basis that she would hold it for another, to allow the trustee to rely on the formalities required by the Wills Act would be to permit the statute to be used as a device to commit a fraud against the testator. Therefore, equity recognized the validity of the fully secret trust.

Equity sees as done that which ought to be done

If an equitable remedy *can* be granted, equity will act as if this has already occurred. While many of the maxims of equity are self-explanatory, this one is rather abstract and is best explained by examples:

- A contract for the sale of land is specifically enforceable as it is a unique type of property for which monetary damages would be inadequate (see chapter 13 on equitable remedies). Therefore, on the completion of such a contract, the vendor is taken to hold the equitable interest on trust for the purchaser until the transfer is formally completed.

. . . .

Walsh v Lonsdale (1882) 21 Ch D 9

A landlord agreed in writing to lease a mill to a tenant. The agreement stated that rent was to be payable in advance if requested. However, such leases required a deed and none was ever made. The tenant entered the property and began to pay rent quarterly. When he fell into arrears, the landlord demanded a year's rent in advance and when the tenant resisted, he sought to use the remedy of distress (which allows the landlord to seize and sell the tenant's property in order to recover the rent). The tenant sought an injunction against the distress on the basis that there was no valid lease *in law* and therefore no provision to allow rent to be demanded annually in advance. The court refused this application, arguing that by allowing the tenant to enter the mill and pay rent, the agreement to lease the mill would have been specifically enforceable. As equity sees as done that which ought to be done, the tenant was to be considered an equitable lessee of the mill *on the terms of the original agreement* and, therefore, the action for distress was legal.

. . . .

✅ Looking for extra marks?

It is sometimes argued that the generality of the maxims of equity can be abused to allow judges to reach a desired result. For example, in *Attorney-General for Hong Kong v Reid* [1994], Lord Templeman used the maxim, *equity sees as done that which ought to be done*, as a basis for holding that a civil servant held bribe money (and the land he bought with it) on constructive trust for his employer. However, this line of reasoning has been criticized as stretching the application of the maxim too far. For an excellent discussion of this case, see Webb and Akkouh, *Trusts Law* (2008), pp 253–8.

Equity is equality

If more than one person claims to be interested in the same property and there is nothing to suggest what their shares should be, equity will assume that they are to have equal shares.

Revision tip

A good discussion of the equitable maxims will recognize that they are not fixed rules but *starting points* for analysing a legal problem. This means that they are not always followed. For example, the maxim, *equity will not assist a volunteer*, discussed more fully in chapter 4, may be said to have generated more exceptions than applications! While this has often led academics to be sceptical of their value, equity has always resisted the application of general rules in favour of a more thorough consideration of all the relevant facts.

Equity today

While equity began life as the King's conscience, it has now become a highly developed body of legal rules which continues to constrain unconscionable behaviour and provides relief from the hardships caused by the strict application of common law rules. Together, equity and its most famous invention, the trust, have continued to develop flexibly and creatively to respond to society's changing needs:

- The development of search orders and freezing orders allows claimants to search for documentation relevant to their claim and to freeze the defendants' assets if there is a real risk that the failure to do so will deprive them of an adequate remedy (see chapter 13 on equitable remedies).

Equity today

✳✳✳✳✳✳✳✳✳✳

- The recognition of constructive trusts of the family home in *Gissing v Gissing* [1971] and subsequent case law has provided financial relief for claimants who do not have legal title. The law of trusts' continuing development of this area of law has been particularly important in the face of the extreme reluctance of Parliament to legislate on this issue (see chapter 9 on implied trusts).

- The development of Quistclose-type resulting trusts has provided the possibility of protecting the money of innocent customers from the creditors of an insolvent company (see *Re Kayford Ltd (in liquidation)* [1975] and, less happily, *Re Farepak Foods and Gifts Ltd (in administration)* [2006]).

- The increasingly flexible approach taken to formality requirements, as illustrated by the 'unconscionability' approach adopted in *Pennington v Waine* [2002] highlights that a lack of statutory formalities should not be used officiously to defeat agreements (see chapter 4 on constitution of the trust).

Revision Tip

Exam questions on this area will invariably be essays. To do well in an essay you must address the terms of the question. Make sure you read the question carefully to identify precisely what it is asking you to discuss – a shorter but tightly focused essay will always be marked higher than a longer general essay on 'everything I know about the history and development of equity'!

Whereas once equitable relief was entirely discretionary (leading to accusations that it was subjective), many forms of equity have now hardened into equitable rights, so that where the relevant criteria are satisfied, equity *will* intervene. The acceptance that beneficiaries have certain rights under a trust, rather than simply at the discretion of the court, is perhaps the most pertinent example here.

While the discretion inherent in equity is no longer unfettered, a continuing debate on the development of equity and trusts is the *extent* of that discretion. Where equity and the common law once clashed over the ideals of fairness and certainty, arguably, this battle now continues to be waged *within* equity and trusts themselves. In all but the first example listed above, each development has been accompanied by great debate over whether the decision can be justified within existing equitable principles. For all that equity has matured into a substantial and detailed body of rules, it seems that it is the underlying impulse towards fairness over a rigid adherence to principle that continues to drive equity today.

Revision Tip

It is tempting to think of trusts law as neatly divided into different topics. However, as you can see, there are many links between different topics. While this chapter discusses major themes and developments in trusts and equity, you should use your knowledge of other topics to build on the basics set out here.

 Key cases

Case	Facts	Principle
Earl of Oxford's Case (1615) 1 Rep Ch 1	Concerned a dispute over a lease and the question of which court prevailed in a conflict.	Equity prevails over the common law in the event of a conflict.
Seager v Copydex Ltd [1967] 1 WLR 923	Claimant sought common law damages in respect of a breach of confidence (which is only protected in equity).	Common law damages awarded as the equitable remedy of account would not be adequate. This case demonstrates the closer relationship of equity and the common law today.
Tinsley v Milligan [1994] 1 AC 340	The defendant argued that the claimant's fraud of the DSS prevented her from claiming that property was held on resulting trust for them both.	While *one must come to equity with clean hands*, the court will only examine past conduct relevant to the equitable relief sought.
Walsh v Lonsdale (1882) 21 Ch D 9	Whether the claimant could enforce a *legal* remedy in respect of an equitable lease.	*Equity regards as done that which ought to be done* – the equitable lease was specifically enforceable on the same terms as the legal lease. This case also provides support for the idea that equity and the common law were fused by the Judicature Acts.

🗩🗩 Key debates

Topic	Did the Judicature Acts do more than fuse the administration of equity and the common law?
Academic/ Author	Worthington/Mason
Viewpoint	There is evidence of an increasing willingness to employ both equitable and common law remedies in hitherto unorthodox ways in order to do justice in a given case.
Source	Worthington, *Equity*, 2nd edn (2006). For a more detailed account of Commonwealth developments, see Mason (1994) LQR 238.

Exam questions

Topic	Should more be done to fuse equity and the common law?
Academic/Author	Worthington/Burrows
Viewpoint	It can be argued that neither equity nor the common law now occupies distinctive positions of principle in relation to how they exercise their jurisdiction. However, this increasing closeness runs the risk of creating more confusion than clarity. Therefore the time is right to consider further unification.
Source	Worthington, *Equity*, 2nd edn (2006), ch 10 offers a useful critique of the argument that equity and common law remain distinctive systems of rules. This book and Burrows (2002) 22(1) OJLS 1 offer a helpful analysis of how the two systems could be more closely reconciled.

Topic	What is the role of equity today?
Academic/Author	Watt
Viewpoint	Equity operates in an increasingly wide range of contexts.
Source	Watt, *Trusts and Equity*, 3rd edn (2008), chs 1 & 2 offers a very clear and accessible account of the foundations of equity and the uses of the trust.

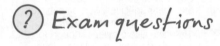 (?) Exam questions

Essay question

It is inevitable that judge made law will alter to meet the changing conditions of society. That is the way it has always evolved. But it is essential that new rules should be related to fundamental doctrine. If the foundations of accepted doctrine be submerged under new principles, without regard to the interaction between the two, there will be high uncertainty as to the state of the law, both old and new. (Glass JA in *Allen v Snyder* [1977])

Discuss.

An outline answer is included at the end of the book.

Essay question

The maxims of equity are unreliable. Though rarely completely meaningless or false, they have a tendency to obscure and mislead, and to stand in the way of analysis of the real principles and policies which shape the law. (Charlie Webb and Tim Akkouh, Trusts Law (2008), p 18)

Discuss.

An outline answer is available online at www.oxfordtextbooks.co.uk/orc/concentrate/

#2
Nature of a trust

- Trusts arise when the legal and equitable interests in property are divided.

- Trusts are either express or implied.

- Trusts create obligations and rights.

- A variety of different interests can exist in trust property.

Introduction

It would be difficult to find absolute agreement on the definition of a trust but in the simplest terms a trust relationship can be identified when the legal title is owned by one person (*the trustee*) and the beneficial interest is held by another (*the beneficiary*). They can be the same people, such as in trusts for land. A key skill to understanding trust law is to visualize the ownership of *all* property as being potentially divided. In chapter 1 you looked at the development of equity, a fundamental feature was the trust. The trust provides for a legal owner to be able to deal with property for the benefit of those who cannot or do not want to deal with it themselves. This is commonly expressed as:

$$\text{S (settlor)} = \frac{\text{T (trustee)}}{\text{B (beneficiary)}}$$

Figure 2.1

Categories of trusts

As a basic introduction, trusts can be broadly categorized as falling into two types: express trusts and implied trusts. This chapter is intended merely to be an introduction and the topics looked at here will be dealt with in more detail in later chapters.

Express trusts

An express trust can be either private or public. Private trusts are created for the benefit of private individuals or classes of individuals. Public trusts are trusts which will benefit members of the public and will be looked at when we consider charitable trusts in later chapters.

Express trusts are trusts which are made expressly by a **settlor** (the person making a trust). Express trusts can be **inter vivos** (made during the lifetime of the settlor) or **testamentary** (made through the settlor's will to take effect upon their death). After death the settlor is referred to as the testator.

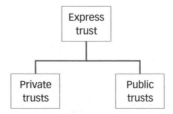

Figure 2.2

Fixed or discretionary express trusts

In a fixed trust, the beneficiaries and their interests under the trust are clearly specified. For example, to my two children Luke and Katie I create a trust of £20,000 in equal parts. They have £10,000 each held on trust.

In a discretionary trust, the property is held on trust by the trustee who has some discretion (choice) over who, within the specified class (see chapter 3), is to benefit, what their share of the trust property will be, or both. For example, 'a trust of £20,000 to my two children, Luke and Katie, as the trustee shall decide', would be a discretionary trust in which there is a discretion as to the share of the property. Under this trust, neither Luke nor Katie has anything more than an expectation in the trust; only when the trustee exercises that discretion will they have a clear interest. However, as this is a trust, the children can require the trustee to exercise that discretion.

An example of a trust in which there is a discretion to choose who is to be benefit would be, '£20,000 to be held on trust for such of my nieces and nephews whom my trustee selects'. The beneficiaries are identified as being part of a class who may benefit.

Bare trusts and protective trusts

Bare trusts

Bare trusts are when property is left on trust and the trustee has no discretion or **contingencies**. The trustee's only duty is to hold the property for the beneficiary. The beneficiary of a bare trust will be a sole beneficiary who is **sui juris**: adult and of mental capability. A simple example is a stockbroker who holds the shares on behalf of another.

Protective trusts

Protective trusts are trusts aimed at preventing an irresponsible beneficiary from wasting trust property. **Section 33 Trustee Act 1925** simplifies the method by which the beneficiary is given a life interest which is **determinable** (can be forfeited) on given events, for example bankruptcy or sale. At this point the protective trust ends and the property is then held on a discretionary trust for the beneficiary, their spouse, and children, or those who would inherit had the beneficiary died.

Classifications of interest under a trust

An important point to understand is that trusts can contain different types of interests. Interests can be either **vested** or contingent.

Revision tip

Understanding what type of interest a person has under the trust is important when considering the powers trustees have in relation to maintenance and advancement which are explored in chapter 11. Make sure that you understand the difference between a vested interest and a contingent interest.

Categories of trusts
✱✱✱✱✱✱✱✱✱✱✱✱

An interest under a trust is said to vest in the beneficiary when the beneficiary has a present right over the trust property. However, this vested interest can be either to a present right to a present interest, or a present right to a future interest. It is important as a vested interest is owned by the beneficiary. This means that if the intended beneficiary dies this interest will pass with their estate.

Example 1

I leave my home Heath Farm to my husband Dell for life then to my son Luke. Dell's interest is a *present* right to a *present* interest; it is said to be *vested in possession*. He has the property for his lifetime. This is particularly important when we look at trustee powers. Luke's interest is a *present* right to a *future* interest; it is said to be *vested in remainder*. Luke has the home when Dell dies, but at this time he has the right to expect the trustee to ensure that he has a home to take possession of.

This must be distinguished from a contingent interest. A contingent interest is one that is conditional.

Example 2

I leave my home Heath Farm to Dell for life and then to Sumita should she reach 25.

Dell's interest is the same as in example 1 but Sumita's is contingent. She has no interest until she reaches 25.

Note: Students often mistake Luke's interest as contingent. But death is something that will happen and this is not a contingent interest. Sumita may not reach 25, so her interest is conditional.

Implied trusts

Implied trusts are those which are not expressly created. There are three broad types of implied trusts: resulting, constructive, and statutory.

Most courses on trusts will spend a lot of time on implied trusts. This chapter only introduces the broad differences between different types of trusts. You should refer to chapter 8 for a more detailed account of implied trusts and their operation.

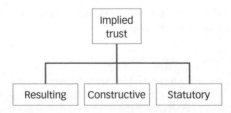

Figure 2.3

Statutory trusts

In certain circumstances statutory provisions impose a trust. For example, a trust for land is created under the **Trust of Land and Appointment of Trustees Act 1996** where joint owners hold the legal title on trust for themselves.

Another area of statutory implied trusts is in dealing with intestate estates, when a person dies without leaving a valid will. The **Administration of Estates Act 1925** provides for **settlement** of the estate to family members on the assumed intention of the deceased. The deceased person's personal representative will be appointed by the courts; they are called administrators not executors.

Resulting trusts

Resulting trusts arise either when:

- there has been a failure to validly create a trust. This means that the beneficial interest exists in a vacuum. Equity, like nature, abhors a vacuum and the vacuum is filled by creating a resulting trust; *Vandervell v IRC* [1967]. This situation has been called an automatic resulting trust because it happens regardless of the intention of the settlor. Indeed, in *Vandervell v IRC* a resulting trust arose contrary to the express intention of the settlor to give away property;

- property is voluntarily transferred to another or purchased (either wholly or partly) in the name of another; *Tinsley v Milligan* [1994]. This category is based on the presumed intention of the resulting beneficiary. Lord Browne-Wilkinson said in *Westdeutshe Landesbank Girozentrale v Islington LBC* [1996] that resulting trusts were based on the intention of the parties.

Constructive trusts

Constructive trusts are based on the presumed intention of the parties. This intention is found by the courts in a variety of situations, increasingly where they feel that it would be unconscionable for a person to deny that another has an interest in the property. The table below provides some examples of when constructive trusts have been found by the courts. This subject is considered in further detail in chapter 9.

Figure 2.4

Factual situation	Case
Breach of a fiduciary duty	*Keech v Sandford* (1726): the special relationship as trustee between the claimant and respondent meant that any benefit was held for the claimant
Unauthorized profit	*Attorney General for Hong Kong v Reid* [1994]: where the receipt of bribes which arose from a position of responsibility was found to be held on constructive trust for the state

Figure 2.4 *Continued*

Factual situation	Case
Receipt of property belonging to another	*El Ajou v Dollar Land Holdings* [1994]: when property is transferred to another without consideration then it was held that the recipient holds the property on constructive trust for the real owner
Immoral receipt	*Re Sigsworth* (1935): receipt by killing
Family home	*Grant v Edwards* [1986]: where home held in the name of one party where the other contributes to the home on the express/implied understanding that they have an interest in home

Distinguishing trust, fiduciary, and mere powers

A trust creates a legally enforceable right for the beneficiary and a legally enforceable obligation for the trustee. However, a power provides for the **donee** of the property to have the power to use property in a certain way but this power is not legally enforceable. The language of this area of law leads to confusion as textbooks will talk of a trust power, fiduciary powers, and mere powers.

Revision tip

Identifying the difference between these categories of interests will be clearer once you have understood the three certainties.

Trust powers

A trustee has powers within the trust, such as the power to invest, s 3 Trustee Act 2000, or to appoint agents. There are also powers to appoint (give), meaning that the trustee can give (appoint) property to beneficiaries from the trust property.

Example

Luke is the trustee of a discretionary trust. He holds £10,000 on trust for such of the settlor's grandchildren that need financial help.

In this situation Luke has the power to invest the money to generate a greater income for the beneficiaries. It is important that the trust fund works for the trust. He could appoint an agent to look after the money, perhaps a stockbroker or accountant. These are powers under the Trustee Act 2000. He also has the power to appoint (give) money to any of the grandchildren he thinks needs the money. As the trust is for the grandchildren the power must be exercised for a beneficiary in that class. Each potential beneficiary can enforce the exercise of the power of appointment but may not receive anything once exercised. This is a power of appointment.

Fiduciary powers

Fiduciary powers are powers in a different sense. They are not part of a trust but a 'pure' power, ie something that can be done but does not need to be done, valid but unenforceable. The person who may benefit from the power cannot make the fiduciary exercise the power but they can make sure that they consider exercising the power. A fiduciary power is a power that is held by a person who is in a fiduciary relationship with the potential recipient of the benefit of the power.

Example

Katie makes the following bequest:

> To Winston, my family solicitor, I give my shares in Bestbits plc in the hope that he uses the income to help my nieces, Sofia and Lauren.

There is no clear intention to create a trust but there is a wish (power) that Winston use it in a certain way. Sofia and Lauren cannot make him give them any benefit. What they can do is ask him to prove that he has considered making the appointment. However, he can consider and decide not to.

Mere/bare power

This is a **power of appointment** given to a person who has no fiduciary obligation. If, in the example above, Winston had only been Katie's friend then the power is entirely without an obligation, unless it is a moral one. In that case it will be a matter for Winston's conscience but not for the law.

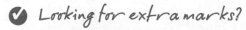 Looking for extra marks?

The distinction between trusts and powers may be blurred by the decision in *Mettoy Pensions Trustee v Evans* [1990] where the court held that an unexercised power could be executed by the court. Warner J saw no reason why the fiduciary power could not be enforced in the same way as a discretionary trust. Consider if this is solely because the decision not to exercise was capricious?

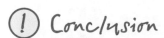 Conclusion

The nature of trusts is a question of becoming familiar with the language of trust law. Good trust lawyers will think of property rights in relation to who holds the interest at law and in equity. It is important in reviewing this chapter that you see this as an introduction to the ideas which

Conclusion

will be developed in later chapters. Ensure that you feel comfortable with the different types of trust which can be created and the different types of interest which can exist within a trust. The language of trusts can often confuse and therefore overcomplicate; understanding the terms and what they mean will pay dividends.

Key cases and key debates will be discussed in detail in later chapters.

The three certainties

Key facts

- All trusts must satisfy the three certainties (but charitable trusts do not need to satisfy the certainty of objects requirement).

- Certainty of intention is a question of fact and the courts will consider the whole context of the case.

- Certainty of subject matter requires certainty as to what property is held on trust and the beneficial interests involved.

- Complicated issues arise concerning trusts of part of a bulk of unascertained goods – the approach taken by the courts depends on whether the property is tangible or intangible.

- A fixed trust will be certain as to its objects if a complete list of beneficiaries can be compiled.

- A discretionary trust will be certain as to its objects if it can be said with certainty that any given individual is or is not a member of the class.

Introduction

Every trust (except for charitable trusts, see chapter 6) must satisfy the three certainties of intention, subject matter, and objects; *Knight v Knight* (1840).

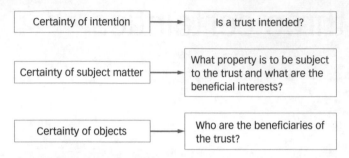

Figure 3.1 The three certainties

It is important that a trust satisfies the three certainties for two reasons:

- Trustees must know what their obligations are under the trust – remember that trustees will be liable for breach of trust if they fail to carry out their obligations correctly. The three certainties therefore provide a trustee with a degree of protection by ensuring that their obligations are clear.
- Satisfying the three certainties ensures that, if necessary, the court itself will be able to administer the trust.

Revision tip

Trusts can be declared orally or in writing. While the three certainties apply to all but charitable trusts, you should remember that every trust will also have to satisfy the formality requirements in respect of the type of property involved. So, for example, a trust of land may satisfy the three certainties. However, if the trust does not comply with s 53(1)(b) Law of Property Act 1925 by being written or evidenced in writing, it will still be unenforceable.

Certainty of intention

Intention is established by considering *all* the circumstances of the case – *equity looks to intent rather than form*. In working out what was intended, there are a number of indicators of intention that you should look out for:

Imperative or precatory language?

Since the case of *Lambe v Eames* (1871), the courts have generally made a distinction between the use of precatory and imperative words.

- Precatory words express a hope, a wish, or a moral obligation. The use of precatory words typically indicates that a gift is intended.
- Imperative words express a command, a duty to do something. The use of imperative words indicates that a trust (or power) is intended.

Figure 3.2

Case	Precatory wording
Lambe v Eames (1871)	'to be at her disposal in any way *she may think best*, for the benefit of herself and her family'
Re Adams and Kensington Vestry (1884)	'*in full confidence* that she would do what is right'
Re Diggles [1888]	'*it is my desire* that [my daughter] allows Anne an annuity of £25 during her life'

While the courts will be guided by the language used, you should remember that just as there is no magic in the use of the word 'trust' (*Kinloch v Secretary of State for India* (1882)) the presence of precatory words will not necessarily prevent the court from finding that a trust exists, as long as it is satisfied that this was the intention of the donor:

Comiskey v Bowring-Hanbury [1905] AC 84

The **testator** left his wife the whole of his estate 'in full confidence that she will make such use of it as I should have made myself and that at her death she will devise it to such one or more of my nieces as she may think fit...' These words sound precatory and would suggest a gift. However, the will continued, '...in default of any disposition by her thereof by her will or testament I hereby direct that all my estate...shall at her death be equally divided among the surviving said nieces'. When read as a whole, the court concluded that the testator had intended a trust, under which the wife held a life interest.

The court may also take into account surrounding evidence which sheds light on the intentions of the parties. In *Staden v Jones* [2008], the Court of Appeal looked to a solicitor's covering letter to conclude that a divorcing couple's arrangement that the wife transferred her share in the family home to her husband on the basis that their daughter should ultimately be entitled to her share amounted to a constructive trust.

Conduct

An intention to create a trust can also be inferred from the conduct of the donor.

....

Paul v Constance [1977] 1 WLR 527

When Mr Constance died, a dispute arose regarding whether his wife (from whom he was sepa-rated but not divorced) or his new partner, Mrs Paul, was entitled to money held in a bank account in his sole name. During their relationship, Mr Constance had made arrangements for Mrs Paul to be able to withdraw money with his written permission. Only Mr Constance withdrew money once, which was split evenly between them and he often told Mrs Paul that the money was 'as much yours as mine'. In addition, they had also paid some joint winnings from bingo into the account. It was held that these actions were sufficient to infer that Mr Constance had made a declaration of trust of the money in the bank account and Mrs Constance was entitled to half of the account.

....

A similar approach has been taken in some commercial contexts. For example, in *Re Kayford Ltd (in liquidation)* [1975], the separation of customers' money in a different bank account was deemed sufficient to demonstrate an intention to create a trust.

However, not all conduct can lead to the inference to create a trust: see, for example, *Jones v Lock* (1865).

The effect of lack of certainty of intention

If there is no intention to create a trust (or power), the donee will take the property abso-lutely, as a gift (*Lassence v Tierney* (1849)).

Certainty of subject matter

There are two elements to certainty of subject matter:

- it must be clear what property is held on trust; and
- the beneficial interests must be clear.

The property held on trust must be certain

Vague or general descriptions of the trust property

The donor must make it clear what property is to be held on trust or the trust will be void as the trustees, beneficiaries and, ultimately, the court will be unable to know what is held on trust. (See Figure 3.3 overleaf.)

Trusts of part of property

This situation arises where there is an attempt to create a trust over part of a bulk of **tangible property**, eg the furniture in a home or a warehouse filled with desktop computers. Where there is a trust of *part of a bulk of tangible property*, the trust property will only be certain if it has been separated from the rest.

Figure 3.3

Case	Uncertain description of property to be held on trust
Palmer v Simmonds (1854)	'the bulk' of the testatrix's estate
Peck v Halsey (1720)	'some of my best linen'
Jubber v Jubber (1839)	'a handsome gratuity'
Re Kolb's WT [1961]	An instruction to purchase 'blue chip' investments

· ·

Re London Wine Co [1986] PCC 121

LWC stocked cases of wine in various warehouses. When wine was purchased by customers, they received a certificate of title which indicated that the wine would be held on trust for them until dispatched. When LWC went into liquidation, the question arose whether the wine was held on trust for the customers or was to be considered part of LWC's general assets available to creditors. It was held that there was no trust as the wine ordered by customers had not been separated from the general stock and therefore the subject matter of each trust could not be identified.

· ·

Note: **s 20A Sale of Goods Act 1979** (inserted by the **Sale of Goods (Amendment) Act 1995**) now offers protection to purchasers of an unsegregated part of a larger bulk of property. As soon as they have paid, they will be considered tenants in common of the whole property. This has the effect of protecting their purchases from creditors in the event of liquidation or receivership.

However, where there is a trust of part of some intangible property, such as shares, there is no need to identify the specific shares to be held on trust:

· ·

Hunter v Moss (1994) 1 WLR 452

Moss owned 950 shares in a company and was found to have declared himself trustee of 50 of those shares for Hunter. However, Moss sold all his shares and kept the proceeds for himself. When Hunter sought a share of the proceeds, Moss argued that the trust was void because he had not separated or identified the specific shares to be held on trust for Hunter.

Certainty of subject matter
✱✱✱✱✱✱✱✱✱✱✱✱

Dillon LJ distinguished *Re London Wine Co* on the basis that, unlike cases of wine or other tangible property, these shares were indistinguishable from one another. Therefore, no segregation was required as holding any 50 of the 950 shares on trust would achieve the same thing.

Revision tip

Remember that this case applies to trusts of a part of a *homogeneous* larger whole. When approaching a problem question on this matter, pay close attention to the facts. If, for example, the question relates to a portion of shares where the shares are of different types or relate to shares in different companies, the rule in *Hunter v Moss* will not apply and the trust will be void if there is no further identification of the relevant property (*Re Harvard Securities Ltd (in liquidation)* [1998]).

✅ *Looking for extra marks?*

Despite the fact that *Hunter v Moss* (1994) has been followed in *Re Harvard Securities Ltd (in liquidation)* [1998], there have been many criticisms of the law in this area. Hayton in (1994) 110 LQR 335–9 raises a number of significant criticisms of which you should be aware:

- Is Dillon LJ's argument that there is no difference between a testator giving 50 shares to a legatee in his will and a settlor declaring himself trustee of 50 of his shares correct?

- Hayton also argues that difficult questions may arise in the event that the 'trustee' sells part of his holding – eg has he sold his own shares or the beneficiary's or, if the transaction is taxable, who is liable, the seller or the beneficiary? Consider this argument in light of Worthington's argument in 'Sorting out ownership interests in a bulk: gifts, sales and trusts' (1999) JBL 1, that such issues could be resolved through the rules of tracing (see chapter 12).

- Is the broad distinction in the cases between trusts of parts of unascertained bulks of tangible and intangible property convincing?

The beneficial interests under the trust must be certain

The beneficial interests under the trust must also be clear. Two cases can help to illustrate the problems that may arise in this context:

Boyce v Boyce (1849) 16 Sim 476

A testator established a trust of four houses for his daughters, Maria and Charlotte. Maria was to choose which house she wanted and the other houses would be held on trust for Charlotte. However, Maria died before making her choice. The trust failed as it was no longer possible to say which houses would be held on trust for Charlotte.

The property had been clearly identified but the beneficial interest had not. The trust would have succeeded if the trustees had been given the power to choose the house, but in the absence of this power, neither the trustees nor the court could determine the beneficial interest.

In the following case, the question was whether the instructions given to the trustees were certain enough to allow them to carry out the terms of the trust:

···

Re Golay's WT [1965] 2 All ER 660

A trust was set up whereby the beneficiary was to 'receive a reasonable income' from the testator's properties. The court held that this was a valid trust as the phrase 'reasonable income' allowed the trustees (and the court, if need be) to make an *objective* assessment of what that might be, based on the beneficiary's circumstances. Therefore, the trust was sufficiently certain as the income the beneficiary would receive would be based on her circumstances – while this might vary over the years, the trustees would always have an objective yardstick by which to act. On the other hand, the trust would have failed if the properties were to be sold in order to provide a reasonable one-off sum of money for the beneficiary. This is because the trustees would have no way of determining what a 'reasonable' payment would amount to: arguably, the wording of the trust suggests that the beneficiary would not receive all the money, but then what portion of the proceeds would be reasonable?

···

Note: the legal issues surrounding the certainty of beneficial interests will not apply in respect of discretionary trusts. This is because the class to benefit merely hold a *spes* (hope) of benefiting – the extent to which they can benefit, if at all, is at the absolute discretion of the trustees.

A link between certainty of intention and certainty of subject matter

If there is a lack of certainty as to the subject matter of the trust, this will cast doubt on whether the settlor truly intended to create a trust (*Mussoorie Bank Ltd v Raynor* (1882)).

The effect of lack of certainty of subject matter

If there is a lack of certainty as to the subject matter, the trust fails and the property will return to the settlor or estate on resulting trust.

Certainty of objects (beneficiaries)

Certainty of objects relates to the question of who are the beneficiaries of a trust. Every trust – with the exception of charitable trusts – must satisfy the certainty of objects requirement. The certainty of objects test is different for fixed trusts and discretionary trusts.

- *Fixed trusts* – the beneficial interests are fixed, eg a trust to benefit Razia and Shahana in equal shares.

Certainty of objects (beneficiaries)

✷✷✷✷✷✷✷✷✷✷

- *Discretionary trust* – this is a type of trust in which the trustees are given the power to appoint people as beneficiaries of the trust. Members of the class of potential beneficiaries do not hold any beneficial interest until trustees exercise their discretion to appoint in their favour. The amount they receive is at the discretion of the trustees.

Fixed trusts

In order to satisfy the certainty of objects requirement, a full list of the beneficiaries must be able to be created (*IRC v Broadway Cottages Trust* [1955]), ie all the beneficiaries must be able to be identified. (See chapter 11 for a discussion of the trustees' options if the whereabouts or continued existence of a beneficiary cannot be ascertained.)

Discretionary trusts

A different approach was taken in respect of discretionary trusts in the key decision of *McPhail v Doulton*:

··

McPhail v Doulton (Re Baden's Trusts (No 1)) [1971] AC 424

The settlor set up a fund for the benefit of employees of Matthew Hall & Co Ltd and their relatives and dependants at the 'absolute discretion' of the trustees. The House of Lords had to decide (a) whether this was a trust or a power and (b) the appropriate test for the certainty of objects requirement. While all the judges agreed that this was a discretionary trust rather than a power, they were split regarding the appropriate test. On a 3:2 majority, Lord Wilberforce, who delivered the leading judgment of the majority, held:

1. The complete list approach adopted in *IRC v Broadway Cottages* [1955] was overruled in respect of discretionary trusts.

2. The test for certainty of objects in discretionary trusts is the same as the test for fiduciary powers in *Re Gulbenkian's Settlement* [1970], namely *whether it could be said with certainty that any given individual is or is not a member of the class.*

··

Applying the test in *McPhail v Doulton*: *Re Baden's Trusts (No 2)*

Having decided on the test for certainty of objects for discretionary trusts, the case was returned to the court of first instance for the test to be applied. Despite the court deciding that it satisfied the new test, the **executors** of Baden's will relentlessly continued to contest its validity, and the case came before the Court of Appeal for the second time:

··

Re Baden's Trusts (No 2) [1973] Ch 9

The trust set up by Baden was to benefit 'employees of Matthew Hall & Co Ltd and their relatives and dependants'. The issue in this appeal was whether the groups 'relatives' and 'dependants' satisfied the new test set out in *McPhail v Doulton* – ie could it be said with certainty that any given individual is or is not a member of these classes?

The Court of Appeal held that *only if a class of beneficiaries is conceptually certain* will it be possible to satisfy the test of whether it can be said with certainty that any given individual is or is not a member of the class.

....

What is conceptual certainty?

Conceptual certainty has been described as 'linguistic or semantic certainty' – in other words, a class of beneficiaries will be conceptually certain when the description enables you to define the group clearly. Consider the following examples:

Example

1. A discretionary trust of £100,000 for members of the British Army who served in the Gulf War.

2. A discretionary trust of £50,000 for morally upstanding residents of Gloucester.

The first trust can be said to be conceptually certain as the group to benefit can be clearly understood. However, it is unlikely that the second trust would be valid as it is extremely difficult to define what exactly would be meant by 'morally upstanding'. For example, X may attend church regularly but may also cheat at poker. Y might give regularly to charity but cheat on her husband. If Z is in favour of same-sex marriage, does this mean he is morally upstanding or not? Where exactly can the line be drawn?

Gifts subject to a condition precedent

Gifts subject to a condition precedent do not require the same degree of conceptual certainty as discretionary trusts.

Terminology tip

A gift made subject to a condition precedent is one to which the donee will not be entitled unless they satisfy the condition, eg £10,000 to each of my children who graduate from university.

....

Re Barlow's WT [1979] 1 WLR 278

A testatrix provided that a number of her paintings could be sold at a reduced price to 'any members of my family and any friends of mine'. The gift in question here was the difference in price between their market value and the reduced price. The central issue was whether the condition precedent – ie that they be family members or friends – rendered the gift void for uncertainty. The court upheld the gift. Whereas the objects of a discretionary trust must be conceptually certain, a condition precedent will be valid if *at least one person can be said to satisfy the condition*.

....

Certainty of objects (beneficiaries)

****

In a gift to a class, as the objects are only entitled to a *share* of the property, it is vital to be able to say whether any given individual is or is not a member of the class. However, in this case, the 'family and friends' were each given an *individual opportunity* to purchase the paintings. Therefore, a greater degree of uncertainty as to who satisfied this condition did not affect the opportunity they received.

> ### Revision Tip
>
> While a gift to 'friends' may be valid as a gift subject to a condition precedent, a discretionary trust for 'friends' will be void for uncertainty, as it is impossible to define friends so that it could be said that *any* individual *is or is not* within the class.

Distinguishing conceptual uncertainty from evidential uncertainty

It is important to distinguish 'conceptual uncertainty' from 'evidential uncertainty'. Conceptual certainty relates to the certainty of the *class*; evidential certainty relates to the issue of whether an *individual* can be found or proven to be a member of the class or not. If a class is conceptually uncertain, the trust will be void, but evidential uncertainty will not defeat a trust.

Having discussed the meaning of conceptual certainty in general terms, it is important to return to the case of *Re Baden's Trusts (No 2)*. The Court of Appeal was asked if the groups 'dependants' and 'relatives' were conceptually certain. All the judges agreed that 'dependants' was conceptually certain. However, while they also agreed that 'relatives' was conceptually certain, the three judges each reached this conclusion by different reasoning!

Sachs LJ: the liberal approach

Sachs LJ started by defining 'relatives' to mean 'descendants of a common ancestor'. He argued that this was conceptually certain as its meaning was clearly understandable. He then stated that trustees have a fiduciary obligation to survey the range of possible beneficiaries. This involves the trustees gaining a sense of the general width of the class – it does not require an exhaustive list. Beyond that survey, anyone who can prove that they are a member of the class can be included.

Sachs LJ's approach clearly separates the question of evidential uncertainty by stressing that an exhaustive list is not required. Moreover, in response to the problem that a potentially limitless number of people could be included within the definition 'descendants of a common ancestor', he makes three points:

1. The trustees should exercise their discretion in a sensible way, thus making it more likely that they would choose close relatives in the general course of events.

2. Proof of one's relationship to another soon becomes very difficult, providing a natural limit on who could establish their membership of the class.

3. Most importantly, these issues are evidential and the fact that it will not always be possible to prove that any given individual is not a member of the class will not render the trust void.

This approach is arguably the purest interpretation of conceptual certainty. The only drawback is that Sach LJ's reasoning provides no simple way for the trustees to work out whether the class to benefit under the trust is conceptually certain. Simple common sense can be a dangerous path for trustees who could be liable if they distribute the money wrongly.

Megaw LJ: the middle ground

Megaw LJ also defined 'relatives' as 'descendants of a common ancestor'. However, he argued that a class would be conceptually certain if it could be said with certainty that *a substantial number of objects fell within the class*, even if there were a substantial number of others of whom it could not definitely be said that they were within or without the class.

- Megaw LJ's approach offers trustees more guidance in that the conceptual certainty of the group can be tested by seeking a substantial number of individuals who definitely come within the class.
- However, what exactly is meant by 'a substantial number'? Megaw LJ suggests that this is a question of common sense but wary trustees will still find themselves questioning whether they have done enough, especially should the situation arise where there are definitely a substantial number about whom they *cannot* say with clarity that they are within the class.
- Despite it being said that evidential certainty will not defeat a discretionary trust, Megaw LJ's approach rests on being able to provide *evidence* that a sufficient number come within the class.

Stamp LJ: the strict approach

Stamp LJ takes a literal approach to the test set out in *McPhail v Doulton* that to be conceptually certain it must be possible to say of *any given individual* that they are or *are not* within the class. On this basis, Stamp LJ rejected the idea that 'descendants of a common ancestor' could be conceptually certain and argued that the discretionary trust could only be valid if 'relatives' was defined as 'next-of-kin'.

- Stamp LJ's reasoning seems determined to undermine the liberal implications of the decision in *McPhail v Doulton*. Applying his approach, there would be no real difference between the new test adopted in *McPhail v Doulton* and the previous complete list approach of *IRC v Broadway Cottages Trust* [1955] as every individual's membership of the class would have to be capable of being established.
- It is questionable whether this approach would be followed in the future, particularly as Lord Wilberforce's full expression of the test states that a trust 'does not fail simply because it is impossible to ascertain every member of the class'.

Certainty of objects (beneficiaries)

✱✱✱✱✱✱✱✱✱✱

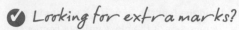 ✔️ *Looking for extra marks?*

The issue of certainty of objects for discretionary trusts is complex. If you want to do well in this area, there is no substitute for reading *McPhail v Doulton* and *Re Baden's Trusts (No 2)* and taking your own detailed notes. You should particularly focus on how well the Court of Appeal in *Re Baden's Trusts (No 2)* use 'conceptual certainty' in their judgments. Once you have done this, you can deepen your understanding of some of the problems in this area by reading Emery's discussion of this issue at (1982) 98 LQR 551.

Can conceptual uncertainty be cured?

There is some debate over whether conceptual uncertainty can be cured by reference to the decision or opinion of the trustees or a third party.

··

Re Tuck's ST [1978] Ch 49

A trust was established to benefit future baronets on the condition that they were of the Jewish faith and married to a wife of 'Jewish blood', as determined by the Chief Rabbi. The court upheld the trust: any conceptual uncertainty regarding the conditions was cured by the power given to the Chief Rabbi.

··

While Denning LJ simply argues that reference to the trustees' or a third party's opinion may cure conceptual uncertainty, Eveleigh LJ's reasoning rests on the narrower ground that there was no conceptual uncertainty because the settlor was 'in effect saying that his definition of "Jewish faith" is *the same as the Chief Rabbi's definition*' (a conceptually certain class).

Note: *Re Tuck's ST* addresses the validity of *conditions precedent*. It remains unclear whether:

1. the same approach would be adopted in respect of a *discretionary trust* with conceptually uncertain objects; and

2. whether the courts would adopt the broad approach of Denning LJ or the more restrictive approach of Eveleigh LJ.

Both approaches remain problematic. Whereas Denning LJ's approach would ensure the validity of many more discretionary trusts, it would also seem to empower individuals named by the settlor to cure conceptual uncertainty in circumstances where the court would otherwise declare the trust void. On the other hand, Eveleigh LJ's approach maintains the need for conceptual certainty but rests on a very fine factual distinction that many settlors will not appreciate (see, Webb and Akkouh, *Trusts Law* (2008), p 72). Compare the following examples.

Example

1. Bradley leaves £10,000 in his will to be held on discretionary trust for 'the men and women who have given me pleasure over my long and happy life'. He adds, 'in the event of any doubt, my wife can choose who qualifies'.

2. Bradley leaves £10,000 in his will to be held on discretionary trust for 'those men and women whom my wife considers have given me pleasure over my long and happy life'.

In the first version, the group to benefit lacks conceptual certainty. Giving someone the ability to decide who comes within the class will not cure this uncertainty as there is no objective way to determine what Bradley meant.

However, in the second version there is no conceptual uncertainty as the class in question is not 'those who have given me pleasure' but 'those whom *my wife considers have given me pleasure*'. As membership is to be decided by Bradley's wife, there is no difficulty in understanding how the class is to be determined.

Administrative unworkability

A trust may be void if the class to benefit is *so wide* that the trust would be administratively unworkable, eg Lord Wilberforce's example of a trust for all the residents of Greater London in *McPhail v Doulton* [1971].

The classic example of this problem can be seen in *R v District Auditor, ex parte West Yorkshire Metropolitan County Council* (1986) where a trust 'for the benefit of any or all or some of the inhabitants of the County of West Yorkshire' (some 2.5 million potential beneficiaries) was held to be void for administrative unworkability.

Note: administrative unworkability will also render a fiduciary power void because the fiduciary obligations of the holder require that the power is capable of being exercised in a responsible manner and that the selection of one person over another can be meaningfully justified. However, administrative unworkability will not affect the validity of a mere power (ie a power given to a non-fiduciary) (*Re Hay's Settlement Trusts* [1982]).

The effect of lack of certainty of objects

A trust which lacks certainty of objects will be void and return on resulting trust to the settlor or his estate.

Comparing discretionary trusts and fiduciary powers

As you have seen, following *McPhail v Doulton* [1971], the test for certainty of objects for discretionary trusts and fiduciary powers is now the same. However, it is important to remember that there are still important differences.

Certainty of objects (beneficiaries)

✷✷✷✷✷✷✷✷✷✷

The duties under the discretionary trust/fiduciary power

Discretionary trusts

McPhail v Doulton [1971] establishes that trustees have the following duties:

- to survey the field to identify the width of the class; and
- to distribute the income from the trust.

Note: watch out for *non-exhaustive discretionary trusts* which expressly allow the trustees to accumulate the income. In such trusts, the trustees may delay distributing for some time but must still ultimately distribute at some point.

Fiduciary powers

The donee of a fiduciary power is *not* under a duty to distribute the property. However, under *Re Hay's ST* [1982] fiduciaries have the following duties:

- to consider periodically whether to exercise the power;
- to consider the range of possible objects (beneficiaries); and
- to consider the appropriateness of appointments made – ie they cannot pick at random or without reason.

> *Revision Tip*
>
> If an arrangement refers to a 'gift over in default of appointment' or a direction that remaining money is to return to the settlor's estate, this will be a fiduciary power as the wording demonstrates that there is not a duty to distribute.

Example

- Discretionary trust: 'I leave £100,000 to my wife to be held on trust at her absolute and unfettered discretion for the employees of Brillington Engineering Co Ltd.'
- Fiduciary power: 'To my trustees I leave £50,000 to share amongst those of my relatives who are most in need. *In the event that all the money is not used up*, any remainder will pass to my gardener, Ted.'

As there is a duty to distribute in a discretionary trust, there are no directions about what should be done with any remaining money. Compare this with the fiduciary power, where a beneficiary in default of appointment is indicated.

The rights of members of the class

Discretionary trusts

Members of the class are not beneficiaries until they are appointed to the trust – until that time they merely hold a *spes* (hope) of benefiting. This means that members of the class may challenge the decisions of the trustees but they *cannot* claim that they are entitled to be appointed, as this is at the absolute discretion of the trustees.

Decisions may be challenged on the basis that the trustees have:

- appointed outside the class;
- failed to consider their reasons for appointment; or
- acted in bad faith in making an appointment (eg appointing only to close friends within the class).

Note: if all the beneficiaries are *sui juris*, they may act together to wind up the trust under the rule in *Saunders v Vautier* (1841) (see chapter 10).

Fiduciary powers

As with discretionary trusts, members of a class under a fiduciary power cannot claim to be entitled to be appointed. However, decisions may be challenged on the basis that the fiduciaries have:

- appointed outside the class;
- failed to carry out their fiduciary obligations under *Re Hay's ST* [1982].

Unlike discretionary trusts, the court will not intervene to compel the fiduciary to exercise their power.

 **Key cases**

Cases	Facts	Principle
Hunter v Moss (1994) 1 WLR 452	An attempt to create a trust of 50 of 950 shares owned by the trustee was upheld.	Trusts of part of an unascertained bulk of intangible property do not require segregation or specific identification to satisfy the certainty of subject matter requirement.
Knight v Knight (1840) 3 Beav 148	Concerned a will which included the statement 'I trust to the liberality of my successors to reward any others of my old servants and tenants according to their deserts'. The successor took the deceased's property absolutely.	Originating case for the three certainties requirement of intention, subject matter and objects.

Key debates

****

Cases	Facts	Principle
Lambe v Eames (1871) 6 Ch App 597	Concerned money left to a wife 'to be at her disposal in any way she may think best, for the benefit of herself and her family'. Wife took property as a gift.	Emphasizes the difference between imperative words (which suggest a trust is intended) and precatory words (which suggest a mere moral obligation).
McPhail v Doulton [1971] AC 424	Concerned the validity of a discretionary trust established for employees, relatives, and dependants.	The certainty of objects requirement for discretionary trusts is whether it can be said with certainty that any given individual is or is not a member of the class.
Palmer v Simmonds (1854) 2 Drew 221	A gift of the 'bulk' of the testatrix's estate failed.	The vagueness of the wording meant there was no certainty of subject matter.
Re Baden's Trusts (No 2) [1973] Ch 9	Concerned whether the groups 'relatives' and 'dependants' satisfied the certainty of objects test for discretionary trusts.	In order to satisfy the test set out in *McPhail v Doulton*, the groups to benefit must be conceptually certain. 'Conceptual certainty' refers to whether the group can be meaningfully *defined* (as opposed to meaning that all the beneficiaries can be *identified*).
Re London Wine Co [1986] PCC 121	An attempt to create a trust of part of an unascertained bulk of tangible property (cases of wine) failed.	Trusts of part of an unascertained bulk of tangible property must be segregated or specifically identified to satisfy the certainty of subject matter requirement.

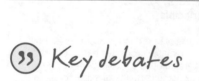 Key debates

Topic	How defensible is the current approach to trusts of part of an unascertained bulk of intangible property?
Academic/ Author	Hayton/Worthington
Viewpoint	The current approach in *Hunter v Moss* raises problems in respect of legal principles and remedies in the event of a breach of trust.
Source	Compare Hayton (1994) 110 LQR 335–9 and Worthington (1999) JBL 1.

Topic	How can the complicated decisions on certainty of objects be unravelled?
Academic/ Author	Emery
Viewpoint	The reasoning of the different judges in *Re Baden's Trusts (No 2)* demonstrates that there is still some confusion around the meaning of conceptual certainty and evidential certainty.
Source	(1982) 98 LQR 551.

 Exam questions

Problem question

Anna was the managing director of a multinational company. She died in 2007 and her will contains the following bequests:

1. £50,000 to my sister, Ruth, whom I trust will use the money to continue supporting her daughter, Joanna.

2. £150,000 to Alistair and Fraser, to be held on trust for any of my trusted work colleagues in any amount at their absolute and unfettered discretion.

3. My favourite jewels are to be held on trust for my beloved granddaughter, Lucy, until her 21st birthday.

Discuss the validity of these bequests.

An outline answer is included at the end of the book.

Essay question

The current approach to certainty of objects in discretionary trusts creates more uncertainty than it resolves. Discuss.

An outline answer is available online at www.oxfordtextbooks.co.uk/orc/concentrate/

#4
Constitution

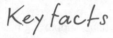

Key facts

- There are three ways to benefit another with property.
- There are legal rules for validly transferring an interest in property.
- When the legal rules fail equity has developed methods to prevent the intention of the transferor being defeated.
- Key principles can be found in the cases:
  - *Re Rose* [1952]
  - *Strong v Bird* [1874]
  - *Cain v Moon* [1896]
  - *Gillett v Holt* [2001]

Introduction

When a person transfers legal title to another the legal title is said to **vest** in the other person. This chapter will consider the rules for the transfer of title (ownership) in property in relation to different types of property. The general principle is that unless the property has been transferred by the correct legal rules then the transfer fails, it is said to be **imperfect**. The equitable maxim that 'equity will not perfect an imperfect title' would be the starting position for the courts. If the person to whom the transfer is intended to be made has not given valuable consideration they are said to be a **volunteer**. A transferee who has given valuable consideration may be able to have the contract specifically enforced. Failing to validly 'vest' title in the volunteer means that the volunteer has no enforceable legal rights. This is reflected in the equitable maxim that 'equity will not assist a volunteer'.

Terminology tip

It is sometimes the language of equity that students struggle with so at a *basic* level this may help.

When a person has property he is said to be the 'absolute owner'. In a simple way it can be said that he has the legal title and the beneficial (equitable) title. A person who gives a gift is referred to as the donor. If the same person was creating a trust of the same property they would be called a settlor. If the same transactions were being created by a will the person would be called the testator (or a testatrix if they are female).

The person who receives the property can be a donee; you will see this in a person being called a donee of a power. A person who is given property under a will or by trust is called a legatee, devisee, or a beneficiary. Don't be put off; just for now the person giving the property will be called the transferor, the person who is intended to get the property the transferee.

Although the maxim 'equity will not perfect an imperfect gift' refers to perfect gifts, it also applies to a transfer of legal title to a third party to hold on trust.

This chapter will begin by briefly considering the legal rules in relation to validly transferring property to another person. It then deals with equitable rules which have developed to overcome the strict application of the legal rules of vesting. This may seem contradictory to the maxim above. However, equitable maxims are the guiding principles of equitable rules and in certain circumstances 'equity looks upon as done that which ought to be done' or 'equity looks at the substance rather than form'.

Equity is a gloss on the common law, and as such has implications beyond the creation of trusts. The rules for transfer of ownership as a gift overlap with the transfer of legal title to the trustee. This chapter is closely linked with chapter 5, the formalities for creating a trust.

Benefiting another with property

Milroy v Lord (1862) identified three ways in which an absolute owner of property could benefit another with their property:

- an outright gift;

Benefiting another with property

- a transfer of legal title to a third person to hold on trust for the benefit of another; or
- declaring that the absolute owner now holds that property on trust for another.

1. Gift

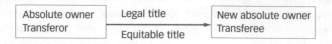

2. Transfer to third person to hold on trust

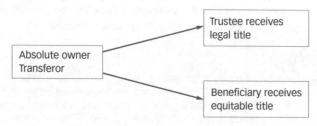

3. Absolute owner declares that they hold property on trust for another

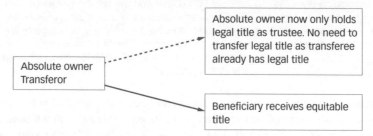

Figure 4.1 Three ways to benefit another with your property

Figure 4.1 shows that it is artificial to talk of the absolute owner having legal and equitable title. The legal and equitable interests have not been separated. However, as with the terminology tip above, as a device for learning the principles it may help to think of the interests in this way.

✅ Looking for extra marks?

A *common mistake* made by students when dealing with constitution issues is either to try and find a trust where the intention was to make a gift or to only consider who has the equitable interest when the transferor intended to create a third person as trustee. Chapter 5 will consider the requirements for dealing with the beneficial ownership of property under a trust. These two topics are closely related but they have been separated out here to help you in your revision. *Keep distinct the legal requirements for constituting the transfer of an interest in property and the formalities for creating and dealing with a trust interest.*

A good plan of the answer usually remedies this, and an answer that has been planned really pays off.

When lawyers talk of the transfer it is said to be 'perfect' if all the legal requirements for a valid transfer have been complied with. If they have not, then the transfer is said to be 'imperfect'.

Revision tip

In answering questions, the focus will be on how equity steps in to modify the legal rules. Do not wander into a long explanation of the legal rules. *Briefly* explain how the legal rule for transfer of title has failed, then explain the equitable rules which may apply.

Different legal rules apply to different types of property. Remember that in talking of property this includes *any* thing, tangible or intangible, that is capable of being owned. Below are the rules for the valid transfer of the most common types of property transfer.

Land

A transfer in land or an interest in land is set out in **s 52 Law of Property Act 1925**.

- It must be by deed (defined in **s 1 Law of Property (Miscellaneous Provisions) Act 1989**).
- Transfer is completed by registration at the Land Registry (**Land Registration Act 2002**).

See *Richards v Delridge* [1874].

Stocks and shares which regulate the ownership of companies

Private Limited Company:

- Memorandum of transfer
- Registration of shares
- **Stock Transfer Act 1963, Companies Act 1985**

Public Limited Company (plc):

- Compliance with the electronic CREST system then the correct instruction will be adequate.

See *Milroy v Lord* (1862).

✱✱✱✱✱✱✱✱✱✱

Chose in action

This includes such things as cheques, debts, or rights under a contract.

- Compliance with s **136 Law of Property Act 1925**, which requires endorsement.

See *Jones v Lock* (1865).

Chattels

This includes such things as paintings, jewellery, etc.

- By deed; or
- Compliance with *Re Cole* [1964]
  - delivery
  - intention that legal ownership is transferred.

.....

Glaister-Carlisle v Glaister-Carlisle (1968) unreported

The owner of a miniature white poodle was upset that his wife had allowed her to mate with the wife's black poodle. He threw the poodle at her and said 'she is your responsibility now'. The court held the language was too vague to transfer the legal title, despite the delivery.

.....

The requirement for delivery can be actual delivery or constructive, this may include delivery of car keys, representing the delivery of the car itself. It can also be informing the intended donee where they can find the chattel; *Thomas v Times Book Co* [1966].

Money

A valid transfer of money merely requires delivery.

Transfer of an equitable interest

Another type of property that can be transferred to another is the ownership of a beneficial interest. The legal requirements to transfer this interest to another are set out in s **53(1)(c) Law of Property Act 1925**. This applies to the beneficial interest in *any* type of property, *not* just interests in land. This type of transfer will be dealt with in detail in the next chapter.

Revision Tip

These clear legal rules, from either statute or common law, for the valid transfer of property rights provide the necessary certainty in dealing with property ownership. Learn the legal requirements for each type of property covered in this chapter. Explain this first in an exam before moving on to say that equity has developed means to overcome problems of imperfect title transfer.

Equitable principles which perfect a transfer

Where legal title has not vested correctly then equity has established exceptions to the legal rules outlined above. It is important to establish the legal rules *first*, then consider which – and there may be more than one – of the equitable rules applies to perfect title.

Legal title vests in another capacity

Where the legal owner promises to transfer property (or promises that they will not enforce the repayment of a debt) but they fail to do this in their lifetime then the gift should fail. However, if the promised property vests in the potential transferee in another capacity then the courts have held that the transfer has been perfected; *Strong v Bird* [1874]. To be able to rely on the 'Rule in *Strong v Bird*' the requirements are:

- there is a clear intention to make an *inter vivos* gift to the **transferee**;
- there is a present intention to give; *Re Freeland* (1952);
- the intention continues until death; *Re Gonin* [1977]; and
- the intended transferee obtains legal ownership by appointment as executor or personal representative; *Re James* [1935].

Intention

The intention must be a clear intention to give immediately and there has only been some practical barrier to the transfer. It must not be an intention to give in the future. The rule originated in the release from debts but it has been extended:

- to chattels; *Re Stewart* [1908]; and
- to an intention to transfer legal title to hold as trustee; *Re Ralli's WT* [1964].

Revision tip

When reading the exam question ensure that you note who the executors are. This is usually at the end of the question. Ensure that you read the whole question.

Donatio mortis causa

Property transferred under a will must comply with the Wills Act 1837. Section 9 requires that the will be in writing, signed by the testator, and witnessed by two people who are not beneficiaries. However, a deathbed bequest can supersede the will if it complies with the requirements of a *donatio mortis causa* (DMC) as set out in *Cain v Moon* [1896]. If the bequest is made:

- in contemplation of imminent death;
- contingent (conditional) on death; and
- there is actual or constructive delivery of the property.

Equitable principles which perfect a transfer
✳✳✳✳✳✳✳✳✳✳✳

Contemplation of death

This is more than contemplation of death which everyone must face. It can be in contemplation of hazardous undertakings, active service during war, or a dangerous trip. It will not apply in the contemplation of suicide; *Re Dudman* [1925].

Contingent on death

If the transferor recovers, then the intended gift fails; so the gift is revocable should death not occur. It can also be expressly revoked or by taking back **dominion** of the property.

Actual or constructive delivery

This means that the transferor hands 'dominion' to the transferee, by giving them the means to control the property. This will be dependent on the nature of the property. Where the goods are tangible it may not be difficult but where the property is intangible, such as money, then there may be evidential problems. In the latter situations the courts look for the relevant evidence which will indicate the transfer of dominion.

Examples

Figure 4.2

Property	Case examples of constructive delivery
Safety deposit box	*Re Lillingston* [1952]: this included handing the key to a trunk which held the keys to a safety deposit box, which had another key to a further such box
Car	*Woodard v Woodard* [1995]: giving the keys to a car
Bank accounts	*Re Dillon* [1890]: the relevant passbook will be adequate
Unregistered land	*Sen v Headley* [1991]: the relevant title deeds
Registered land	Although the Land Registration Act 2002 states that the land certificate is merely evidence of ownership it may form sufficient evidence of delivery of 'dominion' (see Pearce and Stevens, *Land Law,* 3rd edn (2005), p 79)
Shares	*Staniland v Willott* (1852) suggests that handing the executed share transfer form will suffice

Additionally, the property must be capable of forming the subject matter of a DMC. A cheque made by the transferor cannot be the subject matter of a DMC as it is a mandate that ends on death; *Re Beaumont* (1902). However a cheque payable to the transferor can be; *Re Mead* (1880).

Every effort has been taken by the transferor

The property has failed to vest despite every effort of the transferor to perfect title in the transferee; *Re Rose* [1952]. The principle to be gained from this exception is that where power to complete the transfer is out of the hands of the transferor then equity will 'look upon as done that which ought to be done'. In *Re Rose* [1952] the forms for transfer of shares were completed and sent to the company. There was a three-month delay between sending the forms to the company and registration at the company of the transfer. The court held that transfer was effective when the transferor had done all that he could to complete the transfer.

It seems from this case that the transferor must have 'gone beyond the point of no return'. In effect, the transferor has practically lost dominion of the property. Compare *Re Rose* to *Re Fry* [1946] where the transferor had completed forms to transfer title and sent the forms to be registered. The company needed the consent of the Treasury to make the registration. The transferor had completed all the forms to get this consent but had died before the consent was given. The court held he still held power of the shares and they had not done all that was required to transfer them.

If a rule can be gleaned from the cases, it seems from *Mascall v Mascall* (1984) that it is when the transferor can no longer change their mind, that the property has been taken out of the control of the transferor, that the courts will perfect the transfer.

These rules seemed to be quite clearly defined until the decision in *Pennington v Waine* [2002] below.

Unconscionability

Recent decisions have developed a further equitable gloss to the legal rules. The move can be seen to begin in *Choithram International v Pagarani* [2001] where Lord Browne-Wilkinson said that while 'equity will not aid a volunteer, it will not strive officiously to defeat a gift'. In *Choithram International v Pagarani* [2001] Mr Pagarani died after orally declaring the transfer of his property to a trust foundation, of which he was one of the trustees. The Privy Council found that there was sufficient oral and written evidence of his intention to make an immediate unconditional gift to the foundation. As he already had legal title and was one of the trustees, the transfer could be perfected.

Lord Browne-Wilkinson considered that the situation fell between the typical *Milroy v Lord* (1862) criteria for transferring an interest to another. It was not a gift, neither was it actually a transfer to a third party. It can only have been an intention to transfer the property on trust. As the settlor was one of the trustees then the courts of equity could require the executors to transfer the interest to the trust foundation.

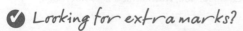 **Looking for extra marks?**

This area is one where there has been much academic criticism. Consider if the ownership by one trustee should automatically provide for a transfer to the other trustees. See key debates below.

Equitable principles which perfect a transfer

****

However, this decision has been used as a basis to extend the equitable jurisdiction of the principles from *Re Rose* [1952] considerably by Arden LJ in *Pennington v Waine* [2002]. The owner of shares wanted to transfer them to her nephew. The relevant forms were completed but not registered, being on file at her solicitors. Her nephew took on some responsibility for the running of the company, which the transfer gave him. All parties acted as if he had the shares. On her death the court were asked to perfect the transfer.

It appears from the decision in *Pennington v Waine* [2002] that where:

* there has been a promise to transfer property to a transferee,
* the transferee has then acted, in relation to that property, as if it had been transferred to the transferee, and
* it is unconscionable to rely on the strict rule of law to deny the transferee the promised property,

then the courts will require that the property be validly transferred.

Arden LJ in a comprehensive judgment reviews the history of the law on perfecting legal title. She felt unconstrained by the decisions in *Re Rose* [1952] and relied on the comments by Lord Browne-Wilkinson as providing the authority to perfect the transfer where it would be unconscionable for the transferor to recall the gift; however the decision is not without criticism.

✅ *Looking for extra marks?*

A *common mistake* is for students to see the principle of *Pennington v Waine* [2002] as the remedy for all failure in vesting. On the facts of the case there was a catalogue of relationships which Arden LJ felt created the relevant equity. Equity is not about doing what may appear morally right regardless of principle. Equity develops on clear principles and will, unless equity demands otherwise, 'follow the law'. After all, remember *Jones v Lock* (1865): the father had promised in front of witnesses that the cheque was for the child and yet the child was denied the property. It is suggested that this decision may be restricted on its facts.

Estoppel

Estoppel is the equitable principle which enforces promises which are unsupported by valuable consideration. Proprietary estoppel, unlike promissory estoppel, can form the basis of a claim (*Pascoe v Turner* [1979]), so it can act as a sword, not only a shield. The requirements are that:

* there be a clear promise, this can be by acquiescence; *Ramsden v Dyson* (1866);
* there be reliance; and
* it be inequitable not to enforce the assurance.

Promise

The promise must be unequivocal, which means that the courts must be able to identify the property over which the equity arises. In *Yeoman's Row v Cobbe* (2008) the House of Lords held that in the commercial agreement the promise in a 'gentleman's agreement' meant that there was no property over which the estoppel could be raised. The situation may be different if there had been an enforceable contract.

Reliance

The burden is on the claimant to prove a causal link between the assurance and the act in reliance. In *Gillett v Holt* [2001] the claimant had worked for the defendant since he was 16. The claimant had rejected opportunities to work elsewhere and better himself on assurances by the defendant that he would leave the farm to the claimant. Over 40 years later they fell out and the defendant made a new will leaving the farm to another. The claimant had relied on the assurances.

However, in *Coombes v Smith* [1986] the claimant moved into a house owned by Smith when she became pregnant by Smith, leaving behind an unhappy marriage. The court held that both these acts were not in reliance of any assurance by Smith but the actions of a woman in love with a man and unhappy in her marriage.

This case illustrates the need for reliance but has been criticized in its narrow view on Coombes' motives.

If a promise and reliance can be proven then evidentially the courts can find the necessary basis on which to raise a remedy in equity. Reliance can be a variety of actions and is for the court to apply the minimum equity to do justice. Figure 4.3 shows some examples where the courts have found sufficient equity.

Figure 4.3

Detriment or change of position	Authority
Improvements to land	*Pascoe v Turner* [1979] – decoration and repairs *Matharu v Matharu* [1994] – installing new kitchen *Gillett v Holt* [2001] – substantial improvements
Working for low pay	*Wayling v Jones* [1995] – working in café for partner on promise of having property left to them by will *Gillett v Holt* [2001] – worked for 40 years on low wages
Personal disadvantage	*Greasley v Cooke* [1980] – caring for the family *Re Basham* [1986] – not buying own property, or leaving employment to live nearby *Gillett v Holt* [2001] – not taking employment elsewhere

Conclusion
✳✳✳✳✳✳✳✳✳✳

Illustrative cases

Remedies on finding an estoppel will be the 'minimum equity to do justice'. This is an unclear situation, based on the extent of reliance, how much detriment has been suffered, etc. This can range from an absolute transfer to the promisee in *Thorner v Major* [2009], a licence to remain on the property in *Greasley v Cooke* [1980], or merely financial compensation in *Jennings v Rice* [2002].

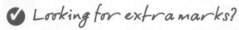 Looking for extra marks?

In addressing a possible estoppel argument it may be better, in the light of the criticisms of *Pennington v Waine* [2002], to demonstrate your knowledge of both the unconscionability argument and estoppel by moving from a claim on general unconscionability, with its ill-defined application, to one based upon estoppel. They share the principles of unconscionability but estoppel has a better pedigree and clearer principles on which to base the advice.

In another direction it would be worth reading the judgment of Lord Scott in *Thorner v Major* [2009] where he felt that the remedy would be better as a remedial constructive trust. In chapter 9 the issue of constructive trusts is discussed in more detail.

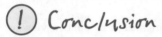 Conclusion

The law requires evidential certainty in relation to the transfer of ownership. Many of the rules set out in this chapter are there to satisfy this evidential burden. The first step in addressing this issue is to establish the legal rules in relation to all property. However, sometimes the legal rules have not been complied with and this failure will cause some injustice. The application of the legal rules in this situation can be particularly harsh. The intervention of equity to remedy the harshness of the legal rules is based on clear principles and clear criteria. It is sometimes assumed by students that equity is merely to achieve some general concept of 'justice'. This is too wide a view of the aims of equity and the principles on when equity will intervene with the legal rules are relatively certain. In an answer plan, you should be able to identify the legal rules and any (there may be more than one) equitable interventions.

 Key cases

Case	Facts	Principle
Cain v Moon [1896] 2 QB 283	The daughter gave her mother a deposit note worth £50. Contradictory evidence suggested that it had been a gift for the mother's care for the daughter during an illness. But later the daughter said 'Have you got the deposit note safe? Never part with it. The bank-note is for you if I die.'	For a valid DMC there should be three elements, a transfer in: 1. contemplation of imminent death 2. conditional on death 3. delivery.

Case	Facts	Principle
Choithram International v Pagarani [2001] 1 WLR 1	The transferor set up a trust foundation, of which he was one of the trustees. He made an oral declaration that he intended the bulk of his remaining wealth to the trust foundation. There was both oral and written evidence of the intention to transfer the property to the trust foundation companies. Mr Pagarani died before title was transferred to the trust foundation. Mr Pagarani was one of the trustees of the foundation.	Privy Council said that as he intended to make an immediate unconditional gift to the foundation, as he was one of the trustees of the foundation, as such he had legal title in the property, that although the court will not perfect an imperfect gift, neither will it 'strive officiously' to deny the intention of the transferor. The legal title in the property would be transferred to the trust foundation. (See key debates below.)
Gillett v Holt [2001] 1 Ch 210	Claimant had worked for the defendant since he was 16. The claimant had rejected opportunities to work elsewhere and better himself on assurances by the defendant that he would leave the farm to the claimant. Over 40 years later they fell out and the defendant made a new will leaving the farm to another.	Where there was a clear unequivocal promise, express or by acquiescence by the transferor; followed by reliance by the transferee; which meant it was inequitable to allow the transferor to go back on the promise, then the court would do the minimum equity to do justice. The facts had created an estoppel for the claimant, which in proprietary estoppel can found a cause of action (ie be a sword).
Jones v Lock (1865) 1 Ch App 25	A father had wanted to transfer the interest in a cheque made out to the father, to his infant son. He had made an oral declaration to that effect but had failed to endorse the cheque.	The transfer as a gift had failed as it required endorsement and the court would not create a trust out of an imperfect gift.
Milroy v Lord (1862) 2 DE G F & J 264	An attempt to transfer property to be held on trust. Although the transferor had made the transfer by deed and delivered them to the respondent, the failure of the transfer to be registered in the bank's books meant that the transfer was imperfect.	Where the transfer has failed because the transferor has failed to do all they could to perfect title the courts will not complete the transferor's actions.
Pennington v Waine [2002] 1 WLR 2075	The owner of shares wanted to transfer them to her nephew. The relevant forms were completed but not registered, being on file at her solicitors. Her nephew took on some responsibility for the running of the company, which the transfer gave him. All parties acted as if he had the shares. On her death the court were asked to perfect the transfer.	Based on principles of unconscionability the court would perfect the transfer to the nephew. (See key debates below.)

Key cases

✳✳✳✳✳✳✳✳✳✳✳✳

Case	Facts	Principle
Re Cole [1964] Ch 175	Husband took wife through home and said 'look it is all yours'. On his bankruptcy she claimed legal ownership of the furniture.	A transfer of chattels not by deed requires a delivery of the chattel with unequivocal words of transfer to be valid.
Re Fry [1946] Ch 312	The transferor wanted to transfer share but to do this he needed permission from the Treasury. He had not obtained this.	The transferor had not done all that was required of him to make good the transfer. Equity would not perfect the transaction.
Re Gonin [1977] 2 All ER 720	A mother had promised her daughter that she would have her house. But the mother believed that she would not be able to leave the house to the daughter, as she was illegitimate. She then wrote a cheque to her daughter.	The writing of the cheque was evidence that the intention did not remain unchanged until death.
Re Rose [1952] 1 All ER 1217	Rose transferred shares to wife and trustees on 30 March. To complete the transfer it had to be registered with the company; they were registered on 30 June.	Where the transferor has done all in his power to make the transfer, and the only fault is a third party inaction, of whom the transferor has no control, then equity will perfect the transfer.
Richards v Delridge (1874) LR 1 HL Eq 11	A grandfather wanted his leasehold interest in land to be held for the benefit of his grandson. He assigned the lease to the boy's mother but did not make the transfer by deed which is required under s 52 Law of Property Act 1925	Failure to complete the necessary legal requirements will mean the transfer fails.
Sen v Headley [1991] 2 All ER 636	The transferor was terminally ill with cancer; he told the transferee, with whom he had had a long-term close relationship, that he wanted her to have his house, saying 'you have the keys. They are in your bag. The deeds are in the steel box'.	Confirming that land could be the subject of a DMC, the Court of Appeal confirmed the decision in *Cain v Moon* that a valid DMC required transfers made: 1. in contemplation of death 2. conditional on death 3. with actual or some indicia of the transferor giving 'dominion' (control) of the property to the transferee (sometimes this is called symbolic delivery).
Strong v Bird (1874) LR 18 Eq 315	A promise to forgo the payment of a debt (unenforceable at law for want of consideration). The promisee was appointed as the executor of the will of the promisor.	Where there has been a failure of the legal requirements of a valid transfer but the transferee in appointed as executor or administrator of the transferor's estate, then equity will perfect if there has been a continuing intention to give during the transferor's lifetime.

Case	Facts	Principle
Thorner v Major [2009] UKHL 18	A young farmer, David, worked for an elderly relative, Peter, for many years on a farm. There were several comments by Peter that David would inherit the farm. The statements were vague and imprecise. Peter was a 'man of few words' and little formal education. Peter died intestate and David claimed the estate were estopped from denying him an interest in the farm.	Although the extent of the farm was imprecise the property itself (the farm) was clear. Although the evidence was imprecise as to the assurance it was clear on the first instance evidence that David and Peter had proceeded on the understanding the David would inherit the farm. The estate were estopped from denying this. Per Lord Scott the decision is better decided as one of remedial constructive trust rather than estoppel as the property was of a future interest under a will rather than a present property.
Yeoman's Row Management Ltd v Cobbe [2008] UKHL 55	A property owner entered into a 'gentleman's agreement' to sell property to Cobbe when he had obtained planning permission, sharing the proceeds by an agreement they would draw up legally at a later date. After expending a great deal of money on the planning application the property owner refused to complete the agreement. Cobbe claimed they were estopped from doing this.	There was no clear property over which the estoppel could be raised. The agreement was not a valid contract, which could form the basis of an estoppel. Both were commercially experienced people who took the risks in the 'gentleman's agreement'.

⑼⁾ Key debates

Topic	Unconscionability
Academic/ Author	Pearce and Stevens
Viewpoint	The decisions in *Choithram* and *Pennington v Waine* are problematic. While the decision in *Choithram* may be based on a valid development of equity acting on the conscience of the parties and on the particular facts justified, it is suggested that the decision in *Pennington v Waine* has strayed too far. There is a lack of guidance on what makes a transaction unconscionable from Arden LJ and it has left the principle of *Re Rose* uncertain.
Source	Pearce and Stevens, *The Law of Trusts and Equitable Obligations*, 4th edn (2006) comments on pp 177–8 on the decision, offering a good, concise criticism of the decision.

Exam questions

✱✱✱✱✱✱✱✱✱✱

Topic	Proprietary estoppel
Academic/ Author	Andrew Robertson
Viewpoint	A review of the reliance issues in finding an adequate remedy in estoppel cases.
Source	[2008] Conv 295.

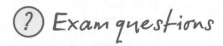 Exam questions

Problem question

Charles says to his brother James 'you can have my shares in DDD Ltd'. Before Charles has time to transfer title in the shares to James he dies and James has been appointed as executor of Charles' will.

Sumita has been run over by a car and is seriously ill. She has been told that she will die soon. Her friend Ellie comes to visit her and Sumita says 'I think I am going to die, I want you to have my car. Here are the keys and registration documents'. Sumita then dies.

Advise James on who owns the property.

An outline answer is included at the end of the book.

Essay question

The decision in *Pennington v Waine* has introduced a much needed degree of flexibility in the strict rules on transfer of legal interests. Giving effect to the intention of the settlor should be the primary concern of the courts. Discuss.

An outline answer is available online at www.oxfordtextbooks.co.uk/orc/concentrate/

#5
Formalities

- There are rules in relation to the creation of an express trust over property.

- A trust can be created *inter vivos* (during the settlor's life) or by will.

- There are different rules in relation to trusts over an interest in land and property other than land.

- It is important to remember that when creating an express trust, the settlor must satisfy the formalities required for both the transfer of the legal interest in property and the creation of the trust itself.

- There are different rules for the creation of an express trust and the transfer of the legal interest in property.

- There are formalities in transferring an equitable interest in *any* property.

Revision tip

This is a complex area of law and commonly examined, especially with the issues raised in chapter 4. It is possible to do very well in this topic if you understand these issues.

However, be cautious, as it is also easy to do *very* badly if you do not understand the link between formalities and constitution. Ensure that you understand the previous chapter which is dealing with how the ownership of property is transferred (constitution). This chapter will deal with how a trust is created in property, creating an equitable interest.

Introduction

This chapter discusses the formalities necessary to create a testamentary (made by a will) and an *inter vivos* trust and the formalities regulating the transfer of an existing equitable interest. There are different formalities in relation to the *creation* of trust dependent on the type of property which is subject to the trust. The main formalities considered in this chapter are set out in **s 53 Law of Property Act 1925 (LPA)** which is discussed in detail below. There are three types of trusts of property that will be relevant to this chapter:

- trusts of property other than land, including trusts of personal property;
- trusts of land or an interest in land; and
- dispositions of an equitable interest.

The need for formalities

One of the purposes of formalities is to create certainty of transactions and prevent fraud. It needs to be clear from the outset who has the benefit of an equitable interest. The certainty created by the formalities has advantages for several parties.

For the trustee

A trustee will need to be certain who the beneficiaries are; the trustees have duties and powers in relation to the trust property. If these powers and duties are performed incorrectly then the trustee may be held personally liable for any breaches.

For the beneficiary

Additionally, the beneficiary must be certain as to their actual interest in property. This will prevent fraud by the trustee. The clearer the allocation of property rights the easier for the trustee, the beneficiary, and ultimately the court to allocate the correct interest to the parties.

For the courts

In certain circumstances the courts may need to intervene with the trust, such as in its variation or exercise of powers. The court will need to ensure they act correctly in relation to competing interests.

For Revenue & Customs

A further purpose of the formalities is to be clear who has the benefit of property for the purposes of tax. The trustee will hold the legal title and would appear to be the person who should pay tax on any income that it produces. The Revenue & Customs will seek to recover tax which is due, hence why so many cases involve the HM Revenue & Customs Commission (HMRC, formerly the IRC).

Testamentary trusts

Many trusts are created by will. A requirement of all wills is that they must comply with the requirements of the Wills Act 1837 to be valid. Section 9 states that it must be:

- in writing;
- signed by the testator, or someone acting at his direction in his presence; and
- in the presence of two witnesses who sign and attest the will in the testator's presence.

The reasons for these requirements are evidential and to prevent fraud or coercion. All testamentary documents must comply with this, so any amendments made by **codicil** must also comply with these requirements. These requirements will satisfy any need for the evidence of transfer of equitable interests or the creation of trusts. The main purpose of s 53 Law of Property Act 1925 is evidential so the Wills Act 1837 requirements satisfy this.

Creation of an *inter vivos* trust in property other than land

The creation of trusts of an interest in property other than land requires no formalities, other than the three certainties, for the *creation* of a trust. This will apply to such property as shares, money, paintings, etc. The most important thing that must be established is the certainty of intention to create a trust. Remember that this is a question of fact which must be established on a case-by-case basis. The certainty of intention can be demonstrated by words, written statements, or by conduct; *Paul v Constance* (1977). In establishing certainty of intention, the court will take the whole situation into account.

However, where the courts fail to find the sufficient certainty required for trusts (see chapter 3) they will not impose a trust to achieve justice; *Jones v Locke* (1865). This is a clear example of the maxims that 'equity will not perfect an imperfect gift' and 'equity will not assist a volunteer'.

Remember that creating a trust is a 'cruel kindness' as it creates such onerous obligations for the trustee. The courts are happy to create a trust on informal statements but they must be clear that this is the true intention of the settlor.

Creation of an *inter vivos* trust of an interest in land

An express trust of an interest in land can be declared orally or in writing, but until it is in writing it is unenforceable. The statutory requirements for creating such a trust in land or interest in land are set out in **s 53(1)(b) Law of Property Act 1925**:

> A declaration of trusts respecting land or any interest therein must be **manifested** and proved by some writing signed by some person who is able to declare such trust or by his will.

So two formalities must be satisfied:

- there must be evidence of the trust in writing; and
- the evidence must have been signed by the settlor.

Interests affected

This rule applies to freehold, leasehold, and equitable interests in land (see below).

Note: s 53(1)(b) deals only with the *creation* of a trust over an interest in land. It does *not* deal with the transfer of legal title in land, nor does it deal with the creation of a trust in anything but an interest in land.

Evidenced in writing

While a valid trust will come into existence from the moment it is declared, until the requirements of s 53(1)(b) are satisfied the trust will not be enforceable. It is valid at the *moment* that it is declared with sufficient certainty, which can have important tax implications for the settlor and the beneficial claimant. It also means that should the trustee exercise his powers under the trust he will not be in breach. Although it is valid, it is unenforceable; the beneficiary cannot enforce the trust, for example they could not use their powers to vary a trust. The evidence, when it is written, must contain all the relevant terms of the trust, ie the three certainties.

The writing required by s 53(1)(b) does *not* need to be in the form of a *deed*. Written evidence signed by the settlor will suffice. This can be a letter or other informal document. Written and signed evidence of the trust can be provided at a later date; *Gardener v Rowe* (1828). In this situation there is a gap between validity and enforceability.

Signed by the settlor

Unlike s 53(1)(c) (see below), the written evidence must be signed by the settlor; it cannot be signed by an agent. This is a matter of construction of s 53(1)(b) read with s 53(1)(c), which specifically states that an agent can sign the written evidence, whereas s 53(1)(b) states it must be a person 'who is able to declare such a trust or by his will'.

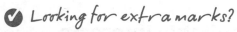 *Looking for extra marks?*

Examiners may have the intention to create a trust communicated by email or perhaps text. This is to stimulate a discussion on the need to have the declaration signed. There is no need to conclude on this but make a reasonable argument on *if* it would satisfy the requirement. Perhaps compare with the principle of e-conveyancing in land.

Revision tip

In dealing with an exam question in this area remember to keep the legal transactions explained in the last chapter separate from the equitable formalities. Figure 5.1 may help your understanding of this.

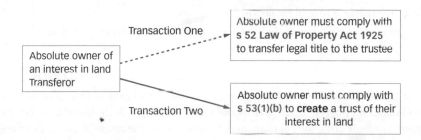

Figure 5.1

However, where a settlor declares herself trustee of her interest in land for a beneficiary, remember that the settlor will only have to declare the trust of land and complete the required formalities of s 53(1)(b) as the settlor as trustee already has her legal title to the land (See chapter 4 on constitution to remind yourself of these issues.)

Avoiding the formalities of s 53(1)(b)

Formalities play an important role in tracking the correct ownership of property. For that reason, the courts are extremely reluctant to allow the required formalities to be avoided. However, the case of *Rochefoucauld v Boustead* [1897] provides an exception to the rule that writing formalities must be completed. If the settlor has transferred legal title to a trustee effectively, intending that it be held on trust but has failed to evidence this in writing, then the courts will usually not consider the trust to be enforceable.

If the result of this would be to allow the relevant statute to be used as an instrument of fraud, then the court may accept oral evidence as proof of the transaction. 'Equity will not permit a statute to be used as an instrument of fraud' and it is commonly thought that the unenforceable trust is given validity by means of a constructive trust, imposed against the conscience of the person trying to misuse the relevant statutory provisions for their own fraudulent ends.

Dealing with existing equitable interests

The first point to remember is that an equitable property interest is property in the same way as land is. It is intangible, forming a **chose in action**, but nevertheless capable of being treated in the same manner as all property. It can be mortgaged, sold, and transferred. If you bear this in mind, you will be able to grasp this topic more easily.

Timpson's Executors v Yerbury [1936] identified four ways to benefit another person with a beneficial interest:

1. Directly assign to a third party.

2. Contract for valuable consideration to assign to another.

3. Direct the trustees to hold for another.

4. Declare that the interest is held by the beneficial owner on trust for another.

Direct assignment of equitable interest to a third party

Section 136 Law of Property Act 1925 allows for the direct assignment of a chose in action, which can include an interest under a trust; *Re Pain* [1919]. The assignment must be of the whole interest and not just a part of the beneficial interest. For example, if you have an absolute equitable interest in property you cannot directly assign the **life interest** but retain the **remainder interest**.

✅ *Looking for extra marks?*

The application of s 136 LPA 1925 to an interest under a trust has been doubted. See Snell's *Principles of Equity*, 31st edn (Sweet & Maxwell). In developing an argument on this issue read what is said on this matter.

The formalities for a direct assignment are:

*   the assignment must be in writing;

*   it should be signed by the assignor; and

*   express notice should be given to the trustee of the assignment.

If the formalities are not complied with there may still be an assignment in equity which needs no particular formalities; *William Brandts' Sons & Co v Dunlop Rubber Co* [1905]. An assignment in equity requires:

- a clear intention to assign, manifested by words or conduct;
- a clear transfer of the interest from the assignor to the assignee; and
- the interest transferred must be clearly identifiable.

There is no need to notify the trustee of the transfer. However, if notice is given to the trustee then the assignee is protected from third party claims and fraudulent receipt by the assignor; *Kekewich v Manning* (1851).

Contract for valuable consideration to assign to another

Where there has been a valid contract to **assign** an equitable interest the contract may be capable of specific performance (see chapter 13 on equitable remedies). For such a transfer there must be a valid contract; note that, for equity, marriage will be valid consideration; *Pullan v Koe* (1913). Then it may be possible that such a disposition need not be in writing. The argument is based upon the application of s 53(2) which states that implied trusts do not need to comply with the requirements in s 53(1).

Implied trusts are considered in detail in chapter 9. One type of implied trust is a constructive trust. This is a trust that is 'constructed' around property when the courts believe that it would be unconscionable to deny an interest in property to a person who does not have legal title. In a contract, which is specifically enforceable – note that *not all* contracts are specifically enforceable – then the parties, consciences are affected by the contract. 'Equity looks upon as done that which ought to be done' and the courts may force perfection of title.

✅ *Looking for extra marks?*

In *Oughtred v IRC* [1960] Upjohn J at first instance and Lord Radcliffe in the House of Lords considered that the benefit of the contract, a chose in action, was held by the legal owner for the benefit of the person who had provided valuable consideration. The Court of Appeal in *Neville v Wilson* [1997] endorsed this view. This is an area of academic debate as the House of Lords majority should be binding on the lower courts, and therefore a popular topic for exams.

Direct trustee to hold the beneficial interest for another

The beneficial owner of property may direct the trustee to hold that beneficial interest for another person. The legal requirements to transfer a beneficial interest to another are set out in s 53(1)(c) Law of Property Act 1925:

> a **disposition** of an equitable interest or trust subsisting at the time of the disposition must be in writing signed by the person disposing of the same or by his agent thereunto lawfully authorised in writing or by will.

This applies to *any* type of property held beneficially *not* just interests in land.

Dealing with existing equitable interests

****

- The wording of the section refers to **subsisting** equitable interests at the time of the disposition. This means that it applies *not* to the creation of a trust but where one is in existence (subsisting) and a person wants to transfer that benefit to another.

- The transfer must be *in writing* which means that it is not a valid disposition unless it is in writing *Grey v IRC* [1960].

- The transfer may be signed by the person making the transfer *or* by a person who is lawfully authorized to do so. This may be the agent of the equitable owner.

The examples below may help set the scene.

Example 1

Johan declares that he will hold his shares in DDD Ltd on trust for his nephew Hendrick.

- No need to comply with s 53(1)(c) as this is an original declaration of trust.

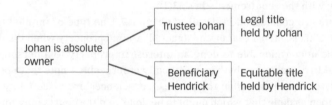

Figure 5.2

Example 2

Hendrick, who now owns the beneficial interest in the shares, asks his trustee, Johan, to hold his beneficial interest in DDD Ltd for the benefit of his wife Precious. He later writes a memorandum to confirm the transfer.

- He must comply with s 53(1)(c) as he only holds the beneficial interest, which is subsisting at the time he intends to give the interest away (a disposition) to Precious. The legal title remains with the trustee.

- The transfer is void until it is actually in writing. A claim that the writing is evidence of a previous oral disposition is invalid. As the transfer is void *ab initio*, you cannot have written evidence of a non-existent transfer. The transfer is said to be void for want of writing; *Grey v IRC* [1960].

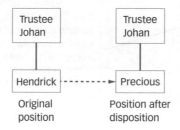

Figure 5.3

The Vandervell exception to section 53(1)(c)

The requirements of s 53(1)(c) are to ensure that the ownership of beneficial interest can be clearly identified by the trustee, beneficiary, the courts, and the Inland Revenue; *Grey v IRC* [1960]. Before going on to see how the *Vandervell (No 1)* exception operates it is important to remember the following principle. A beneficiary who is absolutely entitled and competent can ask that the legal title to the trust property is transferred to them so that they become the absolute owner, this is the rule from *Saunders v Vautier* (1841).

Figure 5.4 shows how the sequence of events would occur.

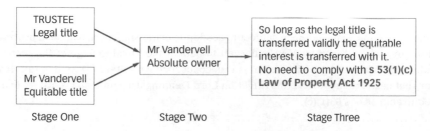

Figure 5.4

Once the title is held absolutely, at Stage Two, then the owner only has to comply with the legal requirements to transfer the legal title. Understanding this will make the principle in *Vandervell v IRC (No 1)* easier to understand.

Where a beneficial owner who is *absolutely* entitled and *competent (sui juris)* makes an *oral declaration* to the trustee that the trustee transfer *the legal title to a third party, intending that at the same time the beneficial title shall transfer to the same third party* then there is no need to comply with s 53(1)(c).

Dealing with existing equitable interests

✶✶✶✶✶✶✶✶✶✶✶✶

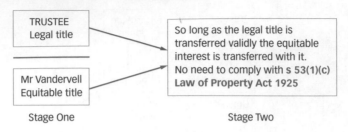

Stage One   Stage Two

Figure 5.5

Looking at Figure 5.5 you can see that it simply removes the *Saunders v Vautier* (1841) step and can be justified on that basis.

> ### Revision tip
> Examiners often use words that are ambiguous, such as 'give', 'transfer', 'convey'. This is because they want students to consider *if Vandervell* applies.

Formalities are required to protect the trustee from any claim for breach of duty. This exception can be justified as the trustee, in transferring the legal title to another person, has no further obligations to the beneficiary.

Vandervell v IRC (No 2) [1974]

This case is complex and has been subject to academic criticism. There had been protracted litigation over the attempt by Mr Vandervell to benefit the Royal College of Surgeons and his children's trust settlement. Much of it was concerned with Stamp Duty and tax. It may appear that in an attempt to end this litigation Lord Denning used judicial creativity to avoid the requirements of s 53(1)(c).

....

Vandervell v IRC (No 2) [1974] Ch 269

On the advice of his accountant when he had transferred the shares to the Royal College of Surgeons an option to repurchase was granted to a trust company. At the time, Mr Vandervell had failed to specify the objects of the trust and therefore it was held on resulting trust for Mr Vandervell.

The option was then exercised and declared to be held for the benefit of the children's settlement. The Court of Appeal held that when the option was exercised the resulting trust of that property ceased to exist. Therefore the property now held for the children was a new trust which required no formalities.

....

The Court of Appeal made a distinction between the option as one form of property which when exercised had ceased to exist. So when the benefit created by exercising the option was declared to be held on trust for the children this was a completely *new* trust. It was not a 'disposition of a *subsisting* equitable interest'. It was in fact a declaration of trust in shares and required no formalities.

Declare that the interest is held by the beneficial owner on trust for another

As with all property, an equitable interest can be held on trust. It can be argued that this is not a disposition but merely a declaration of trust, creating a sub-trust.

Example 1

Anne is the beneficial owner of a bank account at Bigs Banks plc. Herbert is the trustee of the account. Anne wants her son, Luke, to benefit from the account and she states to Herbert that she now holds the interest on a discretionary trust for Luke.

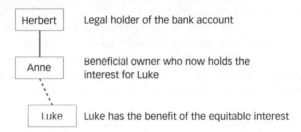

Herbert	Legal holder of the bank account
Anne	Beneficial owner who now holds the interest for Luke
Luke	Luke has the benefit of the equitable interest

Figure 5.6

When dealing with a sub-trust it is important to identify what property is being held on trust because if the equitable interest is in land then, as it is the creation of a new (sub) trust in land or an interest in land, it must also comply with the requirements of s 53(1)(b).

It is a question if the beneficial owner who declares a sub-trust is 'dispossessing' themselves of an equitable interest. One argument is that they are not dispossessing themselves as they are merely holding the interest on trust.

Example 2a

Rishi is the beneficial owner under a bare trust of a house called 'Gills Farm'.

| T | Trustee holds the legal title for benefit of R |
| R | R holds the beneficial interest |

Figure 5.7

Dealing with existing equitable interests

****

This is the starting position, with trustee holding for Rishi. He wants to give this interest to his son, John. He writes to John telling him of his intention.

```
    T     Trustee holds the legal title for benefit of J
    ----
    J     J now holds the beneficial interest
```

Figure 5.8

This would be the classic situation where Rishi is giving away (dispossessing himself of) his equitable interest and as such he must comply with s 53(1)(c).This is the normal trust position students are familiar with but there are also situations where the beneficiary does not intend that the beneficial interest should be given to another but that they intend to hold this interest for the benefit of another person.

Example 2b

Rishi is the beneficial owner under a bare trust of a house called 'Gills Farm'. He wants to hold this interest on trust for his son, John.

In this situation (see Figure 5.9) it appears that Rishi has not dispossessed himself of his interest; he has merely decided to hold this property on trust for another person. In this situation there is a sub-trust created. If this is the situation on a literal reading of the statute, as there is no 'disposition' then there should be no requirement that Rishi comply with s 53(1)(c). However, this seems contrary to the intention of the statute, which is to prevent fraud and allow the trustee to know to whom he owes an obligation. In fact it appears that in creating the sub-trust above, Rishi *effectively* disposes of his interest as he can no longer exert any real control over the trust property other than to hold it for John in exactly the same way as the trustee held it for him. In fact it is John who has the power to decide how the property should be treated.

```
  Head     T     Trustee holds the legal title for benefit of R
           ----
  Trust    R     R holds the beneficial interest
  _____

                 Rishi wants his whole interest to be held for the
  Sub      R     benefit of John
           ----
  Trust    J     John receives the exact interest that R had
```

Figure 5.9

Implications

If the property produces an income then the trustee would have paid this money to the benefit of Rishi. Now the trustee would be required to pay the money to the benefit of John. He may do this by paying it to Rishi who then pays it to John but this is merely a procedural step, it is John who is the real beneficiary of the trust.

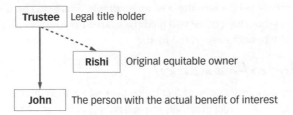

Figure 5.10

This situation illustrates the reason that formalities are required: if the trustee pays the money to Rishi when in reality the benefit belongs to John then the trustee may be in breach, risking the possibility that they may be personally liable for any losses which John suffers as a result. Remember, one of the purposes of formalities is to enable the trustee to be sure to whom they owe a duty.

In this situation it in fact appears that Rishi has disposed of his equitable interest and therefore must comply with s 53(1)(c); *Grainge v Wilberforce* (1889). The reason for this is well explained by Upjohn LJ in *Grey v IRC* [1958] where he said that the original beneficiary (Rishi in our example) would effectively 'disappear from the picture'. The court should look at the substance of the transaction and in all equity the certainty required by the trustee to carry out their duties.

However, an alternative argument is that there is no need to comply with s 53(1)(c) when the beneficial owner retains some control of the beneficial interest.

Example 3

Annabel is the beneficial owner under a bare trust of shares. She wants to hold this benefit for her nieces and nephews. However, as Annabel is unsure which of them she wants to help, she would like to hold the equitable interest in the shares on a discretionary trust.

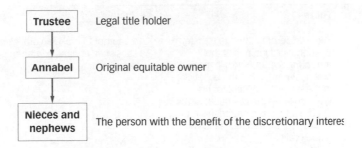

Figure 5.11

In this situation Annabel has not 'disappeared from the picture' as she retains power over the property. In this situation the reasoning by Chitty J in *Grainge v Wilberforce* (1889) and comments by Upjohn LJ in *Grey v IRC* [1958] would suggest that there is no need to comply with s 53(1)(c) as this is not a disposition of an equitable interest. The distinction from the previous examples is that the trustee will hold the shares for Annabel and she still exercises some control over the benefits generated by it.

 **Looking for extra marks?**

In our example, as the property that is subject to the trust is land then this should also comply with s 53(1)(b) as Rishi is creating a trust of an 'interest in land', his equitable interest, which will be valid but unenforceable until it is done.

Good students will note that if we assume that Rishi has stated all the terms of the trust in his letter and has signed it, the requirement of s 53(1)(c) *and* s 53(1)(b) will by default be satisfied. *Although note that* s 53(1)(b) requires that the person creating the trust sign the document and no reference is made to any other authorized person. So if it is signed by an agent it will not comply with s 53(1)(b).

 **Conclusion**

This chapter has considered the formalities which are required to create a trust in property, any property, including an equitable interest. Additionally there are formalities for the transfer of beneficial interests. The purposes of these formalities are evidential. The requirements of a trust in land or an interest in land are particularly stringent, which reflects the importance the law places on land transactions. This chapter should be read with the preceding chapter on constitution. Also in relation to a trust of personalty, remember that there is a close link with the requirements of certainty of intention.

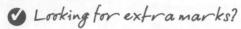 **Key cases**

Case	Facts	Principle
Grey v IRC [1960] AC 1 HL	The transferor wanted to transfer the beneficial interest without attracting Stamp Duty. He made an oral declaration that the beneficial interest was to be held for his grandchildren. He claimed that the documents which stated this merely confirmed the transfer, which he made orally.	An attempt to make an oral disposition of a subsisting equitable interest is void for want of writing.

Case	Facts	Principle
Jones v Locke (1865) LR 1 Ch App 25	A gentleman returned home from a trip and being chastised by his wife for bringing no gift for their new son took a cheque from his pocket. The cheque was made out to the father and he said 'look here it is all for baby'. The father died before he could transfer legal title to the baby.	That this was not a valid declaration of trust as there was insufficient certainty of intention. They will not create a valid trust out of an imperfect gift.
Oughtred v IRC [1960] AC 206 HL	Mrs O had the life interest in shares, then to her son P. She was also the absolute beneficiary of shares. To avoid death duties P and O agreed to exchange their interests. This was later evidenced in writing.	The House of Lords by a 3:2 majority did not uphold this argument. Viscount Radcliffe for the minority held that the exchange happened orally, there was no need for any written evidence. The interest was held on constructive trust, and under s 53(2) Law of Property Act 1925 it was outside the scope of s 53(1). The minority view has, however, found favour in the Court of Appeal in such cases as *Neville v Wilson* [1996].
Rochefoucauld v Boustead [1897] 1 Ch 196	The Comtesse de la Rochefoucauld owned land in Ceylon which she transferred to the defendant intending that he hold on trust for her benefit. This intention was not evidenced in writing. He mortgaged the land and she sought a declaration that he held on trust for her.	Court of Appeal held that evidence other than writing could be admitted otherwise the instrument (at that time the Statute of Frauds) could be used as an instrument of fraud.
Vandervell v IRC [1967] 1 All ER 1	Mr V was the beneficiary under a bare trust of shares. He wanted to endow the Royal College of Surgeons with the shares. He directed that the shares be transferred to the Royal College of Surgeons. At the same time an option to purchase the shares was granted to a trust company. At the point of creation the objects of the trust of the option were unspecified.	Where an equitable owner, absolutely entitled and capable of doing so, makes an oral declaration to the trustee to transfer legal title to a transferee, intending at the same time that the equitable title be transferred to the same transferee, then there is no need to comply with s 53(1)(c) Law of Property Act 1925. Failure to specify the objects of the trust of the option meant that the trust company held on resulting trust for Mr V.

Key debates

****

Case	Facts	Principle
Vandervell v IRC (No 2) [1974] 3 All ER 205	The option was held for Mr V on resulting trust. It was exercised in 1961 in favour of his children's settlement. Between 1961 and 1965 dividends were declared for the benefit of the children's trust. At Mr V's death in 1967 his executors claimed that the dividends should have been held on resulting trust for Mr V and should not have been paid to the children's settlement.	The exercise of the option had ended the resulting trust of the option and a new trust had been created of the shares for the benefit of the children. A creation of a trust of shares required no formalities. Per Denning MR and Lawton LJ, in any event Mr V would have been estopped from denying the children's claim for the benefit: 1. their money had been used to exercise the option; 2. V had approved the paying of the dividends to the settlement.

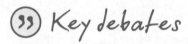 *Key debates*

Topic	The decision in *Rochefoucauld v Boustead* (1897)
Academic/ Author	Pearce and Stevens
Viewpoint	The authors refer to several views. The rule allows other evidence to be used despite the clear words of the statute. Would this still be valid in light of the updating of the principle in the Law of Property Act in 1925. Is it better to see this as a constructive trust rather than an exception to the principle of s 53(1)(b).
Source	Pearce and Stevens, 4th edn, pp 196–7.
Topic	**The constructive trust created around a valid contract to assign a beneficial interest**
Academic/ Author	Pearce and Stevens
Viewpoint	The authors refer to several views. The majority of the House of Lords felt that a constructive trust did not arise and the transaction was within s 53(1)(c) but only by 3:2. A strong minority was followed by the Court of Appeal in *Neville v Wilson* [1997]. What should the court do in these situations?
Source	Pearce and Stevens, 4th edn, pp 205–7.

Exam questions

Problem question

Kirsty wins the lottery and feels very generous. On 1 March, Kirsty calls George to tell him that she intends to hold her leasehold over Blackacre on trust for him.

On 31 March Kirsty writes to her friend Hari. In the letter, Kirsty explains what she has done with Blackacre. The letter is signed.

She then writes to Sanjeev asking him to be the trustee of her freehold cottage, Whiteflower, for the benefit of her friend, Hester.

Kirsty is the absolute beneficial owner of shares in Telico Ltd. She calls her trustee Jose and tells him to transfer the shares to Charlie.

Advise the parties as to the ownership of the property.

An outline answer is included at the end of the book.

Essay question

The confusion created by the decision in *Neville v Wilson* [1997] is contrary to the clear requirements of s 53(1) Law of Property Act. Discuss.

An outline answer is available online at www.oxfordtextbooks.co.uk/orc/concentrate/

#6
Charitable trusts

Key facts

- Charitable trusts differ from private trusts in a number of ways.
- A charitable trust:
    1. must be for a recognized charitable purpose;
    2. for the 'public benefit'; and
    3. for exclusively charitable purposes.
- The public benefit requirement raises different issues under each head of charity.
- The Charities Act 2006 has reformed the law in this area.
- *Cy-près* is a power which allows failing charitable trusts to be applied to other related charities.

How is a charitable trust different from other types of trust?

The beneficiaries of the trust

In a private express trust, the beneficiaries hold the equitable interest in the property and have the ability to enforce the terms of the trusts against the trustees. Whereas a private trust will benefit certain *individuals*, a charitable trust is said to benefit the *public*, or some part of it. This is significant for two reasons:

- *Enforcement of the trust*: as there are no specific named beneficiaries in a charitable trust, who can enforce the terms of the trust? In general, if there is no one to enforce a trust, it will be void (see chapter 7). However, in the case of charitable trusts, this role is ultimately performed by the **Attorney-General**.

- *Certainty of objects*: generally, all trusts must satisfy the three certainties (see chapter 3). However, charitable trusts are exempt from the certainty of objects requirement; *Morice v Bishop of Durham* (1805).

The advantages of charitable status

The work of charities is highly valued in our society and, as a result, charitable trusts are accorded a number of advantages:

- *Tax advantages*: charitable trusts are exempt from a number of taxes, including income tax, corporation tax, and capital gains tax. The rationale for this is that exemption enables charities to retain more of their assets and further their charitable work.

- *The rule against perpetuities*: in contrast to other trusts, property can be dedicated indefinitely to a charitable purpose (contrast this with the rule against inalienability in relation to private purpose trusts in chapter 7). By allowing charitable trusts to exist indefinitely, they can become better at what they do through the development of greater expertise and resources.

The role of the Charity Commission

The legal rules in relation to charitable trusts have been developed over the years primarily through the courts. However, our understanding of what is 'charitable' is constantly evolving and the courts are ill-suited to keep pace with these changes. For many years, therefore, charitable trusts have been regulated by the **Charity Commission**. As a result, the Charity Commission is constantly involved in decisions about whether a new purpose may be considered legally 'charitable'.

The Charity Commission does not create new legal rules: its decisions remain subject to the final say of the courts. However, the Charity Commission has worked carefully to recognize only those 'new' purposes which may be considered analogous to existing legal principles. While, in practice, this has led to the recognition of many more purposes than have been officially tested by the courts, the reforms contained in the **Charities Act 2006** give statutory recognition to the advances it has made.

Revision tip

The decisions and guidance of the Charity Commission are extremely useful in understanding the law. While there is no substitute for reading original case decisions, the Charity Commission website (http://www.charity-commission.gov.uk) contains useful and accessible information on what it understands the law to mean.

What are the legal requirements of a valid charitable trust?

- The trust must have a recognized charitable purpose.
- The trust must be for the 'public benefit'.
- The trust must have exclusively charitable purposes.

What are the recognized charitable purposes?

All charitable trusts must be for a recognized charitable purpose. Charitable purposes were first defined in the **Preamble to the Statute of Charitable Uses 1601**. While this Act has long since been repealed, the Preamble was for many years retained as a foundation from which the definition of charitable purposes could be extended.

The Pemsel heads of charity

The first modern statement of charitable purposes was set out in the case of *Commissioners for Special Purposes of Income Tax v Pemsel* [1891]. Lord Macnaghten identified four heads of charity:

1. The Relief of Poverty
2. The Advancement of Education
3. The Advancement of Religion
4. Other purposes beneficial to the community

These headings operated as general groupings, within which a wide variety of different activities could take place. 'Other purposes beneficial to the community' included analogous charitable purposes which did not fit easily into the other headings, eg:

What are the legal requirements of a valid charitable trust?

✳✳✳✳✳✳✳✳✳✳✳

Scottish Burial Reform and Cremation Society Ltd v Glasgow Corpn [1968] AC 138

A trust supporting the maintenance of crematoria was upheld as charitable under the fourth heading because the maintenance of crematoria was analogous to the 'repair of churches', which is expressly mentioned in the 1601 Preamble.

Section 2 of the Charities Act 2006

As an increasingly diverse range of purposes were approved it became clear that the *Pemsel* categories were in need of review. **Section 2 Charities Act 2006** updates the *Pemsel* categories by creating 12 new statutory charitable purposes and one miscellaneous category which reflect both advances in the law and current Charity Commission practice. These heads are discussed in detail below.

The trust must be for the public benefit

As charitable trusts enjoy significant tax advantages, it is important that charitable status is not abused. The public benefit requirement plays an important role in ensuring only genuinely charitable trusts are recognized. The general rule is that the charitable trust must be of benefit to the public or to some section of the public; *Re Scarisbrick* [1951]. This rule guards against trusts which seek to benefit specific private individuals by masquerading as charitable trusts.

✔ Looking for extra marks?

The effect of the Charities Act 2006 on the public benefit requirement has been hotly debated, making it a likely essay topic. Improve your marks by reading the Charity Commission's view in 'Analysis of the Law underpinning Charities and Public Benefit' (available from their website).

The trust must have exclusively charitable purposes

If a trust is to benefit from the advantages of charitable status, it must operate for exclusively charitable purposes:

The construction of the gift

It must be clear that a gift or trust is made for charitable purposes.

Re Atkinson's Will Trust [1978] 1 WLR 586

A gift to be divided among 'worthy causes' was held to be void because 'worthy causes' could not be said to be limited to exclusively charitable purposes.

So, for example, it might be considered 'worthy' to provide flowers for hospital patients. However, this would not be seen as charitable.

And/or

If a gift is made for several purposes, the use of 'and' or 'or' can be crucial in determining whether it is held for charitable purposes.

- If a gift is for 'charitable *and* benevolent' purposes, the use of the word 'and' allows the court to interpret the second word as being included within the meaning of 'charitable'; *Re Best* [1904].

- Where a gift is left for 'charitable *or* other purposes', this will not be exclusively charitable, as the use of 'or' implies that the other purposes will be something *other than* charitable; *Re Macduff* [1896].

Ancillary non-charitable purposes

Section 1(1)(a) Charities Act 2006 defines a 'charity' as one which 'is established for charitable purposes *only*' (emphasis added). However, it will not be fatal if the trust also carries out *incidental* non-charitable purposes. Whether a non-charitable purpose is ancillary to the main purpose of the trust is a question of fact and a matter of degree, depending on the circumstances of each case; *Attorney-General v Ross* [1986]. A non-charitable purpose which is linked to the overall charitable aims of a trust will be more likely to be acceptable; **Re Coxen** [1948]. However, the more resources or time a charitable trust spends on non-charitable purposes, the less likely it will be held to be merely ancillary.

Revision tip

Examiners often include this issue in problem questions as it is a good way to test whether students are paying attention to the facts of the question. Remember to think about all three requirements when answering a question on charitable trusts.

The heads of charity under the Charities Act 2006

This section considers how the basic principles discussed above have been applied under the different heads of charity. Sections 2(2)(a)–(c) Charities Act 2006 preserve the first three *Pemsel* categories. The remaining categories (d)–(m) mainly comprise purposes previously recognized as 'other purposes beneficial to the community' and analogous purposes recognized over the years by the Charity Commission.

Section 2(2)(a): charities for the relief or prevention of poverty

Defining 'poverty'

Poverty is defined relatively and has a wider meaning than destitution – it includes those who might be said to 'go short'; *Re Coulthurst* [1951]. It is important to analyse each situation carefully to determine whether the trust is truly aimed at the relief of poverty. Compare the following cases:

Re Sanders [1954] Ch 265

A gift to provide housing for the 'working classes' of Pembroke Dock was held not to be for the relief of poverty. Although the 'working classes' may have relatively low incomes, this did not mean that they could not afford housing. The use of the phrase 'working classes' did not sufficiently restrict the gift to a class of the poor.

Re Niyazi's Will Trusts [1973] 3 All ER 785

A gift to build a working men's hostel in Cyprus was upheld as a trust for the relief of poverty. This case is different from *Re Sanders* because it involved building a hostel. The court believed that such temporary accommodation would only be used by those whose income meant that they could not afford more permanent housing, thus sufficiently restricting the gift to poor working men.

The prevention of poverty

Section 2(2)(a) Charities Act 2006 has expanded the *Pemsel* definition to include the 'prevention and relief of poverty'. This addition reflects the existing practice of the Charity Commission and could include, for example, charities providing financial or debt management advice.

The public benefit requirement

Section 3(2) Charities Act 2006 removes the presumption of public benefit previously enjoyed by trusts which relieve poverty.

The public benefit requirement for such charities is more relaxed than for the other heads. This is because of the value the courts have traditionally attached to the relief of poverty. Thus, charities which relieve the poverty of relatives or those connected to the settlor by an employment relationship are valid. For example, in *Re Scarisbrick* [1951] a charity for 'needy relations' of the settlor's children was upheld:

Dingle v Turner [1972] AC 601

A charity to pay pensions to poor employees was upheld. The House of Lords emphasized the distinction between a charitable trust and a private trust. The key issue is the primary intention of the settlor. If the gift aims to relieve poverty among a particular *description* of poor people, it will be charitable. However, if it was merely a gift to particular poor people with the intention of relieving poverty, it will be a private trust.

However, this generous approach to public benefit has resulted in some dubious decisions:

Re Segelman [1996] Ch 171

A trust for 'poor and needy' relations was upheld as valid even though the class to benefit comprised only 26 people. The trust was upheld only because the trust also included the relatives' future children.

The borderline status of the charitable trust in *Re Segelman* [1996] was undoubtedly aided by the presumption of public benefit which trusts for the relief of poverty had previously enjoyed. The removal of this presumption by s 3(2) will not prevent new trusts for poor relatives and employees from being created. However, any future trust of this nature will have to establish a *clear* public benefit from the start.

Exclusively charitable purposes

Charities which relieve poverty must still have exclusively charitable purposes. In *Re Gwyon* [1930], a trust to provide knickers for boys who lived in Fareham was held not to be charitable because it did not exclude boys who were not poor.

Section 2(2)(b): charities for the advancement of education

Defining 'education'

In *IRC v McMullen* [1981], Lord Hailsham defined education as 'the picture of a balanced and systematic process of instruction, training and practice containing...spiritual, moral, mental and physical elements'. It is clear that, in addition to schools and universities, education can encompass a wide variety of other purposes:

Figure 6.1

Case	Educational purpose
Re British School of Egyptology [1954]	Promoting the study of Egyptology
Re Lopes [1931]	London Zoo
Re Dupree [1945]	A chess tournament for young people
Incorporated Council for Law Reporting v Attorney-General [1972]	Production of the Law Reports
Re Hopkins [1965]	Research into the contested authorship of some of Shakespeare's plays

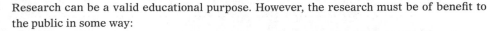
Research

Research can be a valid educational purpose. However, the research must be of benefit to the public in some way:

Re Besterman's Will Trusts, 21 January 1980, unreported

Slade J argued that a trust for research will be charitable if:

- the subject matter of the proposed research is a useful subject of study; and
- it is contemplated that knowledge acquired as a result of the research will be disseminated to others.

The court will also assess the merit of the research. For example, in *Re Shaw's WT* [1957], a trust to create a new 40-letter alphabet was rejected because it did not add anything useful to the sum of knowledge.

Note: particular types of research may now also be valid charitable purposes under s 2(2)(d) and s 2(2)(f) (see below).

Education and sport

Traditionally, the support of sport cannot be charitable in itself; *Re Nottage* [1895]. However, it has been possible to support sporting activities where this is linked to the education of the young, *IRC v McMullen* [1981]. Note: such trusts may now be valid under s 2(2)(g) for the advancement of amateur sport (see below).

The public benefit requirement

- Section 3(2) Charities Act 2006 removes the presumption of public benefit previously enjoyed by educational trusts – now such trusts must be able to prove they are for the public benefit.
- A charitable trust must be for the benefit of the community or some section of the *community* (*Re Scarisbrick* [1951]).

Section of the community?

Oppenheim v Tobacco Securities Trust Co [1951] AC 297

A trust to help pay for the education of the children of employees and ex-employees of British-American Tobacco was held *not* to be charitable. Even though the company employed more than 110,000 people, the majority of the House of Lords confirmed that there are two sections of the community which are not wide enough to satisfy the public benefit requirement:

- where membership is determined by a *personal nexus* with the donor – eg family or other relations; and
- where membership is based on contract – eg a contract of employment.

> As this benefit was supplied by virtue of their employment, the trust did not benefit either the community or a section of it.

In *Oppenheim*, Lord MacDermott delivered a strong dissent in which he argued that the majority's approach takes no account of how much public benefit will be generated by a trust. While a trust which could benefit over 110,000 people is rendered invalid because of the group's nexus with the settlor, a trust for the education of children living in a village of 100 would satisfy the public benefit requirement.

A 'section of the community' is often contrasted with a 'private class of fluctuating individuals'. The former implies an impersonal connection suggesting a benefit to the public while the latter group are personally connected, indicating a private benefit only. However, in *Dingle v Turner* [1972], Lord Cross (*obiter*) argues that while the employees of a small firm might rightly be identified as a private class of fluctuating individuals, it is difficult to say the same of a company employing thousands of workers, many of whom will be entirely unknown to one another.

Rather than relying on artificial personal/impersonal distinctions, Lord Cross argues that it would be better to focus on the financial benefits of charitable status. In other words, however worthy it may be for an employer to establish a trust to help educate her employees' children, it must be considered whether this is merely a 'fringe benefit' that the taxpayer should not be expected to subsidize.

The main thrust of these arguments is that the current approach is artificial and may exclude trusts which ought to be recognized as charitable. Lord Cross argues that while the number which will benefit is significant, ultimately the court should examine the purpose of the trust to assess whether, on its true construction, it is intended to advance education or whether it is a gift to particular individuals with their education in mind.

✅ Looking for extra marks?

While the majority approach in *Oppenheim* provides a solid guide to distinguishing charitable and private trusts, it remains open to a number of convincing criticisms. Read the judgments in *Oppenheim* and Lord Cross's judgment in *Dingle v Turner*. These will help you to assess the strengths and weaknesses of the majority approach in *Oppenheim* and demonstrate a more critical appreciation of the law.

Exclusively charitable purposes

Preferences

Despite the strong line taken in *Oppenheim* against personal connections, there is some authority that a preference for a private class may be allowed. It is not permitted to give an absolute priority to a private class (*Caffoor v Income Tax Commissioner* [1961]) – eg claims by members of my family must be satisfied first – as this puts the public in second place to a private class and therefore cannot be said to be charitable. However a *preference* for a private class may be acceptable:

Re Koettgen [1954] Ch 252

A trust for the education of British-born subjects with a preference for a private class (employees of a company and their families) succeeded. In this case, the testatrix stated that no more than 75% of the trust income was to be applied in any given year to the private class. Upjohn J upheld this trust because it was open to everyone; it was only at the selection stage that the preference took effect. The fact that the trustees did not always apply the full 75% to the private class was also significant.

This decision was criticized in *IRC v Educational Grants Association Ltd* [1967], where it was argued that a trust cannot be charitable merely because it is *potentially* for the public benefit. Instead, it can only be said to be charitable when it is operated for the public benefit. It could be argued that as long as a trust operates for primarily charitable purposes, an ancillary non-charitable purpose should be permissible. However, there are two objections to this argument:

- Ancillary non-charitable purposes are generally more acceptable where they help to further legitimate charitable purposes – allowing a preference for a private class can only be said to accomplish this if one argues that without allowing the preference, there would be no charitable trust in the first place. However, this argument makes charity hostage to a testator's more selfish impulses.

- Is a preference which allows up to *three-quarters* of its income to be used for the benefit of a private class truly an *ancillary* purpose, merely because the trustees had not used the preference to its full extent? A charitable trust should be defined by its operation for the public benefit and not merely its *potential* to do so.

Section 2(2)(c): charities for the advancement of religion

Defining 'religion'

Originally the courts were quicker to recognize different forms of Christianity as religions. However, the modern approach has been more open and all the major world religions have now been recognized either by the courts or by the Charity Commission.

- The law adopts a *neutral stance* between different religions, but assumes that some religion is better than none; *Neville Estates v Madden* [1962].

Thornton v Howe (1862) 31 Beav 14

A gift to promote the religious beliefs of Joanna Southcote, who claimed that she would give birth to the new Messiah, was upheld as charitable – it did not matter if the court believed the religion to be foolish or even devoid of foundation. However, the court will not recognize a religion whose tenets are subversive of all morality.

- The court will not discriminate against religions with only a small number of followers; *Funnell v Stewart* [1996].

While these cases discuss what will *not* be taken into account when deciding what constitutes a religion, the question of what characterizes a religion has been less satisfactorily answered:

....

Re South Place Ethical Society [1980] 1 WLR 1565

The court had to decide whether an organization whose aims were the study and dissemination of ethical principles and the cultivation of a rational religious sentiment was charitable. Its members were agnostics – ie they neither affirmed nor denied the existence of a higher power.

Dillon J distinguished ethical and religious beliefs: the former concerned man's relationship to man while the latter concerned man's relationship to God. He commented (*obiter*) that religion involved two elements:

- faith in a god, and
- worship of that god.

While the court accepted that this was a charity for the advancement of *education*, it rejected the idea that it was a religion as it lacked these two elements.

....

The problem with this definition is that not all faiths, recognized as religions, meet these requirements. Some religions, such as Buddhism, are atheistic – ie they do not require belief in any higher being. Other religions may not involve any form of deity worship at all.

A statutory definition of 'religion'

However, this problem has been addressed by s 2(3)(a) Charities Act 2006, which provides:

'religion' includes—
(i) a religion which involves belief in more than one god, and
(ii) a religion which does not involve belief in a god.

This section confirms that both *polytheistic* religions – ie religions involving the worship of many gods, such as many forms of Hinduism – and *non-theistic* religions – ie those which do not believe in any deity, such as Buddhism – are included within the definition of religion. By dispensing with the need for a godlike figure, the range of beliefs which may qualify as religious is likely to be broadened. However, in order to be charitable, a 'religion' must still involve some form of worship.

The public benefit requirement

Section 3(2) Charities Act 2006 removes the presumption of public benefit previously enjoyed by religious trusts. The public benefit is satisfied if the public have access to the benefits of the religion.

Gilmour v Coats [1949] AC 426

Money left on trust to an order of cloistered nuns was held *not* to be charitable because the public had no access to the nuns and therefore could not be said to benefit. An argument that the public would benefit from the nuns' prayers on their behalf was rejected as too vague and intangible.

Re Hetherington [1990] Ch 1

A trust for the saying of masses for *family members* was held to have public benefit because they were performed in *public* and would have an 'edifying and improving effect' upon those in attendance.

Note: trusts for the performance of purely *private* masses or ceremonies will not be charitable. However, they may be valid as a private purpose trust; *Re Caus* [1934]. (See chapter 7 for more detail.)

Section 2(2)(d)–(m): the other heads of charity

This section will briefly describe the types of purpose included in each head and, where useful, comment on related cases.

Note: the public benefit test in *Oppenheim* applies to all these heads.

Revision tip

Examiners often come up with novel or unusual purposes to test students' ability to identify which head of charity will be relevant. Read the Charity Commission publication 'Commentary on the Descriptions of Charitable Purposes in the Charities Act 2006' (available from their website), which provides practical examples of the sorts of activities covered by each head.

Section 2(2)(d): the advancement of health or the saving of lives

A wide variety of purposes are included under this head, including hospitals and medical research, as well as more lateral purposes, such as the provision of housing for medical staff, the support of lifeboat services, and self-defence classes!

Private medical care

Charities are allowed to charge for their services. However, the charity should not be profit-making, ie any profits should be used to further the charity's purposes. Therefore, a private hospital (and by the same logic under education, private schools) can be charitable.

....

Re Resch [1969] 1 AC 514

A bequest to a private hospital was upheld as charitable. It was not fatal that the beneficiaries were not poor – what was important was that, even though it might be difficult for the poor to afford such treatment, they were not excluded.

The public benefit requirement was satisfied as there was clearly a need for such facilities and medical treatment within the community. Lord Wilberforce also argued that, although there must be a direct public benefit, the court could also take into account indirect benefits. In this case, private medical care freed up hospital beds in the public sector.

....

✅ *Looking for extra marks?*

The continuing charitable status of private education and hospitals was hotly contested during the passage of the Charity Bill 2004 through Parliament. While the Charity Act 2006 does not go so far as to invalidate trusts for such organizations, private education and hospitals raise significant questions about the acceptable levels of public benefit required for charitable status. A useful discussion of these issues can be found in Peter Luxton, 'Public Benefit and Charities: the Impact of the Charities Act 2006' in Dixon and Griffiths (eds), *Contemporary Perspectives on Property, Equity and Trust Law* (2007).

Section 2(2)(e): the advancement of citizenship or community development

Examples of purposes under this head include urban regeneration schemes, good citizenship awards, and charities which encourage volunteering.

Section 2(2)(f): the advancement of the arts, culture, heritage, or science

Examples of purposes under this head include a trust to promote the work of a composer (*Re Delius* [1957]), the performance of choral works (*Royal Choral Society v IRC* [1943]), the preservation of sites of historical interest and scientific research. Purposes under this head will be subject to a test of merit and the courts will often use expert evidence to help determine this. In *Re Pinion* [1965], a trust to preserve the settlor's collection of *objets d'art* was rejected on the basis that it was a 'mass of junk'!

Section 2(2)(g): the advancement of amateur sport

This head of charity gives statutory recognition to the decisions of the Charity Commission, which, for some years prior to the **Charities Act 2006**, had permitted such charities on the basis of the physical and mental benefits to the community.

- This head relates to *amateur* sports; the support of professional sports is not charitable.
- The link to health benefits may mean that some sports may not be included under this head, eg darts.
- Unlike charities under the **Recreational Charities Act 1958** (discussed below), the trust does not have to address some lack among the intended beneficiaries.

Section 2(2)(h): the promotion of human rights, conflict resolution or reconciliation, or the promotion of religious or racial harmony, or equality and diversity

While the wording clearly indicates the types of purposes intended here, it is important that you understand the law's approach to 'political trusts': a political trust cannot be a valid charitable trust; *McGovern v Attorney-General* [1982]. This restriction applies to *all* heads of charity. There are two reasons for this:

- It will be difficult for the court to ascertain whether a political objective will be for the public benefit.
- As the ultimate administrator of trusts, it would be inappropriate for the courts or the Attorney-General to advocate political changes which may conflict with government policy.

Defining 'political purposes'

McGovern v Attorney-General [1982] sets out a non-exhaustive list of political purposes:

- Purposes supporting the interests of a particular political party (eg *Re Hopkinson* [1949]);
- Purposes which seek to change the law of this or foreign countries (eg *National Anti-Vivisection Society v Inland Revenue Commissioners* [1948]);
- Purposes which seek to change government policy or the decisions of governmental authorities, in the UK or elsewhere.

In contrast, encouraging knowledge and debate about politics is acceptable; *Re Koeppler* [1986].

The heads of charity under the Charities Act 2006

✱✱✱✱✱✱✱✱✱✱✱

Compare the following cases:

. . . .

Southwood v Attorney-General [2000] WL 877698

PRODEM, an organization which aimed to educate the public on the evils of war and advocated disarmament was held not to be charitable. While the court did not object to the promotion of peace as an object, PRODEM was denied charitable status because its central purpose was not to encourage discussion of how peace might be achieved, but to act directly to bring about a specific change in government policy.

. . . .

. . . .

Attorney-General v Ross [1986] 1 WLR 252

It was held that the funds of a polytechnic's student union were held on charitable trust. The payment of money to the NUS, a non-charitable organization, was merely ancillary to the acceptable aim of representing the student body.

. . . .

The Charity Commission provides further guidance on the extent to which charities can engage in political activities in 'CC9: Campaigning and Political Activities by Charities' (available from their website):

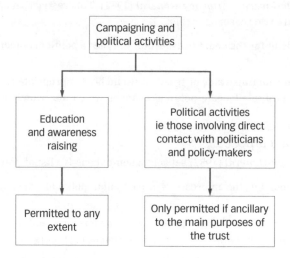

Figure 6.2 Acceptable political activities

- A trust with directly political purposes cannot be charitable.
- However, a trust which engages in political activities as a way of furthering its charitable purposes is more likely to be acceptable.

Section 2(2)(i): the advancement of environmental protection or improvement

This heading will include purposes such as the preservation of plant or animal life or land of particular beauty or scientific interest. Supporting expert evidence may be required to help decide whether such trusts are in the public benefit, eg in deciding whether a trust to preserve badger habitats is charitable, the public benefit in preserving these animals will have to be weighed against the argument made by some that these animals are responsible for spreading disease to livestock. It may also include trusts which aim to promote sustainable development, recycling, or renewable energy sources.

Section 2(2)(j): the relief of those in need by reason of youth, age, ill-health, disability, financial hardship, or other disadvantage

This purpose can be traced back to the **1601 Preamble** which includes charities for the 'aged', 'impotent', and 'the preferment of orphans'. Examples of valid purposes under this head include charities providing meals on wheels for the elderly and homeless shelters.

- The trust must be addressing a need of the identified beneficiaries and not just providing a benefit; *Joseph Rowntree Memorial Trust Housing Association Ltd v Attorney-General* [1983].

- Providing for non-essential or luxury items is not permitted; *Re Cole* [1958].

Example

Compare the following two purposes:

1. £100,000 to improve the range of books in Braille for the blind.
2. £100,000 to provide housing for the blind.

The first purpose would be valid as it addresses a need of the blind. The second purpose would be unlikely to be valid as housing does not address a need of this group *as blind people*. If the second purpose provided the money to help provide housing specially adapted for the blind, this *would* have addressed a need. However, the blind cannot be said to *need* the provision of housing *because* they are blind.

Section 2(2)(k): the advancement of animal welfare

Originally, such trusts were restricted to the welfare of working animals, which were of benefit to man; *University of London v Yarrow* (1857). Today, animal welfare charities have come to be accepted more generally on the basis that they benefit the public by *enhancing public morality and making us better people; Re Wedgewood* [1915]. There is some authority which supports the idea that the public must have access to charities for animal welfare; *Re Grove-Grady* [1929]. However, it is arguable that the public can benefit by more restricted access, remote viewing, educational facilities, or their contribution to science.

Revision tip

It is important to remember that charities under this head are for the welfare of animals or certain types of animals *generally*. If you are presented with a scenario involving a gift for the welfare of specific animals, this will not be charitable, but may be a private purpose trust, subject to the usual perpetuities rules – see chapter 7.

Section 2(2)(l): the promotion of the efficiency of the armed forces of the Crown, or of the efficiency of the police, fire and rescue services, or ambulance services

Purposes under this head are to the public benefit on the basis that they protect the nation or play a key role in activities beneficial to the public, such as the preservation of law and order and protection of the public.

Section 2(2)(m) includes 'any other purposes within subsection 4'

Section 2(2)(m):

- acts as a residual head of charity and contains purposes which do not fit neatly into the other heads (s 2(4)(a)); and

- performs the same role as the fourth head of *Pemsel*, 'other purposes beneficial to the community' by allowing new purposes to be developed by way of analogy with any of the other existing or new purposes (s 2(4)(b)–(c)).

The Recreational Charities Act 1958

Section 2(4)(a) includes those charities valid under the **Recreational Charities Act 1958**. This Act was passed as a result of the House of Lords decision in *Inland Revenue Commissioners v Baddeley* [1955] which held that the recreational purposes of a Methodist Community Centre were not charitable. This decision threw into doubt the charitable status of a number of bodies long-recognized as charitable, such as the Women's Institute and village halls.

The **Recreational Charities Act 1958**, which was passed to solve this problem, sets out the ways in which a recreational charity may be valid:

The heads of charity under the Charities Act 2006

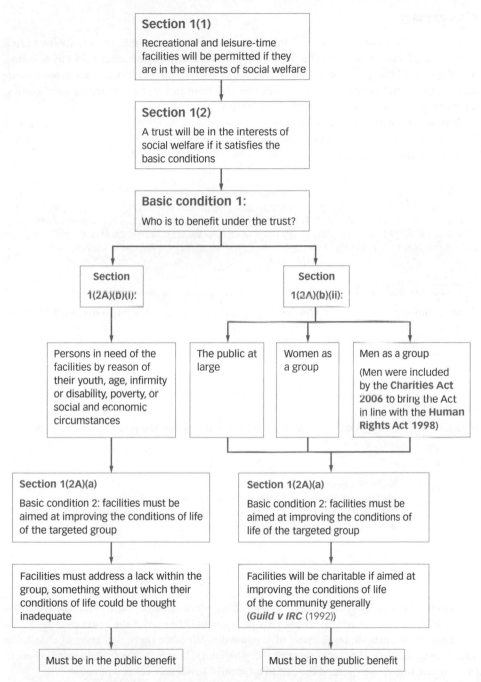

Section 1(1)

Recreational and leisure-time facilities will be permitted if they are in the interests of social welfare

Section 1(2)

A trust will be in the interests of social welfare if it satisfies the basic conditions

Basic condition 1:

Who is to benefit under the trust?

Section 1(2A)(b)(i):

Section 1(2A)(b)(ii):

Persons in need of the facilities by reason of their youth, age, infirmity or disability, poverty, or social and economic circumstances

The public at large

Women as a group

Men as a group

(Men were included by the **Charities Act 2006** to bring the Act in line with the **Human Rights Act 1998**)

Section 1(2A)(a)

Basic condition 2: facilities must be aimed at improving the conditions of life of the targeted group

Section 1(2A)(a)

Basic condition 2: facilities must be aimed at improving the conditions of life of the targeted group

Facilities must address a lack within the group, something without which their conditions of life could be thought inadequate

Facilities will be charitable if aimed at improving the conditions of life of the community generally (*Guild v IRC* (1992))

Must be in the public benefit

Must be in the public benefit

Figure 6.3 The operation of the Recreational Charities Act 1958

Cy-près

Cy-près literally means 'near there'. It is a doctrine which deals with the situation where a charitable gift cannot be applied to the purposes intended by the settlor. It works by allowing the purposes of the gift to be *varied* so that the property can be applied to a related charitable purpose. In this sense, *cy-près saves* the gift from failing and returning on resulting trust to the testator's estate or being given to the Crown.

Section 13 Charities Act 1993 lists the circumstances in which *cy-près* can be used. These include situations where it is impossible, impracticable, illegal, or inefficient to carry out the purposes of the trust.

Revision tip

In an exam, you are most likely to encounter *cy-près* in a context where it has become impossible to carry out the purposes of the trust. This is usually quite easy to spot: look out for facts mentioning the closure of a charity or its facilities. But remember, *cy-près* can only be used in respect of charitable trusts. *Cy-près* cannot be used to 'save' a gift that is not charitable in the first place.

Types of failure

Cy-près can intervene when a charitable trust is failing. There are two different types of failure:

- Initial failure
- Subsequent failure

Initial failure

Initial failure occurs when the purposes of the gift fail *before* the gift has taken effect.

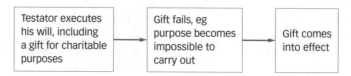

Figure 6.4 An initial failure timeline

In cases of initial failure, the gift will lapse and return on resulting trust to the testator's estate unless it can be saved by *cy-près*. *Cy-près* can only be used if the court can find a general charitable intention on the part of the testator. Whether there is a general charitable intention depends on the facts of each case. The court, in effect, has to determine whether the testator would have wished the gift to be applied to another related purpose.

Factors indicating a general charitable intention

- Where the rest of the will is charitable in nature; *Re Satterthwaite's WT* [1966].

- Where the charity to benefit never existed: if a gift is left to a charity which, in fact *never existed*, the court will take this to mean that the testator's intention was generally charitable; *Re Harwood* [1936].

- Where the gift is to an **unincorporated association**: unincorporated associations do not have legal personality and consequently cannot own property in their own right (see chapter 7). Therefore, if a charitable gift is made to an unincorporated association which has been dissolved, the courts are more likely to construe the gift as being for the *charitable purposes* of the association and apply the money *cy-près* to another body carrying out these purposes; *Re Finger's WT* [1972].

Factors indicating no general charitable intention

- Where the terms of the gift are precise or specific: the more specific the terms of a testator's gift, the less likely it can be said to demonstrate a general charitable intention; *Re Rymer* [1895].

Example

£100,000 to help patients of the Cranford Physical Spinal Injuries Centre purchase equipment that can assist in their continued recovery.

Should the Centre cease to exist prior to the testator's death, *cy-près* would not be used in this case. The terms of this gift are very specific – as there are no longer any patients, the gift will lapse. A *general* gift to help the Centre would have allowed the court to consider whether there were other factors demonstrating a general charitable intention.

- Where the gift is to a corporation: in contrast to gifts to unincorporated associations, corporations have legal personality. This suggests the gift is to a specific body to carry out charitable purposes, rather than a general gift for charitable purposes; *Re Finger's WT* [1972].

Removing restrictions on the purposes of a charitable gift

Sometimes the recipient of a charitable gift will be unwilling to accept the gift because of the testator's restrictions upon its use. In these circumstances, the court may construe the gift as being for general charitable purposes and remove the restrictions:

....

Re Lysaght [1966] Ch 191

The Royal College of Surgeons threatened to disclaim a gift to provide medical scholarships because it excluded women, Jews, and Roman Catholics. The court held that this caused the trust to fail, but concluded that there was a general charitable intention to further medical education and applied the money *cy-près* to the Royal College without the settlor's restrictions.

....

Key cases

Subsequent failure

Subsequent failure occurs when there is a failure in carrying out the purposes of the gift *after* the gift has taken effect.

Figure 6.5 A subsequent failure timeline

In cases of subsequent failure, *cy-près* operates automatically. In effect, as the gift has already been dedicated to charitable purposes, the court can vary the purposes and apply the money to another related charity. To identify cases of subsequent failure, you must be able to identify *when* the charitable gift takes effect:

- A charitable gift takes effect at the time of the death of the testator, ie when the will comes into effect.
- It does not matter if the will has not yet been administered; *Re Slevin* [1891].
- It also does not matter if the gift is a remainder interest which only takes effect after the death of a life tenant; *Re Wright* [1954].

Amalgamation

If a gift is made to a charity which has been amalgamated (ie merged) with another, the gift will be applied automatically to the new organization without the need for the court to exercise its *cy-près* jurisdiction; *Re Faraker* [1912]. This is because the charity is not deemed to have failed; it simply continues to exist in another form. This case will *not* apply where the gift is for specific purposes which can no longer be carried out, eg a gift for the upkeep of the charity's premises which are closed after the amalgamation.

Cases	Facts	Principle
Commissioners for Special Purposes of Income Tax v Pemsel [1891] AC 531	Concerned the validity of various trusts relating to the advancement of religion.	Established four general heads of charity: poverty, education, religion, and other purposes beneficial to the community.

Cases	Facts	Principle
Dingle v Turner [1972] AC 601	Upheld a gift to provide pensions for poor ex-employees.	Trusts for poor employees are charitable. Lord Cross's dissent critiques the *Oppenheim* approach to public benefit as artificial.
Gilmour v Coats [1949] AC 426	Trust for the benefit of cloistered nuns not for the public benefit.	Charities for the advancement of religion require the public to be able to access the religion.
McGovern v Attorney-General [1982] Ch 321	Concerned the validity of Amnesty International as a charitable organization.	Political purposes are not allowed in charitable trusts, but engaging in political activities to further a charitable purpose may be acceptable as ancillary non-charitable purposes.
Oppenheim v Tobacco Securities Trust Co [1951] AC 297	A trust for the education of employees of BAT held not to be charitable.	Apart from charities for the relief of poverty, a charitable trust will not be for the public benefit if it benefits relatives or employees.
Re Scarisbrick [1951] Ch 622	A trust for poor relations upheld as charitable.	Public benefit means for the benefit of the community or some section of it.
Re South Place Ethical Society [1980] 1 WLR 1565	An Ethical Society was held not to be a charity for the advancement of religion.	'Religion' involves faith in a god and worship of a god. (See also s 2(3)(a) Charities Act 2006.)

⟩⟩ Key debates

Topic	How are charitable trusts different from other types of trust?
Academic/ Author	Warburton
Viewpoint	The distinctive treatment of charitable trusts requires them to be treated separately from the main body of rules on trusts.
Source	'Charitable trusts – unique?' (1999) *Conveyancer* 20.

Exam questions

****

Topic	What effect has the Charities Act 2006 had on the public benefit requirement?
Academic/ Author	Charity Commission
Viewpoint	While the Charity Commission argues that the main effect is the removal of the presumption of public benefit, they have also suggested that they will scrutinize certain types of charity, such as independent schools, much more closely.
Source	*Charities and the Public Benefit* (2008) and *Analysis of the Law underpinning Charities and Public Benefit* (2008) (both available from their website).

Topic	How satisfactory is the law's approach to charities with political purposes?
Academic/ Author	Santow
Viewpoint	Even with the further guidance issued by the Charity Commission, the current approach to political purposes is uncertain and may restrict the ability of charities to contribute fully to the development of democratic society.
Source	'Charity in its Political Voice: a Tinkling Cymbal or a Sounding Brass?' in M Freeman (ed), *Current Legal Problems* (1999).

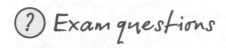 ② Exam questions

Problem question

Oliver James executes his will in 2005, which contains containing the following provisions:

1. £1,000,000 to build a Recreation Centre for the elderly in Lincoln.

2. £100,000 to Broadfield University to provide scholarships to law students, in the hope that they will challenge the increasing attacks by successive governments on our civil liberties.

3. £500,000 to further the good work of the Mountcastle Cancer Hospice.

Oliver dies in 2008. In December 2007, the Mountcastle Cancer Hospice closed.

Discuss the validity of these trusts.

An outline answer is included at the end of the book.

Essay question

Critically discuss the impact of the Charities Act 2006 on the public benefit requirement.

An outline answer is available online at www.oxfordtextbooks.co.uk/orc/concentrate/

#7

Non-charitable purpose trusts

Key facts

- Trusts generally need a human beneficiary.

- There are limited exceptions to the beneficiary principle.

- Transfers to unincorporated associations appear to have extended the exceptions.

- Gifts with a particular purpose have been held valid in commercial situations.

- Valid purpose trusts must comply with the rules on **perpetuity**.

Introduction

Trusts that do not have a human beneficiary are generally void; *Re Astors ST* [1952]. The beneficiary principle requires a valid trust to have human beneficiaries; *Morice v Bishop of Durham* (1804). (See chapter 3 to review the requirement of certainty of objects.) Charitable trusts are the largest exception to the 'beneficiary principle'. However, there are further 'anomalous' exceptions to this rule:

* Monuments: The erection and upkeep of monuments and graves.
* Animals: The upkeep of individual animals.
* Masses: The saying of private masses.
* Miscellaneous: This is a very narrow scope.

Revision tip

There is a correlation between these categories and charitable trusts and in exams good students will note the reason why a particular trust may fail as a charitable trust but succeed as a non-charitable purpose trust. Although both do not need to satisfy the beneficiary principle their objects (objectives) must still be sufficiently certain, either as clearly charitable or within a recognized purpose.

They are 'gifts of imperfect obligation' because the trustee does not have to carry out the obligations and there are no human beneficiaries to enforce it. Because they do not satisfy the beneficiary principle, and have no human beneficiary, the courts have taken a strict approach to the categories of purpose trusts. These 'troublesome, anomalous and aberrant' exceptions have developed historically and they should not be extended; *Re Endacott* [1960]. Despite this strict approach it will be seen later that the categories seem to have been extended.

Requirements of a non-charitable purpose trust

There are general barriers to the enforcement of purpose trusts which will limit their application. They must satisfy these hurdles in addition to falling clearly within the accepted 'anomalous exceptions'.

Perpetuity rules

Any purpose trust which is held to be valid must comply with the rules of perpetuity. The common law rules can be complex and the **Perpetuities and Accumulations Acts of 1964 and 2009** have made some amendments to the common law rules. The two rules relevant to purpose trusts are:

- *Remoteness of vesting*:
  - *Old rules* that apply to wills made and instruments of trust established before the commencement date of April 2010:
    (a) The property must not vest in the beneficiary outside the perpetuity period, which is **a life in being** plus 21 years. The old common law rule was that if this could fail then the trust was void from the start.

    (b) s 15 **Perpetuities and Accumulations Act 1964** which provides that the trustee can 'wait and see' if the property will vest within 80 years.

  - *New rules* The **Perpetuity and Accumulations Act 2009** will set the period for vesting at 125 years and replace the old rules. However this will only apply to trusts made after the date the relevant provisions are implemented.
- *Inalienability*: A settlor cannot rule from the grave, tying up his property once he has died. To prevent this a purpose trust cannot continue for ever, unlike a charitable trust. So a trust for a purpose must not last longer than a human life in being plus 21 years. The **Perpetuities and Accumulations Acts of 1964 and 2009 (s 18)** do not apply to this rule.

The perpetuity period does not have to be legally defined but it must be clear that it is within that period. In *Re Hooper* [1932] the period was lsimited by the words 'so long as the trustees can legally do so'. This was held to be a valid declaration of the perpetuity period.

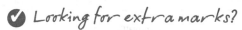
✅ *Looking for extra marks?*

As the law in relation to vesting has recently changed it may be the focus of essays, such as why has the rule on inalienability not been addressed. Look at the Law Commission website for some background and articles by Charles Harpum who was instrumental in devising reform in this area.

Capriciousness

A purpose trust may also be set aside by the courts if the purpose is capricious. This means that the use of the money serves no valid purpose. This may be of no economical value but this is not the only limitation. For example, in *Re Shaw's WT* (1957) the money left for developing a forty letter alphabet served no valid purpose. This principle would apply to all trusts but is particularly relevant to a pure purpose trust.

The anomalous exceptions

Monuments

A trust for the upkeep of a church will be charitable. However, a trust for the upkeep of an individual monument or grave which is not part of the fabric of a church is not charitable.

This is because an individual monument or grave has no public benefit whereas improving the fabric, or body, of a church will benefit those who use the church.

The bequest itself must also be sufficiently certain in its purpose. In *Re Endacott* [1960] a residual gift to North Tawnton Parish Council to provide 'a useful memorial to myself' was invalid as it was too broad. It was unclear what was meant by 'useful memorial'.

The perpetuity period was an issue in *Musset v Bingle* [1876] where a bequest to erect a monument to the testator's first husband was valid but a second bequest for its upkeep was void. It did not fail for perpetuity in relation to the erection of the monument as it was assumed that the monument would be erected within the period. However, as no period was stipulated for the upkeep of the monument this part of the trust failed.

Animals

Trusts for the support and welfare of animals in general may be charitable and enforceable such as a trust to benefit the RSPCA. However, trusts for the upkeep of *particular* animals can only be enforceable as a non-charitable purpose trust. In *Re Dean* (1899) a trust for the upkeep of horses and hounds was held to be valid.

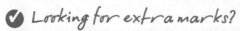 *Looking for extra marks?*

In the above case the period was for 50 years 'if they live that long' and was held to be valid. Presumably, this was because the animals were unlikely to live that long, but perpetuity was not addressed in the case.

It is clear from *Re Kelly* [1932] that the 'life in being' required by the perpetuity period must be a human life. The anomaly between these two decision may be worthy of note.

Masses

The saying of masses (church service) in public will be charitable, even if the object of the masses is dedicated to a private individual; *Re Hetherington* [1990]. The saying of masses in private or cloistered orders can be an anomalous exception; *Gilmour v Coates* [1949].

Miscellaneous

This category is now limited to the case of *Re Thompson* [1934] which was for the promotion of fox hunting. With the ban on fox hunting this is unlikely to be upheld as valid today.

Unincorporated associations

The courts were reluctant to allow trusts to operate outside the accepted 'gifts of imperfect obligation'; *Re Endacott*. However, the courts have been asked to consider how gifts to a group of people should be interpreted. The policy underlying the anomalous exceptions is to encourage community benevolence. If a gift to a small community club is not charitable then it may fail, defeating the intention of the donor and the policy of community benevolence. These small groups often take the form of **unincorporated associations**.

Requirements of a non-charitable purpose trust

An unincorporated association is formed when two or more people come together for a common purpose, such as a gardening club. They will be bound by rules; *Conservative and Unionist Central Office v Burrell* [1982]. These groups can be quite organized, local political groups or informal book clubs.

Unincorporated association have no legal personality, existing in their own right, and therefore cannot own property. There are four accepted ways that the gift of property to an unincorporated association can be interpreted according to *Re Recher's WT* [1972]:

- An outright gift to the members to hold as joint tenant or tenants in common.
- A trust for the association's purpose.
- A trust for the members and future members of the association.
- An outright gift to the members as joint tenants subject to their contractual obligations.

An outright gift

This interpretation states that each member of the association takes the property as an outright gift. They can hold this either as **joint tenants** or as **tenants in common**. This interpretation is possible depending on the nature of the property, but in *Re Grant's WT* [1980] Vinelott J thought that this interpretation would be uncommon without clear evidence of the settlor's intention.

Finding the settlor's intention

The nature of the property and how the property is transferred to the members will be relevant in finding the relevant intention. If they are joint tenants then each member of the joint tenancy holds the entire interest among themselves equally. Should one of the joint tenants sever their interest then they can take their share of the property as an absolute gift. So the property must be capable of being severed.

If the gift is given as tenants in common each member takes their share as an absolute gift immediately; *Cocks v Manners* (1871). If there is an ambiguity in the gift then the courts will look at the nature of the property to infer an intention.

Example 1

A gift of £300 to a gardening club with 30 members. It is perfectly possible that each member could take £10 each. So they can be tenants in common or joint tenants, the property is capable of **severance**.

Example 2

A gift of an acre of land to a gardening club with 30 members. It is possible but unlikely that the donor/settlor intended that each member take 1/30 of the acre for their own use. It is unlikely that the property was intended as an outright gift and this interpretation would fail.

Requirements of a non-charitable purpose trust
✶✶✶✶✶✶✶✶✶✶

A trust for the purpose of the association

This would fail as a purpose trust as it is neither charitable nor within the anomalous exceptions. The courts have tried to make the distinction between the interpretation of the bequest as a gift to the members and for a purpose. If the members can do what they want with the property and it can be held individually then it is likely to be construed as a gift. If the members cannot do what they want with the property then it is likely to be a trust for a purpose and void; *Leahy v AG for New South Wales* [1959].

A trust for the members and future members

This is a possible interpretation in which the current members will hold the property on trust for themselves and for future members subject to the trust complying with the rules of perpetuity. The relevant rule on perpetuity here will be the remoteness of vesting. This interpretation was recognized in *Leahy v AG for New South Wales* [1959].

A gift for the members subject to their contractual obligations

The contractual analysis is the most popular interpretation. It is seen as a gift to the current members who own the property; it is an 'accretion to funds'; *Re Grant's WT* [1980]. This means it is merely a direct contribution to the club funds. How they distribute their interests in the property is regulated by their internal, contractual, rules. This will solve the problem of what will happen when a member leaves as their contract will stipulate the distribution of assets on dissolution of the association or if a member leaves.

Making the 'contractual analysis' work

The association must be in control of their own finances; *Re Grant's WT* [1980]. The association must have within its contractual agreement, which regulates the running of the club, rules on how the finances of the association are held. It must not be subject to control from another organization or superior body.

....

Re Grant's WT [1980] 1 WLR 360

The gift was to a local Labour party committee. The rules of the party meant that the local party were not in control of their own internal rules, or able to decide what happened to funds should the local party cease to exist. The court held that the gift could not be a gift to the members subject to their rules as they were not in control of their own finances.

....

Advantages of this analysis

The contractual analysis is the most popular interpretation for the courts as it raises no problems with perpetuities. This is because the property vests immediately in the members and as it is not a trust the rule on inalienability does not apply.

However, this interpretation will not aid a settlor who wants to ensure that the 'purpose' of the settlement is carried out. As the members are in charge of their own financial arrangements, should they agree to use the gift for a different purpose or divide the property up and take absolutely, the settlor cannot prevent this. The 'purpose' is merely the motive for the settlement.

An alternative approach

This last interpretation seems to satisfy the ownership issue but it may defeat the intention of the settlor. As the members obtain the property as a gift then, subject to the rules of the association, they can deal with the property as they wish. It seems that the categories have been extended by the decision in *Re Denley's Trust Deed* [1969]. Although this case did not refer to an unincorporated association it could be applied to such a gift.

The problem with the gift was that the 'purpose' of use as a sports ground could not be achieved with any of the *Re Recher's* interpretations. If the contractual analysis was applied then the members of the club could defeat the purpose, and the members would need to be identified.

Having established that the purpose was sufficiently clear Goff J considered if it failed the beneficiary principle. He found there was no problem with the beneficiary principle requirement. He felt that the purpose of the beneficiary principle, requiring a human beneficiary, was to prevent possible fraud by the trustee. In the present case there were identifiable persons who would enforce the trust: the members of the sports club. This being the case there should, in principle, be no bar to enforcement of this type of trust. It was assumed by Goff J that the members of the club would act as 'watchdogs' of the purpose.

Terminology tip

Do not refer to the identifiable persons in a Denley trust as identifiable beneficiaries as they do not have any beneficial interest. It seems they merely have a right to enforce the obligation. This will help in explaining the interests.

This type of trust must be limited to the perpetuity period in relation to inalienability.

Requirements of a non-charitable purpose trust
✱✱✱✱✱✱✱✱✱✱

Re Denley was not concerned with an unincorporated association, indeed in *Re Grant's WT* it was said that *Re Denley* was in fact a discretionary trust with an identifiable class of beneficiaries who could be identified by the *McPhail v Doulton* test for certainty. The principle from *Re Denley* was applied to unincorporated associations in *Re Lipinski's WT* [1976].

> *Re Lipinski's WT* [1976] Ch 235
>
> Property was left to construct and improve buildings for the use as a sports and social club for Jewish children, said to be in memory of his late wife. The court held the trust to be valid.

It was interpreted as being a *Re Denley* type of trust with ascertainable individuals (members of the sport and social club). Oliver J said that the 'purpose' of celebrating his late wife was merely a motive for the settlement. However, interestingly he also referred to this as being 'an accretion' to funds, referring to the contractual analysis of interpreting the gift. This was because Oliver J felt that the individuals could, if they wished, use the settlement for any purpose they chose, subject to the social club rules.

✅ Looking for extra marks?

The decision in *Re Lipinski* is a confusing mix of analyses. One view of the decision in *Re Denley* is that the purpose with 'ascertainable individuals' to act as watchdogs is the preferable interpretation should the settlor want to ensure the 'purpose' is carried out. Goff J seemed to assume that the 'ascertainable individuals' would carry out the purpose but without stating just what would make them do this. However, *Re Lipinksi's* interpretation *would* suggest that Goff's assumption of enforcement would not necessarily apply.

Additionally *Re Lipinski* mixes ideas of gifts and trusts. *Re Denley* trusts must comply with the rule on perpetuities but a gift does not have to. It is better to keep these two views separate, the better interpretation is the contractual analysis; *Artistic Upholstery Ltd v Art Forma Ltd* [1999]. In an essay be prepared to comment critically on *Re Lipinski* as it has confused this area.

Quistclose trusts – purpose trust?

A further type of possible purpose trust which has developed is illustrated by *Barclays Bank v Quistclose* [1970]. In this situation loans were made by the bank to the company for the payment of dividends. This was not done and the company went into liquidation. The bank claimed that the money was held by the company on resulting trust for the bank (see chapter 9). It had been lent for a particular purpose and when this was not done the property should then be returned to the lender.

Lord Wilberforce, expressing the view of the court, ruled that the money was transferred on trust, with a power to use for a particular purpose. Therefore it was not a purpose trust. When the trust power was not exercised then a second trust arose to return the money to the bank. Lord Millett has interpreted this situation as a voluntary transfer, creating a resulting trust with a power to apply for a specific purpose; *Twinsectra v Yardley* [2002]. This interpretation may be a method to allow the successful enforcement of a purpose trust. It will, however, require careful drafting.

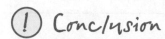 **Looking for extra marks?**

Read the commentaries on *Quistclose* and *Twinsectra*; consider if the analysis of the primary and secondary trust has any validity. A focus for essays may be in identifying the nature of the trust; the language of the judges appears to reference constructive, while also calling them resulting. There is much to commend them as express trusts with a power. Also consider that the trust analysis does protect the lender in a commercial context but does disadvantage other creditors.

① **Conclusion**

Purpose trusts fall into charitable and non-charitable categories and are closely linked. A good student will consider if a trust is valid as a charity, explain why it may succeed or fail, and then consider if it falls into one of the anomalous exceptions. A more complex issue arises with a 'gift' to an unincorporated association. The four interpretations should be explained with the extended *Re Denley* construction

✳ **Key cases**

Case	Facts	Principle
Barclays Bank v Quistclose [1970] AC 567	Money was lent to a company to pay dividends. The money was held in the bank, the dividends were not paid, and the company went into liquidation.	The money was lent with a primary purpose, when that purpose failed then a secondary resulting trust arose for the lender.
Leahy v AG for New South Wales [1959] AC 457	Land and furniture was left for the benefit of nuns of the Catholic church.	The gift was to a group of people for a purpose which would fail.
Re Denley's Trust Deed [1969] 1 Ch 373.	Land was left to be used as a sports ground for employees of a company and any other persons the trustees may allow to use the grounds.	The land was held for ascertainable individuals who would supervise the trust. It was not a purpose trust, not contrary to the beneficiary principle as the individuals would ensure no fraud.
Re Grant's WT [1980] 1 WLR 360	Money was left for the use of a local political party.	The money left to the unincorporated association could not be held on the contractual analysis as the local club was not in control of its own finances but regulated by the National party.

Key debates

****

Case	Facts	Principle
Re Recher's WT [1972] Ch 526	The testatrix left property to the Anti-Vivisection Society.	The gift was not a purpose trust but an accretion to the funds of the association for the members, subject to their contract, to do with as they wished. There was no problem with inalienability as the members could, if they wished, wind up the association and take their property. Note: The gift failed on another point as it had ceased to exist by the time the testatrix died.

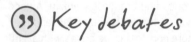 Key debates

Topic	*Re Denley* trust
Academic/ Author	Rickett
Viewpoint	In the *Denley* trust the beneficial interest is held in suspense, enforceable by the settlor and the beneficiary.
Source	(1991) 107 LQR 70. As a starting point for the discussion see Pearce and Stevens, *Law of Trusts and Equitable Obligations*, 4th edn (2006), pp 383–7.

Topic	The *Quistclose*-type trust in commercial context
Academic/ Author	Goodhart and Jones
Viewpoint	The *Quistclose* trust raises questions as to how property is held. The development of the trust is an essential development in commerce.
Source	(1980) 43 MLR 489. Generally see Moffat, *Trusts Law*, 4th edn (2005), pp 772–4 for an excellent summary of the issues.

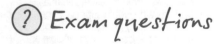 Exam questions

Problem question

Advise on the validity of a bequest, in Johan's will, to the Shannon Gardening Club of £10,000. Johan's will requires that the money should be used to purchase a piece of land to be used as an allotment for local children.

An outline answer is included at the end of the book.

Essay question

Explain how the courts have interpreted a gift to an unincorporated association and outline the problems associated with them.

An outline answer is available online at www.oxfordtextbooks.co.uk/orc/concentrate/

#8
Secret trusts

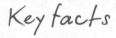

Key facts

- Secret trusts are testamentary trusts which operate outside the requirements of the Wills Act 1837.

- Secret trusts can be either fully secret or half secret.

- All secret trusts have requirements as to communication, acceptance, and reliance.

- There are time differences in the need for communication for the two types of trust.

- A secret trust of land can operate but it is unclear if these are express or constructive.

- There are theoretical problems in justifying the operation of trusts which are unresolved.

Introduction

Secret trusts allow property to be left to someone in a will without explicitly naming that person. This is achieved by a bequest to a person who has previously promised to hold that property as trustee for the intended recipient. The anonymity provided by a secret trust is important, as all wills are public documents and therefore open to scrutiny. They are public to prevent attempts to defraud wills, but this same publicity created problems for those testators who wished to be more discreet in the final disposal of their estate.

Additionally, early statutes (since repealed) prevented bequests to women or leaving land on trust to a charity, so a secret trust was a vehicle to avoid this; *Katherine, Duchess of Suffolk v Herenden* (1560). The secret trust also continues to be of use to the indecisive testator who can defer the final decision about who is to benefit without having to rewrite their existing will.

The Wills Act 1837, s 9, imposes certain requirements for the creation of a valid will:

- the will must be in writing;
- the will must be signed by the testator; and
- the will must be witnessed by two persons.

The requirements imposed by this Act are designed to ensure that a will contains a clear, complete, and formalized record of how a testator's estate should be distributed. Therefore, if the statute were to be strictly applied, secret trusts could not be enforced.

Justifications for secret trusts

Fraud theory

In *Katherine, Duchess of Suffolk v Herenden* (1560) the court held that Herenden was bound by his promise to the Duke of Suffolk to take ownership of his estate for the benefit of his wife, the Duchess of Suffolk. To enforce the statute strictly would allow Herendon to avoid the obligations of his promise. 'Equity will not allow a statute to be an instrument of fraud.'

In the case of *McCormick v Grogan* (1869), Lord Hatherley LC confirmed that secret trusts are imposed to prevent a secret trustee from defrauding a testator, who only left property to the secret trustee in reliance of his promise to carry out the testator's wishes.

Who is defrauded?

- The testator? Difficult to prove that the testator is defrauded as they are dead. It does defeat the intention of the testator but they are trying to avoid the requirements of the Wills Act 1837 so perhaps should not be protected in this way.

Justifications for secret trusts
****

- The secret beneficiaries? If the secret beneficiary is denied her benefit, this is only because the testator failed to comply with the formalities required by the **Wills Act 1837**.

Who commits the fraud?

- The secret trustee by denying the existence of the trust?
- The testator, who left property in a way that contravenes the policy of the **Wills Act 1837**?
- The secret beneficiary is only entitled to assert their claim over the property insofar as it is acceptable for the testator to avoid the legal requirements set out in the **Wills Act**.

Dehors the will

The alternative justification for the enforcement of secret trusts avoids the problem of the **Wills Act 1837**. It can be argued that the trust is declared *inter vivos* (in the testator's lifetime and not through the will) and the will merely constitutes the transfer. If this were the case, the trust would arise **dehors** (outside) the will and therefore would not be contrary to the **Wills Act 1837**.

While this argument may appear attractive initially, there are a number of significant problems which flow from this approach. As soon as the trust has been created, the *beneficial interest* in the property would be transferred to the secret beneficiary. If this were the case, the testator would no longer be able to change their mind, or that part of the will which relates to the property. This goes against the principle that wills are ambulatory (meaning that they can be revoked or amended up until the testator's death).

The testator would no longer be able to do anything with the property as he no longer owns the beneficial interest. It is extremely unlikely that this would have been the testator's intention as the whole idea is that the property is the testator's until he dies! If the *dehors the will* theory were correct, then, in effect, creating a secret trust would be like locking property in a safe to which only the beneficiary has the key.

✔ *Looking for extra marks?*

Arguably the biggest problem is that the *dehors the will* explanation of secret trusts would seem to involve the creation of a trust of future property. This means that at the time the trust is declared, there is no way of knowing whether the property will still be part of the testator's estate when he dies. As such, the trust that is being created is only the trust of an expectancy. Allowing a trust of an expectancy would be like allowing a trust of the wish you make when you see a shooting star! Such trusts of future property are generally considered to be impossible; *Re Ellenborough* [1903].

Neither justification is entirely satisfactory. Contrary to the **Wills Act**, equity has sought to enforce secret trusts in order to give effect to the testator's final intentions. This may be taken to reflect the original purpose of equity – to do justice where a strict application of the legal rules would lead to an unfair result.

While the debate over how secret trusts may be justified persists, the courts have continued to enforce such trusts, and despite arguments that they are no longer required, surveys of lawyers have proved that they are alive and well.

Categories of secret trusts

There are two types of secret trust: *fully secret trusts* and *half-secret trusts*. The case of *Ottaway v Norman* [1972] clearly sets out that to establish a valid secret trust there must be:

- an intention to create a trust;
- communication of that intention; and
- acceptance of the trust obligation.

While the rules governing the creation of valid secret trusts are broadly similar, you must remember that there are some significant differences.

Fully secret trusts

In a fully secret trust there is no evidence on the face of the will that the trust exists. The testator will appear to have left the property as an outright gift.

Intention

In *Kasperbauer v Griffith* (2000), Peter Gibson LJ clarified that in order to create a valid secret trust, a testator must have intended to create a trust, complying with *all* of the three certainties (see chapter 3).

Communication

What must be communicated?

The case of *Re Boyes* (1884) establishes that the testator must communicate to the trustee *both* his intention to establish the secret trust and the terms on which that property is to be held. If the trustee only knows of the testator's intention to create a secret trust but not its terms, the trust will fail. This is a logical result because a trustee must know what he is meant to do with the property he receives.

How can this communication take place?

The intention and terms of a trust may be communicated either orally or in writing. It will also be sufficient if the intention and terms are communicated by an agent of the testator; *Moss v Cooper* (1861). Instructions can be contained in a sealed envelope to be opened on the death of the testator: constructive delivery. This method was approved in the case of *Re Keen* [1937], Lord Wright comparing it with a ship sailing under sealed orders.

Categories of secret trusts

****

When must this communication take place?

Fully secret trusts can be communicated at any time before the death of the testator, when the will comes into effect. In *Wallgrave v Tebbs* (1861) the people who appeared to take property as an absolute gift only found the request to use it for charitable purposes in the testator's papers after his death. The failure to inform them of the trust before the will came into effect meant that they took as a gift.

Revision tip

This is one of the areas where there are different rules. A *fully* secret trust must be communicated before death. One of the main things your examiner will be looking for is a clear knowledge and explanation of the rules relevant to the type of secret trust involved.

Who must be told of the trust?

In general, all secret trustees should be told about the testator's intentions. However, in a fully secret trust, if communication is not made to all of the intended secret trustees, the question of whether they will *all* be bound depends on two things:

* *how* the trustees were intended to hold the property; and
* the *timing* of the communication.

You will know that *all* property can be held as either **joint tenants** or **tenants in common**. In *Re Stead* [1900] the testator only informed one secret trustee of her intention before the will was executed. Farwell J held that only Mrs Witham, the secret trustee who had been informed, was bound by the trust; Mrs Andrew (the other intended secret trustee) took free of the obligation.

This case establishes a complicated set of rules for deciding when communication to only some of the trustees will bind the others. Do not try and justify this set of rules as even the trial judge was not entirely convinced that they made sense!

Revision tip

Warning: it is a common mistake of students to confuse the ordinary use of the term 'tenancy' as referring to the occupation of land with the legal use of this term, which includes the ability to hold any type of property, from a bank account to a palace, in a form of co-ownership. Do not fall into this trap! Look for words such as 'to hold in equal parts' which may mean they are tenants in common, as these are words which indicate separate interests are being created.

To try to make this clearer, have a look at the diagram below:

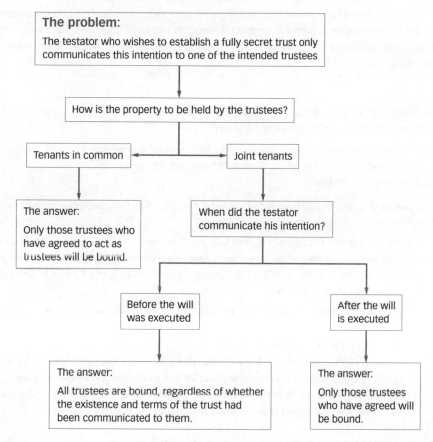

The problem:

The testator who wishes to establish a fully secret trust only communicates this intention to one of the intended trustees

How is the property to be held by the trustees?

Tenants in common

Joint tenants

The answer:

Only those trustees who have agreed to act as trustees will be bound.

When did the testator communicate his intention?

Before the will was executed

After the will is executed

The answer:

All trustees are bound, regardless of whether the existence and terms of the trust had been communicated to them.

The answer:

Only those trustees who have agreed will be bound.

Figure 8.1

Acceptance

The final requirement for the creation of a valid fully secret trust is that the trustee must accept the terms of the trust. The case of *Ottaway v Norman* [1972] states that this can be either:

- expressly; or
- by **acquiescence** (silence).

Categories of secret trusts

****

Moss v Cooper (1861) 4 LT 790

The secret trustee who had been informed of the testator's intentions told the other two intended trustees; one expressly accepted but the other remained silent. The court held that having learned of the trust, his silence amounted to acceptance. The key point here is that he knew of the trust but failed to object.

What happens to property in the event that a fully secret trust cannot be established?

If the three requirements of intention, communication, and acceptance are not satisfied, the fully secret trust will fail. However, what will happen to the property?

There are two possibilities:

1. If the person who was intended to be a secret trustee had no knowledge of the trust, he will be able to take the property for himself.

2. If the person knew that property was being left to him to hold on trust but had no idea what the purpose of that trust was to be, that person cannot keep the property for himself. Instead, the legatee will hold the property on resulting trust back to the estate. There are two reasons for this:

   - Because the testator has failed to satisfy the communication requirements the secret trust will fail and therefore he is not bound to pass the property on to the person the testator wanted to benefit.

   - Because the legatee also knew that the testator never intended him to have that property for himself, his conscience is affected and he cannot keep the property for himself. As it has not been proven that the property *must* be passed to the intended beneficiary of the secret trust, it must go back to the testator's estate.

Re Boyes (1884) 26 Ch D 531

The testator left the residue of his estate to his solicitor, who had been told that he was to hold it on trust and that he would be informed of the terms of that trust by letter. However, the solicitor did not learn of the terms of the trust until after the testator's death when a letter was found indicating that the property was to be held for a woman who was not the testator's wife. Despite the solicitor's willingness to carry out the terms of the trust, it was held that the solicitor held the property on resulting trust for the estate.

Half-secret trusts

In a half-secret trust the will contains reference to the existence of a trust, but the beneficiaries and the terms of the trust remain secret. In *Blackwell v Blackwell* [1929], the House of Lords held that a half-secret trust must satisfy the same basic requirements as a fully secret trust. Therefore, a half-secret trust must establish:

- an intention to create a trust;
- communication of that intention;
- acceptance of the trust obligation.

Intention

The rules here remain the same. The testator must have had the intention to create a trust and that trust must satisfy the three certainties (certainty of intention, certainty of subject matter and certainty of objects).

> ### Revision tip
>
> In a half-secret trust, the will shows that certain property is to be held on trust. Remember that the trustee may not see the will until much later. Therefore, the testator must have made it clear to the half-secret trustee that he is to hold the property on trust.

Communication

Many of the basic requirements under this heading remain the same as for fully secret trusts. Therefore:

- the testator must communicate both his intention to create a trust and its terms (*Blackwell v Blackwell* [1929]); and
- this communication may be made orally, in writing (including by way of a sealed envelope to be opened on death), or by an agent of the testator.

When must this communication take place?

The major difference between fully secret and half-secret trusts relates to *when* the communication must take place. In a half-secret trust, communication must take place before or at the time that the will is **executed**. The basis of this rule were *obiter* comments by Lord Sumner in *Blackwell v Blackwell* [1929] which were later applied in the case of *Re Keen* [1937] and *Re Bateman's WT* [1970].

The communication must be consistent with the will

In *Re Keen* [1937], before the execution of his will the testator had given one of his trustees instructions contained in a sealed envelope to be opened on his death. However, after he died the relevant bequest in his will stated that the property was left to the trustees for purposes that *would be communicated* to them in his lifetime. The Court of Appeal held that this did not create a valid half-secret trust for two reasons:

1. By saying that he *would* instruct the trustees he suggested that he would give his instructions *after* the will had been executed. In other words, the will suggests that

instructions would be given in the future. Therefore, the only logical construction of the will was that the instructions the trustees had received were *not* the instructions referred to in the testator's will. On this basis, the half-secret trust failed as the trustees did not know the true intentions of the testator.

2. By attempting to leave his instructions until after his will had been executed, the testator was clearly trying to avoid the requirements of the Wills Act 1837.

The first reason given by the court may seem harsh, but you can see its logic. A will is a formal legal record of the testator's intentions and therefore its interpretation is taken very seriously by the courts to make sure those wishes are fulfilled. Therefore, it is vital that the words in the will and the actual communication correspond. Any inconsistency will be fatal to the trust.

All secret trusts offend against the policy behind the Wills Act 1837. However as a half-secret trust, with unknown purpose, is referred to in the will the attempt to avoid the Wills Act is clear. (Other jurisdictions, such as the Republic of Ireland, have the same rules on communication for half-secret trusts as for a fully secret trust.)

Revision tip

Remember to check for consistency between the will and the actual instructions as this is a popular issue for examiners to see how carefully the student is reading the facts.

Who must be told of the trust?

All trustees of a half-secret trust should be told of the testator's intentions. What will happen if communication only takes place to one of the trustees? Unlike a fully secret trust the half-secret trustee *cannot* claim the property as their own. This is because the will makes it clear that the property is not intended as an outright gift but is to be held on trust. Instead, the property will be held on resulting trust back to the estate.

Acceptance

The rules of acceptance are the same as for a fully secret trust. Trustees of a half-secret trust must accept their position and may do so expressly or by acquiescence; *Blackwell v Blackwell* [1929].

Proving the existence of a secret trust

The burden of proof

The burden of proof lies on the person trying to establish that the trust exists. Remember, in this respect the same rules apply to fully secret and half-secret trusts.

Standard of proof

Although originally the standard of proof was very high (that required to rectify a written instrument; *Ottaway v Norman* [1972]) over the years, it has become less stringent. *Re Snowden* [1979] states that the standard of proof required is the 'ordinary civil standard of proof'. Remember that a very practical issue lies behind the legal rules on how the existence of a fully secret trust can be established. The nature and purpose of many fully secret trusts means that many testators will wish to keep knowledge of their true intentions limited to as few people as possible. There is always the risk that an unscrupulous fully secret trustee will claim the property as their own, so it may be advisable to inform another person other than the secret trustee. The table below recaps the general rules applicable to the creation of fully secret and half-secret trusts.

Figure 8.2

	Fully secret trust	Half-secret trust
Appearance	Appears as gift on the face of the will.	Appears as trust on the face the will (purpose and beneficiaries unknown).
Intention	Must intend to create a trust and satisfy the three certainties (*Kasperbauer v Griffith* [2000]).	Must intend to create a trust and satisfy the three certainties (*Kasperbauer v Griffith* [2000]).
Communication	**What?** Existence of the trust and its terms (*Wallgrave v Tebbs* [1855]). **How?** Orally or in writing • Terms of the trust can be in a sealed envelope if the trustee knows it contains the existence and terms of the secret trust (*Re Keen* [1937]).	**What?** Existence of the trust and its terms (*Blackwell v Blackwell* [1929]). **How?** Orally or in writing • Terms of the trust can be in a sealed envelope if the trustee knows it contains the terms (*Re Keen* [1937]) as long as the letter is given before the will is executed. • Communication must be consistent with the will – not a future communication (*Re Bateman's Will Trust* [1970]. • Sealed instructions must be delivered before the will is executed.

	When? Before death of testator (*Wallgrave v Tebbs* (1855)).
	
	If communication not to all trustees?
	• Tenants in common: only those who accept the trust are bound.
	• Joint tenants:
	  (a) If communication before will executed, all bound.
	  (b) If communication after the will is executed, only those who accept are bound.
	
	(*Re Stead* [1900])
		When? Before or at the time of the execution of the will (*Blackwell v Blackwell* [1929]).
		
		If communication not to all trustees?
		• Trustees cannot claim property as their own.
		• If will allows communication to some trustees, all bound if communication before will is executed.
		• If will says all trustees know, if this is not the case, the entire trust fails.
		
		(*Re Keen* [1937])

Figure 8.2 *Continued*

	Fully secret trust	Half-secret trust
Acceptance	Express or inferred by acquiescence (*Moss v Cooper* (1861)).	Express or inferred by acquiescence (*Moss v Cooper* (1861)).
Failure	• If trustee has no knowledge of trust, he takes beneficially. • If the trustee knows a trust was intended but not its terms, trustee holds on resulting trust (*Re Boyes* (1884)).	• Trustee cannot claim property as his own – holds on resulting trust.

Developing understanding

These issues have been kept separate to help you focus on the core requirements for secret trusts before considering some of the more unusual questions that arise in this area.

Can the secret trustee change his mind?

During the lifetime of the testator this causes no problems; they merely inform the testator who can simply amend the will. However, there may be problems if the change of mind is after death or on finding they will not or cannot perform the instructions contained in a sealed envelope. A valid trust has been created and as the trustee knows there is no intention of an outright gift, he cannot claim it. There are two contrary views on the result:

- *Re Maddock* [1902] suggests *obiter* that the trust will fail (to be held on resulting trust to the estate).
- *Blackwell v Blackwell* [1929] *obiter* comments by Lords Buckmaster and Warrington suggest that as equity will not allow a trust to fail for want of a trustee, the courts can appoint a replacement, willing, trustee.

The possibility of the trustee's claiming the property as a gift increases in fully secret trusts but the principle above should still apply.

Can the testator change the terms of the secret trust?

This issue was considered in the context of a half-secret trust in the case of *Re Colin Cooper* [1939]. The testator left £5,000 on a half-secret trust the purposes of which had been communicated to trustees before his will was executed. The testator later added a codicil to his will which increased the amount to £10,000. However, he failed to communicate this to the secret trustees before his death. The Court of Appeal held that only the original £5,000 was subject to the obligations of the trust. The remainder was held on resulting trust to the estate.

As this was a half-secret trust, the trustees could not claim the additional amount as their own property. It is unclear if the same reasoning would apply to a fully secret trust. As the trustees know that the property is subject to a trust, *Re Boyes* (1884) would presumably apply; additional property would be held on resulting trust for the estate.

If the amount to be held on secret trust was reduced, Sir Wilfred Greene MR argued, *obiter*, that the greater sum would be considered to cover any lesser sum that was substituted.

Problems caused by the 'dehors the will' explanation of secret trusts

As the trust is created outside the will there are several consequences of this:

* A witness to a will can benefit from a secret trust:

. . . .

Re Young [1951] Ch 344

Mr Young left his estate to his wife; before his death he told her that their chauffeur should receive £2,000. This established a fully secret trust, with his wife as the secret trustee. However, the chauffeur was a witness to the will and s 15 Wills Act 1837 prohibits witnesses from benefiting from a will. Therefore, if the benefit passed by the will it would be void. The court held that the trust was established when the terms were communicated to Mrs Young.

. . . .

* A beneficiary of a secret trust who dies *before* the testator may still benefit from the trust.

. . . .

Re Gardner (No 2) [1923] 2 Ch 230

A testatrix left all her property to her husband for life; the remainder to be split by way of a fully secret trust among her nephew and nieces. One of the nieces died, *two years before* the testatrix. Section 25 Wills Act 1837 establishes the doctrine of lapse; if a beneficiary under a will dies before the testatrix, the bequest fails and lapses back into the residue of the estate. If the niece took under the Act, her share would lapse. However, Romer J held that the secret trust took effect *dehors* the will and had come into existence as soon as the husband had accepted. Therefore, the trust took effect free of the Wills Act and the deceased niece's estate was held to be entitled to her share.

. . . .

If this decision is correct, a testator would not be able to change his will. This is because when the secret trustee accepted the trust, an *inter vivos* trust would be established over all her property. This is contrary to the ambulatory nature of a will and therefore can be changed or revoked at any time until the testatrix's death.

✔ Looking for extra marks?

Re Gardner [1923]: this case illustrates all the problems with the *dehors the will* theory and is arguably incorrect. While it remains an authority, the weight of academic opinion suggests that it should not be followed. See key debates below.

Conclusion

✱✱✱✱✱✱✱✱✱✱✱✱

Can you have a secret trust of land?

Section 53(1)(b) Law of Property Act 1925 requires an enforceable declaration of a trust of land to be manifested or evidenced in writing. As the communication of the terms of a secret trust may be made orally, even a half-secret trust, this merely indicates the trust's existence. Thus it appears not to comply with s 53(1)(b). There are conflicting views of this problem:

- *Re Baillie* (1886): a half-secret trust of land was held to fail because it was not evidenced in writing.
- *Ottaway v Norman* [1972]: the oral communication of a fully secret trust of a bungalow was accepted (although the formalities question was not explicitly raised).

This has led a number of commentators to speculate on whether secret trusts are express trusts or constructive trusts. It is arguable that secret trusts of land are acceptable on the basis of the rule in *Rochefoucauld v Boustead* [1897], which states that legal formalities will not be insisted on if they are being used to perpetrate a fraud (equity will not allow a statute to be an instrument of fraud). In other words, a legatee who is using the requirement of s 53(1)(b) to make the trust fail so that he can claim the property for himself will not be allowed to succeed.

 (!) **Conclusion**

Secret trusts are characterized by conceptual uncertainty and inconsistency, therefore a topic ripe for examination. The development of secret trusts aims to give effect to the final intentions of the testator. The development of secret trusts echoes, perhaps, the decision in *Choithram v Pagarani* [2001], in which Lord Browne-Wilkinson stated that equity will not 'strive officiously to defeat the intention of the testator'. While the origins of secret trusts lie many years in the past, secret trusts still appear to be in use, reflecting their continuing usefulness in today's society.

 (✱) **Key cases**

Case	Facts	Principle
Blackwell v Blackwell [1929] AC 318	The testator gave legacies to five people to apply the income 'for the purposes indicated by me to them'. Instructions to the trustees were made orally, to benefit the testator's mistress and their illegitimate son.	House of Lords established the validity of a half-secret trust, satisfying the same basic requirements as a fully secret trust. Additionally, *obiter*, that should the secret trustee refuse to carry out the trust that it would not defeat the trust and a willing replacement would be appointed.

Case	Facts	Principle
McCormick v Grogan (1869) LR 4 HL 82	Testator left property to Grogan and as he lay dying instructed Grogan that there was a letter instructing Grogan as to what to do with the property after the testator's death. The terms of the instructions were not obligatory. 'I do not wish you to act strictly on the foregoing instructions, but leave it entirely to your own good judgement to do as you think I would, if living, and as the parties are deserving.' Grogan complied with some of the wishes but not all.	• The wording of the letter was properly constructed as imposing merely a moral obligation upon Grogan. This was not sufficient to create a secret trust and therefore the claimant's action failed. • Secret trusts are imposed to prevent a secret trustee from defrauding a testator, who only left property to the secret trustee in reliance on his promise to carry out the testator's wishes.
Moss v Cooper (1861) 4 LT 790	Testator left property to three secret trustees G, S, and O. The will and details of trust were drawn up by one of the secret trustees, who then communicated the details of the trust to the other two secret trustees, who neither expressly rejected nor accepted. S did accept eventually but O remained silent on the issue.	• It will be sufficient if the intention and terms of a secret trust are communicated to the trustees by an agent of the testator. • Silence can also amount to acceptance; knowing of the trust he failed to object.
Ottaway v Norman [1972] 2 WLR 50	The testator left property to his housekeeper on the understanding that on her death she would leave the property to O. She died and left the property to N.	• Sets out the requirements for a valid secret trust. • That a land can be the subject matter of a secret trust.
Re Keen [1937] Ch 236	The testator had given one of his trustees instructions contained in a sealed envelope to be opened on his death. He did this before his will was executed. However, after he died the relevant bequest in his will stated that the property was left to the trustees for purposes that *would be communicated* to them in his lifetime.	• Details of the secret trust could be in a closed envelope if before the testator's death, the trustee knows of the testator's intention to create a trust and where he can find the terms of this trust (constructive communication). • The will must be consistent with the communication. The testator had already informed the trustees of his wishes while the will referred to future communication.

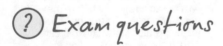 **Key debates**

Topic	Fraud as a justification
Academic/ Author	Critchley
Viewpoint	That the argument for *dehors* is implausible and that fraud is the justification.
Source	'Instruments of fraud, testamentary dispositions and the doctrine of secret trusts' (1999) 115 LQR 631.

Topic	Secret trusts as *dehors* the will
Academic/ Author	Kincaid
Viewpoint	The relationship between the will and the secret trust and the justifications evaluated.
Source	'The tangled web: the relationship between the secret trust and the will' [2000] Conv 420.

Topic	Secret trusts operate outside the will
Academic/ Author	Pawlowski and Brown
Viewpoint	That the secret trust is an express trust which is created outside the will and may be justified on the basis of estoppel.
Source	'Constituting a secret trust by estoppel' [2004] Conv 388.

(?) Exam questions

Problem question

Jasper recently died; his will makes the following bequests:

1. To Kamjit I leave my home, Bushmills.

2. To Jessica and Hamid I leave my shares in Badgers Bridges Ltd to be held on trust, on terms of which they are aware.

The will is dated 12 December 2003. On 11 December 2003, Jasper called Jessica and asked her to be his secret trustee. He also told her that the details of the trust were locked in his safe. Jessica accepted. Two days before his death Jasper met Kamjit and said that he had left his home to her, but it was to be for the benefit of his love child, Hector. Kamjit broke down and cried and said nothing.

Advise Jessica, Hamid, and Kamjit.

An outline answer is included at the end of the book.

Essay question

The fraud theory cannot justify a secret trust as they are in themselves a fraud on the requirements of the Wills Act 1837. Discuss.

An outline answer is available online at www.oxfordtextbooks.co.uk/orc/concentrate/

#9
Implied trusts

Key facts

- Implied trusts can be either resulting or constructive.
- There are no formalities for the creation of implied trusts.
- The law has developed methods of identifying the creation of implied trusts.
- Implied trusts are particularly important in relation to the family home.

Introduction

The flexibility of equity to adapt to the changing demands of society and commercial needs is seen nowhere more clearly than in the use and development of implied trusts. This chapter will deal with the central issues of implied trusts and identify where they link to other areas of study. It is important to see trusts as a whole, rather than separate and discrete areas.

An important area for implied trusts is in relation to allocating rights in a family home. Lord Hope in *Stack v Dowden* [2007] noted that this area was an interest not just to the parties but to society in general. The cases reflect changing social attitudes to family roles and are a topic ripe for examination. The law in relation to implied trusts in this area has been dealt with in a separate section to help understand how the law on implied trusts applies.

Implied trusts

Revision tip

Be aware that implied trusts are a huge subject which can be examined in a variety of areas; as a remedy for breach of trust, enforcing property rights, failure of trusts, and protecting business interests.

Implied trusts fall outside the requirement for formalities required by s 53 (1) Law of Property Act 1925. Section 53(2) Law of Property Act 1925 states:

> This section does not affect the creation or operation of resulting, implied or constructive trusts.

Chapter 2 briefly considered implied trusts; resulting, constructive, and statutory. This chapter will look in more depth at resulting and constructive trusts. Implied trusts arise without the express declaration of trust by the settlor. This chapter will consider how these trusts are identified by the courts. Resulting trusts fall into two categories, automatic or presumed. Constructive trusts are more difficult to define as the scope of their application seems to have been 'left deliberately vague' so that the courts can develop them as needed.

Resulting trusts

Resulting trusts are said to operate independently of the intention of the party but this is not an absolute. The 'settlor' may not intend to create a trust but they may still intend to benefit another person with the property. The courts look at the intention to benefit another person rather than the intention to create a trust: *Twinsectra v Yardley* [2002].

Automatic resulting trust

As stated in *Twinsectra v Yardley* [2002]; the automatic resulting trust arises *despite* the intentions of the parties. They arise in the following situations;

Resulting trusts

✶✶✶✶✶✶✶✶✶✶✶

1. Uncertainty of objects,
2. Failure of a **contingency**,
3. Failure to dispose of whole beneficial interest,
4. Surplus of funds after a valid purpose trust has completed its purpose,
5. Money given for a stated purpose which can no longer be carried out.

Uncertainty of objects

Chapter 3 noted that failure to specify the beneficiaries of a trust means the trust fails. Equity **abhors a vacuum** and the beneficial interest must be owned by someone and should not exist in suspension. So the property is said to be held on resulting trust for the settlor; *Vandervell v IRC* [1967]. Additionally, poor drafting may result in failure (*Re Diplock* [1948]) where a purported charitable trust is actually construed as a purpose which does not fall within one of the accepted **anomalous exceptions** (chapter 7), then the property will result back to the settlor or his estate.

Failure of a contingency

Some interests are contingent (conditional); for example, a trust for Iain, should he reach the age of 25. If he fails to reach that age then the conditions of the settlement have not been fulfilled. A person with a contingent interest has no **vested** interest in the property; if he cannot or does not meet the contingency then the trustee must hold the property for someone. As with the situation above, this problem is resolved by an automatic resulting trust for the settlor; *Re Ames Settlement* [1946].

> *Terminology tip*
>
> A vested interest is a *present* right to property. It is owned by the person who has that interest. But a contingent interest is conditional and the person has no property until the contingency is met.

Failure to dispose of whole beneficial interest

A failure to specify who owns the whole beneficial interest will mean that it is held for the settlor; *Re West* [1900]. For example, Anne leaves her shares to Iain for his lifetime; the trustee is clear that it is for Iain while he lives but who gets the property when Iain dies? The property will result back to Anne's estate.

Surplus of funds after a valid purpose trust has completed its purpose

A valid purpose trust, either charitable or an anomalous exception, may complete the purpose and have money left over. In this situation, the question arises as to what to do with the trust property and/or any donations?

Purpose trust with human objects

Where the purpose is not charitable and there are human objects of the trust then the question arises as to what to do with the donations (see chapter 7). There are two views of this situation:

- A pure purpose which is valid and complete, or there is money left at the end of the perpetuity period with no gift over, then the money is returned to the donors/settlors; *Re the Trust of the Abbott Fund* [1900].

- The money is given to the objects of the trust as an outright gift. The purported purpose is seen as no more than a motive for the donation; *Re Osaba* [1978].

Purpose trust with no human objects

If the purpose has no human beneficiaries but is one of the anomalous exceptions then the property would result back to the estate of the settlor after the completion of the task or the end of the perpetuity period. Different rules will apply to charitable trusts (chapter 6).

Unincorporated associations

A trust for an unincorporated association can be seen as a purpose trust (see chapter 7). When the association ceases to exist there are two main interpretations of how to deal with the property held by the association.

- The property held by the association is held on resulting trust by the association for the individual members and will be divided between them in proportion to their contributions; *Re Printers and Transferrers' Amalgamated Trades Protection Society* [1899]. The problem with this interpretation is that the members and contributors may not be identifiable. So this analysis can only work where the contributors are ascertainable.

- The property held by the association is held for the members of the association according to the contractual obligations in the association rules; *Re Bucks Constabulary Widows & Orphans Fund Friendly Society (No 2)* [1979]. The advantage of this is the ascertainability of the people entitled to the funds.

✅ *Looking for extra marks?*

An interesting view was taken by Goff J in *Re West Sussex Constabulary's Widows* [1971]. He differentiated between contributions made by members and funds raised by donations and fundraising raffles. It was suggested that those who donate to street collections have no intention of retaining an interest.

Money given for a stated purpose which can no longer be carried out

When money is paid to a person on the understanding that it will be used for a certain purpose then if that purpose cannot be carried out the money will be held on resulting trust for the donor; *Barclays Bank v Quistclose* [1970]. It must be clear that the transfer was made *only* for that purpose and with the intention that should that purpose fail then the money will be returned.

The focus for the courts is in finding the necessary intention when lending the money to the recipient. While holding in a separate account is good evidence it is not essential; *Re EVTR Ltd* [1987]. The courts will also look at the agreement between the parties to ascertain the intention. In *Twinsectra v Yardley* [2002] Millet LJ said that as the agreement indicated that the money was not at the free disposal of the recipient it was held on resulting trust for the settlor if not used for the specified purpose.

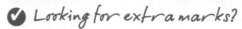 *Looking for extra marks?*

The use of a *Quistclose* trust can create problems on insolvency as it seems to give a preference to certain creditors, which is contrary to the provisions in the Insolvency Act 1986. This could form a basis for an essay, and the litigation in relation to the collapse of Farepak is worth reading to gain an understanding in this area.

Presumed resulting trusts

There are a number of situations in which the conduct of the parties will create a presumption that a resulting trust was intended. These are:

1. The voluntary conveyance of property to another.

2. The purchase of property in the name of another.

Remember that presumptions are only a starting point for the court and can be rebutted by evidence which indicates a different intention.

Voluntary conveyance

A voluntary conveyance refers to a transfer of property where the recipient does not provide **valuable consideration**. The maxim that 'equity presumes a bargain and never a gift' would hold that a party would never give away property. In this situation the presumption (the starting evidential point for the court) is that the property is held by the recipient of the legal title (presuming that the legal formalities for transfer are perfect, see chapter 5) for the benefit of the transferor.

Where the property transferred is real property (land) then this presumption is undermined by s 60(3) Law of Property Act 1925. This states that:

> in a voluntary conveyance, a resulting trust for the grantor shall not be implied, merely by reason that the property is not expressed to be for the use or benefit of the grantee.

It has been suggested that the effect of this section is that a resulting trust will no longer be presumed where the property conveyed is land. In *Lohia v Lohia* [2001] it was said that 'on a plain reading' of the section the presumption of resulting trust was abolished. However, other cases maintain that as a matter of basic equitable principle s 60(3) does not prevent a resulting trust being presumed – see *Hodgson v Marks* [1971]. The position is, as Lord Browne-Wilkinson said in *Tinsley v Milligan* [1993], 'arguable'.

Purchase in the name of another

When one person provides either part or all of the money required to buy a property but is not identified as the legal owner of that property, equity will again assume 'a bargain' and not a gift. In contrast to the voluntary conveyance of property considered above, this presumption applies regardless of whether the purchased property is **personalty** or **realty**.

Where two parties contribute towards the purchase then they will hold the property in proportion to the contribution they made to the purchase price. The contribution must be prior to or at the time of purchase; *Cowcher v Cowcher* [1972].

Rebutting the presumption of resulting trust

As with all presumptions in law, it is for the party who is not relying on the presumption to rebut it.

✅ Looking for extra marks

A basis of essays and problem questions may be the old law in relation to the presumption of advancement.

Before the Equality Act 2010 in certain relationships there was an easily rebuttable presumption that the transfer or purchase was a gift; *McGrath v Wallis* [1995].

The relationships were based on 'inferences of fact...[from the] intention of...the propertied classes of a different social era' per Lord Diplock in *Pettitt v Pettitt* [1970]. Transfers from husbands to wives; father to child and those in *loco parentis* to a child. This presumption will be removed by s 199 Equality Act 2010, when this section is enacted, as it is outdated in current social situations. For further details see the online materials.

The transfer was merely a loan

Evidence can be provided that the grantor intended their contribution only as a loan and there was no intention of gaining an interest in the property merely a contractual right; *Clark v Mandoj* [1998].

The transfer was intended as a gift

Evidence, express or by conduct, which is sufficiently certain as to create the intention to give as a gift will rebut the presumption of a resulting trust; *Fowkes v Pascoe* (1875).

What evidence can be relied upon to rebut these presumptions?

Statements made before or at the time of transfer or purchase: acts or statements made before or at the time of transfer can be relied upon by *both parties* in addressing whether a presumption of resulting trust or advancement is to be rebutted. Statements made after transfer or purchase *cannot* be relied upon by the *maker* of those statements; *Shepherd v Cartwright* [1955].

 **Looking for extra marks?**

Shepherd v Cartwright [1955] suggests that acts or declarations which occur *'so immediately* after [the purchase] as to constitute part of the transaction are admissible' (emphasis added). It will be a question of fact whether later statements made after the transfer are part of the transaction. This may be a point of discussion in an exam.

Evidence of illegal purpose: the person trying to rebut the presumption *cannot* rely upon evidence of an illegal purpose; *Gascoigne v Gascoigne* [1918]. This supports the view that those who seek equity must come with 'clean hands'. However, the situation is not clear cut. In *Tinsley v Milligan* [1993] property was purchased by joint contributions. To avoid losing housing benefits it was bought in Tinsley's name only. When the relationship broke down, Milligan claimed a beneficial share of the property based on her contribution to the purchase.

The House of Lords rejected the Court of Appeal decision based upon 'public conscience' as being too broad. The majority of the House of Lords held that Milligan did not need to rely on her illegal purpose to support the presumption of a resulting trust. She merely had to produce evidence of the contribution to the purchase price.

In *Tribe v Tribe* [1996] the Court of Appeal distinguished the decision of the majority in *Tinsley v Milligan* [1993]. A father voluntarily transferred shares to his son to avoid debtors who had threatened litigation, which never transpired. The father tried to reclaim the shares.

The son, relying upon the old law on presumption of advancement, which required the father to rebut the presumption by reliance on the evidence of his illegal purpose in the transfer, refused to return them.

The Court of Appeal was able to distinguish *Tinsley v Milligan* because he had withdrawn from the illegal purpose; had the illegal purpose been carried out he could not have relied upon it.

 **Looking for extra marks?**

It is unclear from the decision in *Tribe v Tribe* how far the illegal purpose has to progress before it can be said to capable of withdrawal. This creates a lack of clarity in the area. It is also worth reading the judgment of Lord Goff in *Tinsley v Milligan* to get an alternative view of the outcome. Although all rejected the Court of Appeal's public conscience basis of the finding, Lord Goff dissented from the majority on the outcome.

Constructive trusts

Unlike resulting trusts the categories of constructive trusts are not clearly defined. They have been left 'perhaps deliberately vague' (per Edmund-Davies LJ *Carl Zeiss Stiftung v Herbert Smith* [1969]). They have been used as a residuary category of trusts which are imposed by the courts when 'justice…may require'.

It can be simply stated that the courts 'construct' a trust around the conscience of the legal owner. As Lord Browne-Wilkinson said in his judgment in *Westdeutsche Landesbank Girozentrale v Islington LBC* [1996]:

> In the case of a [constructive] trust the conscience of the legal owner requires him to carry out the purposes which the law imposes on him by reason of his unconscionable conduct.

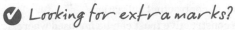 **Looking for extra marks?**

Other jurisdictions have used constructive trusts as a wide-ranging remedy. The English courts have taken a more traditional approach. While there are hints that a remedial trust could eventually develop (see the comments of Lord Scott in *Thorner v Major* [2009]), the current position is that England and Wales do not use a constructive trust as a remedy for a wrong; *Polly Peck International plc (in administration) No 2* [1998].

Traditional constructive trusts

A breach of a fiduciary obligation will give rise to a constructive trust. Fiduciary relationships generally arise where there is a situation of 'trust and confidence' between the parties. A fiduciary relationship can arise in a variety of situations, such as solicitor/client; accountant/client. Where such a relationship exists, the fiduciary owes an obligation to the principal to carry out their fiduciary duties correctly. Below are examples of where a breach of a fiduciary obligation has created a constructive trust.

1. Solicitor: *Lipkin Gorman v Karpnale* [1991]
2. Trustee: *Keech v Sandford* (1726)
3. Company directors: *Guinness v Saunders* [1990]
4. Intermeddlers with a trust: *Mara v Browne* [1896]
5. Recipients of trust property: *BCCI v Akindele* [2000]
6. Persons who assist in the breach of a trust: *Twinsectra v Yardley* [2002]
7. Positions of trust within an organization: *AG for Hong Kong v Reid* [1994]
8. Breach of contractual obligations: *Ashburn Anstalt v Arnold* [1989]

****

> *Revision tip*
>
> Note that the categories above are not closed. Judicial statements indicate that even a thief who obtains property raises the necessary fiduciary relationship; *Westdeutsche Landesbank Girozentrale v Islington LBC* [1996]. If this is the case then it does open the door for the more flexible remedial constructive trust.

Categories 1–7 are dealt with in detail in later chapters so are only identified here for you to see the interwoven nature of equitable principles.

Contractual obligations giving rise to constructive trusts

A contractual relationship does not necessarily create a fiduciary relationship so it would be incorrect to say that it is imposed as a fiduciary. However, the constructive trust has been used as a method of giving a remedy for a breach of contractual obligations.

Ashburn Anstalt v Arnold [1989] stated that a constructive trust can be imposed where 'it was satisfied that the conscience of the owner of the land had been affected so that it would be inequitable to allow him to deny the claimant an interest'. However, this decision is based on its own particular facts and has been doubted in *IDC v Clark* [1992].

✅ *Looking for extra marks?*

The imposition of a trust for the breach of a personal obligation may be a step too far. See the decision in a commercial context of *Yeoman's Row v Cobbe* [2008], which seemed to shut the door on their imposition, although Lord Scott's later statements in *Thorner v Major* [2009] seem to reopen it.

Trusts of the family home

When relationships break up the most common battle is over the ownership of the family home. In this part of the chapter we consider how implied trusts apply to family property. When a home is legally owned by two or more people at law they will own the property as joint tenants. There is a presumption that they will also own the beneficial interest as joint tenants. The burden will be on the person trying to rebut that presumption to prove that the beneficial interest is owned differently; *Stack v Dowden* (2007). If there is only one legal owner then it is for the claimant to establish a beneficial interest first, before it can be quantified; *Lloyds Bank v Rosset* (1991).

Resulting trusts

When a party pays money which is used to purchase a family home the presumptions of resulting trust and advancement explained above will apply. For a resulting trust to be established, the contribution must be made prior to or at the time of acquisition of the property; *Curley v Parkes* [2004]. A point to note is that when there is a mortgage over the property, the person who takes the mortgage out is held to make that contribution on their own behalf; *Cowcher v Cowcher* [1972].

Quantifying the share of the home under a resulting trust

The share is in direct proportion to the contribution. This is the 'bank balance' approach to allocating shares in the home, if there was a 10% contribution to the purchase it will give rise to a 10% interest in the property.

Constructive trusts and the family home

An interest in the family home may be gained when it would be 'unconscionable' for the legal owner to deny that another person should have some claim to the ownership of the home. It was accepted in *Gissing v Gissing* [1971] that contributions other than financial can create an interest in the home. Lord Bridge in *Lloyds Bank v Rosset* [1991] stated that this is based upon the common intention of the parties. This can be found in two ways:

- Express common intention constructive trust.
- Inferred (implied) common intention constructive trust.

As stated in *Stack v Dowden* [2007] it is clear that there is a two-stage procedure:

- Establish a beneficial interest.
- Quantify the beneficial interest.

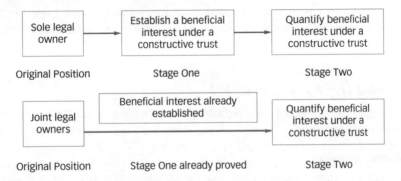

Figure 9.1

Express common intention trusts

An express common intention constructive trust will arise when, at the time of acquisition (but exceptionally later), the parties have expressed a shared common intention to share the interest in the home.

- The intention must be express.
- The intention must be common.

Trusts of the family home

****

- The common intention must relate to the acquisition of a share in the beneficial interest of the family home.

Express

In *Springette v DeFoe* [1992] Dillon LJ said that the interest:

> cannot mean an intention which each happened to have in his or her own mind but had never communicated to each other.

The express agreement can be 'imperfectly or imprecisely remembered' as Lord Bridge said in *Lloyds Bank v Rosset* [1991]. The courts are not looking for legal language, but language clear enough to form the necessary intention on which to base a proprietary interest.

Common

The intention must be common. It must be shared by both parties and not the view of only one of the parties In *Springette v DeFoe* [1992] Dillon LJ continued that as their intention was not expressed it would be difficult to find that their intention was 'common'.

Sharing the home

The intention must be to share the home, not just to share their lives. Thus, an agreement to pay rent would not help to establish an interest in the family home; *Thomas v Fuller-Brown* [1988]. It must concern gaining an interest in the family home. In *Eves v Eves* [1975], lies to the young claimant about why she was not to be registered on the legal title gave the courts enough evidence that there had been a discussion about owning the house and not just sharing a life together.

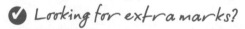 **Looking for extra marks?**

It could be suggested that the fact that one party lies is explicit evidence that there is no intention to share. See key debates below.

Detrimental reliance

Once an express common intention is found, the person seeking to establish the existence of a constructive trust must prove that he relied on that agreement to his detriment. The reliance must be subsequent to the express intention, and not something that was being done before and part of the normal tasks of a couple; *Lloyds Bank v Rossett* [1991]. The conduct from which reliance can be found is broad in *this* category of constructive trust. In cases such as *Eves v Eves* [1975] and *Grant v Edwards* [1986] the courts look for some action that the other would not have done 'but for' believing they had an interest in the home.

Figure 9.2

Case	Conduct which has sufficed to create an interest following an express agreement
Eves v Eves [1975]	Had children, cleaned and decorated home. It seemed significant to the court that she undertook heavy manual work on home
Grant v Edwards [1986]	'made a very substantial contribution to the housekeeping and the feeding and bringing up of the children…[using] her earnings in that way'

In considering if there has been detrimental reliance the courts try to distinguish from actions which are 'truly' detrimental and those which are merely demonstrations of 'love and affection'. In *Lloyds Bank v Rosset* [1991] the actions of Mrs Rosset were no more than would be expected from a wife. See also *Pettitt v Pettitt* [1970].

Revision Tip

A common mistake for students in exams is to leap straight into the discussion of detrimental reliance, using the cases explained above. Students will then note that there has been no express agreement. To an examiner this indicates a poorly thought out answer and perhaps a misunderstanding. If there is no agreement then the relevance of contributions other than directly financial is relevant *only to the quantification* of the interest. See below.

Inferred common intention constructive trusts

In the absence of an express agreement the common intention is to be inferred from the conduct of the parties. There is only one type of conduct which allows the courts to infer that the parties intended to share the beneficial interest in the family home: direct financial contributions.

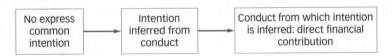

Figure 9.3

Gissing v Gissing [1971] stated that in the absence of express statements, the question of the parties' intention was an objective one. Lord Bridge went further in *Lloyds Bank v Rosset* [1991] where he 'doubted anything else' but contributions which are referable to the acquisition of the property would be sufficient to infer the common intention. Thus, payments at the time of acquisition will apply, such as paying a deposit, but the difference between this and resulting trust is that later payments to the mortgage will also be sufficient. If there is no such payment then this category of trust will fail.

Trusts of the family home

✳✳✳✳✳✳✳✳✳✳✳

Figure 9.4

Case	Conduct that HAS NOT given an interest under an inferred constructive trust
Pettitt v Pettitt [1970]	Husband had laid out the garden, built walls, and done substantial work in the home.
Thomas v Fuller-Brown [1988]	Designing and building a two-storey extension to home. Inferred this was just work in lieu of rent.
Gissing v Gissing [1971]	Contributions to children's clothes, her own clothes, and laid the lawn.
Case	**Conduct that HAS given an interest under an inferred constructive trust**
Hussey v Palmer [1972]	Claimant paid for an extension which increased the value of the house; she gained an interest in the home.

✔ Looking for extra marks?

In *Gissing v Gissing* [1971] although there was a later express agreement the court held this did not reflect their intention at the time of acquisition. Consider if there is a gender stereotype in cases such as *Pettitt v Pettitt* [1970]. Be prepared to comment on cases in essays. Also, the case of *Burns v Burns* [1984] can be seen as the high point of the inferred constructive trust concept and *Lloyds Bank v Rosset* [1991] has firmly rejected this move. Although there have been *obiter* comments in the lower courts (*Le Foe v Le Foe* (2001) that the statement by Lord Bridge, that he 'doubted' that anything other than direct contributions to the acquisition of the property would count, was not a statement that other contributions could *never* count. It was possible that in 'exceptional' circumstances other conduct could be considered. This has also been addressed by the House of Lords in *Stack v Dowden* [2007]. Comments by Baroness Hale and Lord Walker suggest that the time may be ripe to consider other financial contribution to the family home as able to infer a common intention to hold on constructive trust.

Revision tip

It is important to note that the statements in *Le Foe v Le Foe* and *Stack v Dowden* do not change the ruling in *Lloyds Bank v Rosset*, on the issue of *establishing* an equitable interest. As it was not an issue in *Stack v Dowden* the comments of the Lords there are *obiter*. It is a point to consider in giving depth to an answer. *Also note*: the conduct which will create an equitable interest must be kept separate from the conduct which will quantify an interest which we consider below.

Quantifying the share under a constructive trust

Having established the property interest under a constructive trust the courts will then quantify the interest. Unlike the 'bank balance' approach of resulting trusts the issue of quantification in respect of constructive trusts of the family home is more problematic. As the trust is based upon the conscience of the party then the 'equity required to do justice' will vary.

Starting point

If the parties are joint legal owners then the starting position for the courts will be that 'equity follows the law' and they share the beneficial ownership; *Stack v Dowden* [2007]. Where there is sole legal ownership the law presumes that it is owned solely by the legal owner. The person trying to rebut these presumptions can produce evidence to the contrary.

Evidence

While parties may agree to share their home they rarely, in the flush of romance, discuss just how the home will be divided should they separate. If such an agreement is made then the courts will give effect to that express agreement; *Springette v DeFoe* [1992]. This will apply regardless of actual contributions; *Clough v Killey* [1996].

In an inferred common intention constructive trust the evidence will be based upon the contributions made by the beneficial claimant; *Gissing v Gissing* [1971]. However, for both types of constructive trust these are starting positions for allocating interests.

The courts take what has been called a 'broad brush approach' to quantifying the share and will look at the whole course of dealing between the parties to allocate interests. Cases such as *Midland Bank v Cooke* [1995] and *Drake v Whipp* [1996] have suggested that 'the whole course of dealing' between the parties should be considered which 'should not be confined to acts of direct contributions'. In *Oxley v Hiscock* [2004] Chadwick LJ suggested to quantify interests in the family home based on principles of 'fairness' at the end of the relationship or based on principles of proprietary estoppel; *Yaxley v Gotts* [2000].

Stack v Dowden [2007] has reviewed this area, while calling for changes in how to establish a beneficial interest; it has rejected decisions based on fairness (see Lord Neuberger at 144) but Baroness Hale has set out what factors may be considered very clearly in her judgment.

Revision tip

In explaining this area it is essential that students are very clear that it is a two-stage step when there is a sole legal owner. First establish a beneficial interest, using the principles in *Lloyds Bank v Rosset*. The second step, which also applies when there are joint legal owners, is to establish the beneficial share; *Stack v Dowden*.

Proprietary estoppel

If a trust cannot be found then the courts retain the ability to find an estoppel. It is important to note that proprietary estoppel can be the basis of an action (therefore a sword and a shield). The courts look for:

- an assurance, which can be a unilateral statement;
- followed by reliance of the claimant, see *Pascoe v Turner* [1979].

Conclusion

Detriment which makes conduct unconscionable

Assurance can be active or passive, such as allowing another to work on your property, knowing that they believe by such actions they will gain an interest in the home. The reliance can be not seeking alternative arrangements for accommodation or work; *Gillett v Holt* [2001]. This area has been reviewed recently in a commercial context in *Yeoman's Row v Cobbe* [2008] and in a family situation in *Thorner v Major* [2009].

 Conclusion

The imposition of implied trusts has a varied and complex basis. The resulting and constructive trust can be applied to any property but has particular practical relevance in relation to the family home.

However, be aware that implied trusts are a huge area which can be examined in a variety of areas: as a remedy for breach of trust, enforcing property rights, failure of trusts, and protecting business interests.

 Key cases

Case	Facts	Principle
Barclays Bank v Quistclose [1970] AC 567	Money was lent for the payment of dividends. The payments were not made and the company went into liquidation.	The money given to pay dividends was held on a primary trust to pay dividends and when that failed the secondary trust (resulting) was to repay the lender.
Lloyds Bank v Rosset [1991] AC 107	Property was purchased with a mortgage in the name of Mr Rosset only. Extensive renovation work was supervised by Mrs Rosset. The bank claimed possession of the home when the mortgage was defaulted. Mrs Rosset tried to establish an equitable interest in the home by way of constructive trust.	To establish an interest under a constructive trust it must be proved that there was: • an express declaration that the beneficial interest would arise followed by detrimental reliance; or • financial contributions to the purchase of the home, which could be post-acquisition, from which the courts could infer a common intention as to beneficial ownership.
Shepherd v Cartwright [1955] AC 431	Property purchased by a father for his legitimate child.	The court presumes that this is a gift and no equitable interest arises for the father unless he can prove a contrary intention.

Case	Facts	Principle
Tinsley v Milligan [1993] 3 All ER 65	Property was bought in the name of one party but both contributed to the purchase. The reason for the purchase in one name only was to defraud the benefits system.	An equitable right could arise if a party can establish an equitable right without relying on their illegality.

Key debates

Topic	Constructive trusts and common intention
Academic/ Author	Anna Lawson
Viewpoint	That the cases where a party lies to another about their interest such as *Eves v Eves* suggest that the intention is anything but to share beneficially.
Source	'The things we do for love: detrimental reliance in the family home' LS 1996, 16(2), 218–31. See also Gardner, 'Rethinking family property' (1993) 109 LQR 263.

Topic	Reform of trusts in the family home
Academic/ Author	Hughes *et al*
Viewpoint	Excellent summary of the proposals for reform.
Source	'Come live with me and be my love' Conv 2008, 3, 197–225.

Topic	Quantification of share in the family home
Academic/ Author	Martin Dixon
Viewpoint	Does *Stack v Dowden* change anything in the imputation or inference of how the beneficial interest should be shared? Looking at the following Privy Council decision too.
Source	'Never ending story – co-ownership after *Stack v Dowden*' Conv 2007, Sept/Oct, 456–61.

Topic	Commonwealth approaches to sharing the family home
Academic/ Author	Pearce and Stevens; Moffat
Viewpoint	A summary of the approach in other jurisdictions which will form a base for comparative essays.
Source	Pearce and Stevens, *Law of Trusts and Equitable Obligations*, 4th edn (2006), pp 307–15. Moffat, *Trusts Law*, 4th edn (2005), pp 625–41.

Exam questions

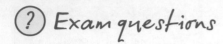

Problem question

Anne and Iain buy a house for £100,000. Anne takes out a mortgage for £80,000 in her name. Anne pays £18,000, while Iain pays the remaining £2,000. When they move in Iain tells Anne that he thinks couples should share everything. Anne replies 'that is a lovely idea'. Iain later wins £18,000 on the lottery and gives this to Anne to buy a car.

Iain takes on all the household duties so that Anne can pursue her career. While Anne is pregnant Iain takes over paying the mortgage. Iain agrees to be the primary carer of their child so that Anne can continue her work.

After ten years Anne now wants to sell the house and travel the world, without Iain.

Advise Iain on his interest in the home.

An outline answer is included at the end of the book.

Essay question

The imposition of a resulting trust for a settlor may be contrary to their every intention. Discuss the situations when a resulting trust can arise and if they are justified.

An outline answer is available online at www.oxfordtextbooks.co.uk/orc/concentrate/

#10
Variation of trusts

- A trust may be varied by a power within the trust itself, the collective consent of the beneficiaries, by the court, through its inherent jurisdiction, or by statute.

- The power of the courts to intervene will depend on whether the variation relates to administrative or managerial matters or a reorganization of the beneficial interests.

- The Variation of Trusts Act (VTA) 1958 gives the courts a wide jurisdiction to vary a trust for the benefit of those beneficiaries unable to consent.

- A benefit under the VTA 1958 will typically be financial but the court can also take into account non-financial benefits.

Introduction

As a trust can operate for many years, there may be occasions where it is useful or necessary to vary the terms of the trust. The most common reason for varying the terms of a
trust is to minimize beneficiaries' liability to pay tax. The key issue in variation of trusts is
consent – either by the beneficiaries or, where necessary, by the courts. Where this consent
does not exist, trustees who do not follow the terms of the trust will be liable for breach of
trust. However, it will often be impossible for all the beneficiaries to consent. Therefore, the
majority of this chapter will focus on the circumstances in which the courts may approve a
variation on their behalf.

Methods of varying the terms of the trust

A trust can be varied by:

- the terms of the trust instrument;
- the consent of beneficiaries;
- the court's inherent jurisdiction; or
- statutory provisions.

The trust instrument

The provisions of the trust may expressly provide trustees with the power to vary the terms
of the trust. This allows trustees to modify the terms of the trust to adjust to changing circumstances without having to receive the consent of the beneficiaries or use trust assets in
gaining court approval for such variations. While this might appear to give trustees free
rein to remould the trust as they see fit, a measure of protection is provided by *Society of
Lloyd's v Robinson* [1999]. Lord Steyn stated that a power to vary the terms of a trust must
be exercised for the purpose for which it was granted and not beyond the reasonable contemplation of the parties. Therefore, the extent to which the trustees are free to vary the terms
of the trust will depend on the terms on which the power was granted.

Example

Richard establishes a trust for Jackie for life, remainder to Eleanor. The trust includes a
power to the trustees to vary the terms of the trust 'where necessary for the efficient administration of the trust'. Suppose that after 20 years' dedicated service the trustees propose to
include a new term in the trust to provide them with an annual salary: would they succeed?

Arguably, they would not. The power to vary refers to changes improving the efficient
administration of the trust. The trustees are already bound by their fiduciary obligations
to carry out their responsibilities – if it is argued that money would 'improve' their efficiency, legitimate questions might be asked about how well they have so far carried out their

responsibilities! The trustees, of course, remain free to pursue remuneration through other methods – eg s 29 Trustee Act 2000 or court-approved payments (see chapter 11).

Beneficiary consent: the rule in *Saunders v Vautier*

Collectively, the beneficiaries can use the rule in *Saunders v Vautier* (1841) to end the trust, at which point they may choose to take the property absolutely or resettle it on more favourable terms. The rule in *Saunders v Vautier* can only be applied where:

- all the beneficiaries are together absolutely entitled to the trust property;
- all beneficiaries agree to ending the trust; and
- all beneficiaries are *sui juris* – ie adults (over 18) with the legal capacity to give consent.

There are two important limitations on the rule in *Saunders v Vautier*:

1. Beneficiaries cannot use the threat of ending the trust as a bargaining chip to force trustees to invest the trust funds in accordance with their instructions; *Stephenson Inspector of Taxes) v Barclays Bank Trust Co Ltd* [1975]. If this were permitted, trustees would effectively be prevented from discharging their fiduciary obligations to the beneficiaries by personally considering and deciding how their best interests are served.

2. *All* beneficiaries must give their consent. If the beneficiaries include children, beneficiaries who cannot legally consent, or others who do not yet exist, the rule in *Saunders v Vautier* will not apply.

As any change to the terms of the trust requires the collective consent of all beneficiaries, variation will not always be possible. However, in certain circumstances the court will be able to provide approval for those beneficiaries who cannot.

The courts' inherent jurisdiction

The courts have an inherent jurisdiction to vary the terms of a trust where the consent of all the beneficiaries cannot be obtained. As Romer LJ stated in *Re New* [1901], this is a jurisdiction which is to be exercised 'with great caution, and the court will take care not to strain its powers'. The central concern of the courts is to act only when it is required and, otherwise, to avoid interfering with the intentions of the settlor.

Revision tip

Reading some of the key cases in this area can really improve your understanding of the area. However, the facts of these cases and the proposals for variation can often be technical and complex. Concentrate on the headnote and the leading judgment. The judgments tend to focus on the central issues and will help you get to the heart of the legal questions.

Methods of varying the terms of the trust
✳✳✳✳✳✳✳✳✳✳✳

What sort of variations could be approved?

The court will only approve variations relating to the administration and management of the trust. It will not generally intervene in situations relating to the reorganization of the beneficial interests of the beneficiaries. (Note: there is one exception to this rule, in relation to **maintenance** provisions, which is discussed below under the emergency jurisdiction of the courts.)

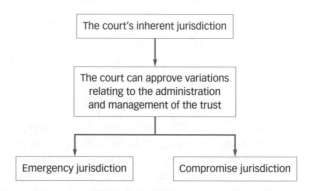

Figure 10.1 The court's inherent jurisdiction

In what circumstances will the court approve a variation?

Following the decision of the House of Lords in *Chapman v Chapman* [1954], the courts' jurisdiction is restricted to two situations, 'Emergency' and 'Compromise'.

'Emergency'

'Emergency' can be understood in its literal context, as in *Re Jackson* [1882], where the trustees needed permission to use trust money to make repairs to a trust property which was about to collapse. However, a more accurate understanding of an 'emergency' is something not anticipated by the settlor; *Chapman v Chapman* [1954]. This means that the court will intervene if, *by not taking action*, it would frustrate or interfere with the settlor's intention.

For example, in *Re Tollemache* [1903], the court refused to approve a variation merely because it was of financial benefit to the beneficiaries. However, it is interesting to contrast this decision with the reasoning of the Court of Appeal in *Re New* [1901]:

··

Re New [1901] 2 Ch 534

It was proposed that a company, in which the trust already had shares, be reorganized to allow for further growth. It was undisputed that this would be of benefit to the beneficiaries. However, the trustees did not have the power to invest in these new shares and applied for a variation to the terms of the trust from the court.

While the Court of Appeal approved the variation, Romer LJ emphasized that it was not within the court's inherent jurisdiction to interfere merely because a change would be of benefit to the beneficiaries. Instead, *as the proposed variation would not alter the trust's property but only its nature* (ie the *type* of holding), the court was satisfied that its intervention actually *supported* the settlor's intention of leaving shares in this company on trust.

. . . .

Maintenance provisions – The court will in general only approve variations to the administration or management of the trust. However, the underlying idea that the court will intervene only in matters unanticipated by the settlor has been used to justify one limited exception. Where a settlor has established a trust and directs that the income should be accumulated for a period of time, the court will approve the insertion of a term providing for the maintenance of a beneficiary, on the basis that a settlor would not establish a trust to benefit a beneficiary in the future but in the meantime allow the beneficiary to go short; *Havelock v Havelock* (1881).

'Compromise'

The second aspect of the court's inherent jurisdiction is in approving compromises where there is a conflict regarding the rights of the beneficiaries. Originally, 'compromise' was defined widely to allow the court to approve variations to the rights of the beneficiaries; *Re Downshire Settled Estates* [1953]. This allowed the court to approve of tax-saving and financially advantageous bargains between different classes of beneficiaries.

However, such a power was difficult to reconcile with the narrower 'emergency' jurisdiction of the courts, and in *Chapman v Chapman* [1954] the House of Lords adopted a more restrictive approach. Lord Morton argued that the court only had the jurisdiction to intervene in *'genuine disputes'* over the beneficial interests. He stressed that in such circumstances, the court could not be said to be interfering with the beneficial interests because the existence of a dispute meant that they were not already clear. Therefore, all the court was doing was *clarifying* the settlor's intentions.

Why is the court's inherent jurisdiction so narrowly defined?

Why did the House of Lords adopt such a cautious approach to their inherent jurisdiction, especially given that an application to vary the trust is usually accepted to be in the best financial interests of the beneficiaries? In *Chapman v Chapman*, Lord Simonds argued that if the courts were to exercise a wider jurisdiction, this should be authorized by the legislature and not claimed by the courts for themselves. This restrictive approach was criticized by the Law Reform Committee in their 1957 Report *The Court's Power to Sanction Variation of Trusts* (Cmnd 310) which provided the impetus for the Variation of Trusts Act 1958. This Act, together with the various other statutory provisions, has now largely replaced the court's inherent jurisdiction with a wider authority to approve changes to the terms of a trust.

Methods of varying the terms of the trust

Statutory provisions

The courts have also been given statutory authority to vary the terms of a trust in a number of circumstances:

Section 53 Trustee Act 1925: allows the court to vary the terms of a trust 'for the maintenance, education, or benefit of the infant'. It both mirrors the court's inherent jurisdiction to provide maintenance from a trust and extends it to authorize changes which support the education or benefit of a child.

Section 57(1) Trustee Act 1925: allows the court to approve changes to the administration and management of trusts where it is 'expedient' to do so. As this section does not require an emergency, it largely renders the court's inherent emergency jurisdiction redundant. However, this section does not allow the courts to interfere in the *beneficial interests* under a trust; *Re Downshire Settled Estates* [1953].

The Variation of Trusts Act 1958

The **Variation of Trusts Act 1958** allows the court to provide consent for certain types of beneficiary where they cannot do so for themselves. Thus, any variation still requires the consent of all other existing *sui juris* beneficiaries. What was striking about the Act was its scope: in *Re Steed's Will Trusts* [1960], Evershed MR described the Act as conferring 'a very wide and indeed revolutionary discretion' to the courts to vary the terms of a trust.

In order to answer a question on the application of the VTA 1958, you will need to consider the following questions:

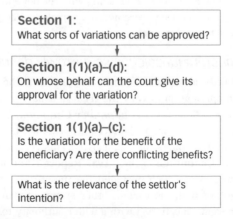

Figure 10.2 The Variation of Trusts Act 1958

What sorts of variations can be approved?

Section 1 VTA 1958 gives the courts the power to approve 'any arrangement...varying or revoking all or any of the trusts, or enlarging the powers of the trustees of managing or administering any of the property subject to the trusts'. Therefore, unlike other methods of variation discussed, the **VTA 1958** allows the court to deal with matters relating to both:

- administrative and managerial aspects of the trust; and
- all other terms, including those relating to the beneficial interests under the trust.

However, there are limits to what the court will approve. The court will *not* give its approval for variations which represent, in effect, a complete **resettlement** of the property on new trusts. In *Re Ball's ST* [1968], Megarry J explained that 'If an arrangement changes the whole substratum of the trust, then it may well be said that it cannot be regarded merely as varying that trust'. In the recent decision of *Ridgwell v Ridgwell* [2007], Behrens J accepted that a variation that created an additional life interest that deferred the entitlement of the remaindermen children did not fundamentally alter the basis of the original trust. Compare this decision with the following case:

Re T's ST [1963] 3 WLR 987

A mother held a life interest in half the trust's property, the remainder going to her two children. The other half of the trust's property was to be split between her two children when they reached 21. The mother believed that one of her daughters was irresponsible and immature and applied for a variation to the trust which would transfer her daughter's quarter share to a new protective trust under which she would hold a life interest. Wilberforce J rejected this proposal as it fundamentally altered the daughter's position under the trust from an absolute interest to a mere life interest.

✅ Looking for extra marks?

The courts' powers under the VTA 1958 are essentially supportive ones. When discussing the VTA 1958 in an essay, it is useful to be able to discuss this policy and not just recite the relevant decisions. If you read the judgment in *Re Ball's ST* [1968] and particularly *Re T's ST* [1963], you will see that the court does more than simply approve or reject proposed variations. In both cases, the court contributes advice on how a successful application can be made. For example, in *Re T's ST* [1963], while Wilberforce J was unwilling to approve the proposed application, he was sympathetic to the applicant's concerns and granted a revised order which *postponed* the vesting of the daughter's absolute interest and created an interim **protective trust** which could be extended should the daughter's behaviour warrant it.

On whose behalf can the court give its approval for the variation?

The **VTA 1958** does not change the fact that all *sui juris* beneficiaries must consent to any proposed change to the terms of the trust. In general, the parties to an application under the

Methods of varying the terms of the trust

✳✳✳✳✳✳✳✳✳✳✳

VTA 1958 should include the settlor (if still alive) and all beneficiaries. The courts can only give consent on behalf of *four* types of beneficiaries identified in s 1(1) VTA 1958:

Section 1(1)(a): infants and those incapable of giving consent

This group will include minors and those persons unable to consent, eg beneficiaries of unsound mind.

Section 1(1)(b): unascertained persons

Under this subsection, the court can give approval for:

> Any person (whether ascertained or not) who may be entitled, directly or indirectly, to an interest under the trusts as being at a future date or on the happening of a future event a person of any specified description or a member of any specified class of persons, so however that this paragraph shall not include any person who would be of that description, or a member of that class, as the case may be, if the said date had fallen or the said event had happened at the date of the application to the court.

While the wording of this subsection is difficult to follow, its meaning can be broken down into two parts:

1. It covers those who *may be entitled* at a future date or on the happening of a future event:

....

Knocker v Youle [1986] 1 WLR 934

Property was held on trust for a woman's children. Under the trust, there was a remote chance that the children's Australian cousins could become entitled. The children sought to vary the trust and approval was sought from the court on behalf of the cousins, as it was impractical to obtain the consent of all of them.

The court refused to give its consent on their behalf. In interpreting the phrase 'may be entitled' in s 1(1)(b), Warner J argued that regardless of how unlikely it was that they would become entitled, they still had an interest and their consent was needed to any change.

....

Section 1(1)(b) does not include those beneficiaries who only have a remote chance of benefiting – they must still consent. Instead, s 1(1)(b) covers those beneficiaries whose future *status* may entitle them to an interest. Therefore, a trust which benefits a future spouse would be included (*Re Clitheroe's ST* [1959]) as the beneficiary may never marry. Likewise, a trust which benefits the **next-of-kin** of a beneficiary would be included (*Re Suffert* [1961]) as it remains uncertain who the next-of-kin will be until the beneficiary dies.

These situations can be distinguished from the unborn beneficiaries dealt with by s 1(1)(c) where the question revolves around their existence rather than a particular status.

2. The proviso to s 1(1)(b):

   The second half of s 1(1)(b) – beginning 'so however' – contains a proviso which provides that at the time the application is made, it will be assumed that the future date or event has occurred. If, on that basis, there are persons who satisfy the contingency, those persons will have to consent personally and the court will not do so on their behalf.

   ....

   Re Suffert [1961] Ch 1

   A woman held a life interest under a trust, with the remainder to be passed either to those appointed in her will or, in the absence of a will, to her next-of-kin under the rules of intestacy. When she sought to vary the terms of the trust, she had three adult cousins who were her next-of-kin. The court applied the proviso and considered who would have an interest if, at that point, the woman was assumed to have died. On that basis, it held that it would not provide consent for the cousins.

   ....

Example

Michael establishes a trust for his wife, Catherine, with the remainder to be divided equally between those members of his family who are members of the armed forces. In default of appointment, the capital is to be divided among his nieces and nephews.

Should Catherine wish to vary the terms of the trust, all of Michael's adult nieces and nephews would have to give their consent. Under s 1(1)(a), the court would have the jurisdiction to provide consent for any infant nieces and nephews. Under s 1(1)(b), consent could be given on behalf of those unknown beneficiaries who may at some future time become members of the armed forces. In addition, the court will assume that at the time of the application Catherine has died. Therefore, if, at that time, one of Michael's brothers is an Army Lieutenant, the court will apply the proviso in s 1(1)(b) and require that the brother also consent to any change.

Section 1(1)(c): unborn beneficiaries

Many trusts seek to provide benefits for future generations of a family. This section allows the court to consent to changes on behalf of those not yet born.

Section 1(1)(d): discretionary beneficiaries under a protective trust

Protective trusts are defined by s 33 Trustee Act 1925. If the principal beneficiary's interest is forfeited due to certain events, eg their bankruptcy, the property will instead be held on discretionary trust for others, such as the beneficiary and his family. As long as the principal beneficiary has not yet forfeited their interest, this section allows the court to provide consent on behalf of those who would be entitled under the discretionary trust.

Methods of varying the terms of the trust
✳✳✳✳✳✳✳✳✳✳

Is the variation for the benefit of the beneficiary?

Section 1 VTA 1958 states that for those beneficiaries under s 1(1)(a)–(c), any variation must be for their benefit.

Note: the benefit requirement does not apply to variations affecting those beneficiaries under s 1(1)(d).

'Benefit' has been broadly defined by the courts to include not only financial advantages (eg the reduction of inheritance tax as in *Re Druce's ST* [1962]) but also non-financial advantages:

Figure 10.3

Case	Non-financial benefit accepted by the court
Re T's ST [1963]	Delay to entitlement approved to protect an 'immature and irresponsible' beneficiary from squandering benefits.
Re Holt's ST [1968]	Delay in entitlement approved to ensure children were advanced in maturity and careers before becoming independently wealthy.
Re Weston's ST [1969]	Proposal to move trust (and beneficiaries) to Jersey for financial advantage rejected in favour of allowing the children to grow up in England.
Re Remnant's ST [1970]	Proposal to remove a forfeit clause for those children who married a Roman Catholic approved as preventing family conflict.

The courts' discretion to assess the 'benefit' of a variation is extremely wide and potentially very subjective. This problem is accentuated when the court has to weigh financial benefits against non-financial ones. While this discretion allows the court to consider all the circumstances of a case, it is an unfortunate feature of variation cases that many are heard in private and not reported. Therefore, it is difficult to establish any clear principles determining how that discretion should be exercised.

What is the relevance of the settlor's intention?

In the case of *Re Steed's WT* [1960], the settlor's intention to protect her housekeeper from her 'sponging brother' was used to refuse an application by the beneficiary to vary the trust.

However, this case was later distinguished in *Goulding v James* [1997]:

....

Goulding v James [1997] 2 All ER 239

The testatrix left her daughter, June, a life interest, with the remainder to go to June's son Marcus, should he reach the age of 40. Marcus's children (of which he had none at the time) would take the remainder should Marcus predecease June. June and Marcus applied to the court under s 1(1)(c) VTA 1958 for approval on behalf of Marcus's unborn children to vary the trust. Under their proposal, Marcus and June would take 45% of the estate absolutely with the remaining 10% held on trust for Marcus's children. While this would benefit the children, evidence was presented that the testatrix had set up the trust specifically to protect June's interest from her husband, Kenneth, whom she mistrusted. She had also delayed Marcus's benefit as she thought him a 'free spirit' who needed first to settle down (Marcus was living in an artistic community in Nantucket at the time).

In approving this arrangement, the Court of Appeal held that the settlor's intention could only be taken into account insofar as it related to the interests of the beneficiary on whose behalf the court was asked to give consent. As the testatrix's concerns related to June and Marcus, her intentions were irrelevant to the question of whether consent should be given on behalf of Marcus's unborn children.

✅ Looking for extra marks?

Goulding v James renders the settlor's intention largely irrelevant. However, it remains unclear what weight the court would give to that intention should it relate to the interest of the beneficiary the court is being asked to consider. You could gain valuable credit in an exam by being able to analyse the conflicting reasoning. In 'Variation of trusts: settlors' intentions and the consent principle in *Saunders v Vautier*' [1997] Modern Law Review, pp 719–26, Luxton argues that if the effect of varying a trust under the VTA 1958 is akin to the operation of the rule in *Saunders v Vautier*, the court is providing proxy consent for the beneficiary and so, logically, it should only consider questions of relevance to that beneficiary. This would exclude the question of the settlor's intention entirely. However, neither *Re Steed's WT* nor *Goulding v James* goes quite that far. Instead, we are left with a compromise, wherein the settlor's intentions may sometimes be relevant but rarely conclusively.

✳ Key cases

Case	Facts	Principle
Chapman v Chapman [1954] 2 WLR 723	Raised the question of the court's inherent jurisdiction to vary a trust to the financial advantage of the beneficiaries.	Defined and narrowed the courts' inherent jurisdiction to vary a trust to cases of emergency and the resolution of 'genuine disputes' over beneficial interests. Led directly to the enactment of the VTA 1958.
Goulding v James [1997] 2 All ER 239	The court approved the variation of a trust under the VTA 1958 on behalf of as yet unborn children, despite extrinsic evidence that the settlor's intentions regarding the *sui juris* beneficiaries ran contrary to the changes.	The settlor's intention is only of relevance insofar as it relates to the beneficial interest of the beneficiary on whose behalf the court is asked to consent. However, it will not necessarily outweigh financial benefits.

Key debates

✱✱✱✱✱✱✱✱✱✱✱✱

Case	Facts	Principle
Re Ball's ST [1968] 1 WLR 899	The court approved a variation dispensing of the settlor's life interest in favour of life interests for his two sons.	The court cannot approve variations which amount to a 'resettlement' of the trust on entirely different terms.
Re Weston's ST [1969] 1 Ch 223	Proposal to move trust (and beneficiaries) to Jersey for financial advantage rejected in favour of allowing the children to grow up in England.	'Benefit' under the VTA 1958 can include non-financial as well as financial benefits.

🢒🢒 Key debates

Topic	How consistent has the courts' approach to variation of trusts been?
Academic/ Author	Harris
Viewpoint	Harris provides an excellent overview of the entire area. There has been relatively little written on this area – some extra reading on your part could really improve your marks.
Source	*Variation of Trusts* (1975).

Topic	What is the relevance of the settlor's intention under the VTA 1958?
Academic/ Author	Luxton
Viewpoint	*Goulding v James* distinguished *Re Steed's WT* to allow a more restrictive approach to be taken to the settlor's intention. However, this still imposes unsatisfactory constraints upon the court's discretion to vary a trust for the benefit of the beneficiaries.
Source	[1997] 60 MLR 719.

? Exam questions

Problem question

Scott and his wife, Laura, have life interests in the Summers Trust. The remainder is shared equally between their four children, Ben, Connor, Deborah, and Eve, on the condition that they are married at the time their interest vests. The trust states that if any of the children do not marry, their share will pass to their siblings.

Scott and Laura are tired of the wet weather in the UK and are seriously considering emigrating to Australia. They would like the trustees to be able to invest in residential property in Australia so that they might spend some time there to decide whether they wish to move permanently.

They also wish to help all their children by removing the marriage condition in the trust and inserting a condition that the children will not become entitled until they are 25 years old.

Ben is 23 and married.

Connor is 20 and gay.

Deborah is 16 and a devout Christian. She has broken off all contact with her gay brother and opposes the change on religious grounds.

Eve is 14 and severely autistic. As she finds it extremely difficult to form close personal relationships, her parents are concerned that she will never marry.

Advise Scott and Laura whether the court will give permission for these variations.

An outline answer is included at the end of the book.

Essay question

Discuss the extent to which the courts should take the settlor's intention into account when deciding whether to approve variations under the VTA 1958.

An outline answer is available online at www.oxfordtextbooks.co.uk/orc/concentrate/

#11
Trustees' duties and powers

Key facts

- Trustees' duties are obligatory and must be carried out.

- Trustees' powers are entirely discretionary.

- Trustees are in general not entitled to **remuneration**, but the Trustee Act 2000 provides for the remuneration of trust corporations and trustees acting in a professional capacity.

- Trustees are the archetypal fiduciary and are subject to strict duties designed to prevent any risk of conflict between their duties and their own personal interests.

- When a beneficiary is entitled to an income from trust property, trustees have a duty to invest. This duty is predominantly dealt with by the reforms of the Trustee Act 2000.

- Trustees have a duty to provide beneficiaries with information about the trust, but this is not absolute.

- Powers of maintenance and advancement allow trustees to assist certain beneficiaries before their entitlement vests.

Introduction

This chapter deals with the main duties and powers of trustees. Rather than rigidly separating duties and powers, this chapter presents the duties and powers of trustees in a way which reflects how they might arise during the operation of a trust. Therefore, after dealing with the initial questions of the appointment, removal, and payment of trustees, the chapter turns to issues arising on appointment to the trust and then those likely to arise during the administration of the trust.

The appointment and removal of trustees

Anyone with the capacity to hold property can be a trustee, eg adults of sound mind and corporations. Trustees are typically appointed by the settlor or testator in the trust instrument or will. If a person is named as a trustee but is unwilling to accept the role, they may disclaim (refuse) the trust. This should be done by a deed. A trustee cannot disclaim *part* of the trust – acceptance of part of the trust is acceptance of the whole; *Re Lord and Fullerton's Contract* [1896]. A trust should typically have no more than four trustees (although the settlor may expressly require more and the court may authorize further trustees where appropriate).

- Trusts of realty – trusts which include land should have a minimum of two trustees.

- Trusts of personalty – a trust which involves only personal property may operate with a single trustee.

How can additional trustees be appointed?

- An express power in the trust instrument.

- **Section 36(6) Trustee Act 1925** – as long as there are no more than three trustees, additional trustees may be appointed by either the person expressly given the power to do so (s 36(6)(a)) or, if there is no such person, the other trustees (s 36(6)(b)).

- **Section 19 Trusts of Land and Appointment of Trustees Act (TOLATA) 1996** – where all beneficiaries are *sui juris* and collectively absolutely entitled to the trust property, they may direct the trustees to appoint an additional trustee of their choosing. This power cannot be exercised where (i) the trust instrument has expressly conferred a power to appoint trustees to someone else or (ii) there are already more than three trustees.

- **Section 20 TOLATA 1996** – beneficiaries may direct trustees to appoint a substitute if a trustee becomes mentally incapable of carrying out their role. (**Section 20** only applies where the power under **s 36 Trustee Act 1925** is not exercised.)

- **Section 41 Trustee Act 1925** – the court may appoint an additional trustee where it is impracticable or inexpedient for others to act without the court's involvement.

How can trustees be removed?

Retirement

Trustees can only retire in certain circumstances. If their retirement is ineffective, their liability to the trust will continue. Trustees can retire in the following ways:

- Where the trust instrument expressly allows trustees to do so.
- Where it is intended to *replace* the retiring trustee (considered below).
- **Section 39 Trustee Act 1925** – a trustee may retire if:
  - there are at least two remaining trustees or a trust corporation;
  - the remaining trustees or person with the power to appoint trustees consents by deed to the retirement.
- **Section 19 TOLATA 1996** – unless the trust instrument expressly confers the power to appoint trustees to someone else (s 19(1)(a)), where all beneficiaries are *sui juris* and collectively absolutely entitled to the trust property, they may direct a trustee in writing to retire (s 19(2)(a)). Section 19(3) places conditions on the use of this power:
  - reasonable arrangements must have been made to protect any rights of the trustee in connection with the trust;
  - there must be at least two remaining trustees or a trust corporation;
  - the trustee is either to be replaced by another or the remaining trustees consent by deed to his retirement; and
  - the retiring trustee has made a deed declaring his retirement.
- The court may exercise its inherent jurisdiction to supervise trusts to permit a trustee to retire. This jurisdiction does not require the consent of the remaining trustees.

How can trustees be replaced?

- **Section 36(1) Trustee Act 1925** – lists eight situations in which a trustee can be replaced, eg death, retirement, unfitness to act. The power can be exercised by a hierarchy of persons in the following order:
  - person expressly given the power (s 36(1)(a)) or, if there is no such person,

– the surviving trustees or the personal representative of the last surviving trustee (s 36(1)(b)).

- **Section 19 TOLATA 1996** – beneficiaries may direct the trustees in writing to appoint a trustee of their choosing, subject to the same conditions set out in relation to retirement (above).
- **Section 41 Trustee Act 1925** – the court may replace a trustee where it is impracticable or inexpedient for others to act without the court's involvement.

Removal by the court

The court may exercise its inherent jurisdiction to remove a trustee. Its primary motivation will be the welfare of the beneficiaries. Therefore, a trustee's dishonesty may warrant their removal, as might hostility between the trustees and beneficiaries, even though in the latter case, the trustee has committed no wrong; *Letterstedt v Broers* (1884). However, as each case is decided on its facts, minor errors (*Isaac v Isaac* [2005]), or the expense to the trust of replacing a trustee (*Re Wrightson* [1908]) may persuade the court not to remove a trustee.

Payment of trustees

Generally, trustees are not entitled to be remunerated for their services. The rationale for this rule is that financial motives should not be allowed to intrude upon the trustee's fiduciary obligations to beneficiaries. However, it is common practice for trust instruments to include an express remuneration clause. Where there is no express remuneration clause, trustees will be entitled to remuneration in the following circumstances:

***Sui juris* beneficiaries collectively consent to trustees' remuneration**	**Court's inherent jurisdiction to remunerate trustees** Note: this is only used in exceptional circumstances (*Re Duke of Norfolk's ST* [1982])
Section 29 Trustee Act 2000 Trustees acting in a **professional capacity** are entitled to **reasonable** remuneration, provided the other trustees consent in writing. Note: **lay trustees** are still **not** entitled to payment unless authorized by other means.	**Section 31 Trustee Act 2000** **All** trustees may recover expenses properly incurred in the course of their duties.

Figure 11.1 The remuneration of trustees

Duties on taking up the role of trustee

Upon accepting a position as trustee, the trustees must do the following:

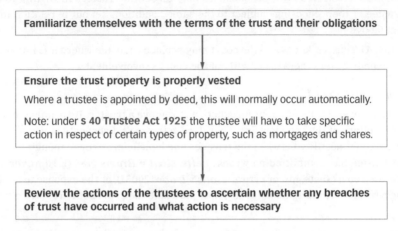

Figure 11.2 Duties on taking up role of trustee

The administration of the trust

In administering a trust, the trustees must act unanimously, unless the trust instrument allows otherwise; *Luke v South Kensington Hotel Co* (1879). This rule offers a degree of protection to beneficiaries by preventing majority decision-making.

Fiduciary duties

In *Bristol and West Building Society v Mothew* [1996], Millett LJ described the fiduciary relationship in the following terms:

> A fiduciary is someone who has undertaken to act for or on behalf of another in a particular matter in circumstances which give rise to a relationship of trust and confidence. The distinguishing obligation of a fiduciary is the obligation of loyalty.

As fiduciaries, trustees have a number of duties designed to prevent any conflict arising between the interests of the trustee and those of the beneficiaries. These duties are strictly enforced by the courts. While this can sometimes be said to lead to the unfair treatment of innocent fiduciaries, the exacting nature of these duties discourages trustees from undertaking any action which might be said to conflict with their paramount duty of loyalty to beneficiaries.

Unauthorized profits

Trustees (and fiduciaries generally) cannot retain any unauthorized profits generated by their connection to the trust; *Bray v Ford* [1896]. Any profits will be held on constructive trust for the beneficiaries (see chapter 9 on implied trusts):

Keech v Sandford (1726) Sel Cas Ch 61

The trustee held a lease of the profits of a market for a minor. When the lease was approaching its end, the trustee sought to renew the lease for the beneficiary. The landlord refused because he would not be able to enforce any of the covenants against a minor. The trustee then took the lease on his own behalf. Despite the fact that the landlord would not have renewed the lease for the minor, the court held that the lease was held for the benefit of the trust.

It will not make a difference if the trustee generates a profit for both himself *and* the trust:

Boardman v Phipps [1967] 2 AC 46

In his fiduciary capacity as solicitor to a trust, Boardman obtained information about a company in which the trust had invested. He realized that the company could be made more profitable and purchased a controlling share to enable him to carry through his plans. All of the competent trustees and the beneficiaries had been made aware of this opportunity, but due to the trust's restrictive investment powers, the trustees could not make the purchase themselves. Through his hard work, the company made substantial profits for both himself and the trust. Despite this, the House of Lords held on a 3:2 majority that Boardman held his profits on constructive trust for the trustees.

Note: Boardman was able to retain a portion of the profits on a **quantum meruit** basis for his efforts. However, this does not alter the fact that all of the profits were held on trust.

If a trustee makes a profit from his company's dealing with a trust, his share of the profits will be subject to a constructive trust for the trust; *Williams v Barton* (1927).

The strict approach taken by the courts in relation to the duties of fiduciaries is illustrated by the following recent decision:

O'Donnell v Shanahan [2009] EWCA Civ 75

The appellant and respondents were directors and equal shareholders of a company providing financial advice and assistance. A client approached the company for assistance in finding a purchaser for a property. The respondents identified a prospective purchaser who paid for solicitors' fees and a valuation report in relation to the property. For their part in arranging the sale, the company were to be paid a commission of £30,000. Before completion, the original purchaser withdrew from the transaction. Another purchaser was identified, but he would only buy 50% and was unwilling to pay the commission. The respondents, relying upon the valuation report, agreed to purchase the other 50%. The appellant alleged the respondents had breached their fiduciary duties and should be held to account. The Court of Appeal agreed: a conflict of interest was created when the respondents agreed to the deal that deprived the company of its commission. Moreover, an unauthorized profit had been made as the respondents had failed to offer the company the opportunity to invest in the property deal. The correct course of action would have been to obtain the consent of the company shareholders first. The fact that the trial judge had found that the appellant was risk averse and unlikely to have agreed to such a venture was immaterial. Furthermore, the respondents' profit was only made possible through their role as directors to the company and their reliance on the valuation report that was more correctly seen as the property of the company.

Trustees' dealings with trust property

Trustees who sell trust property have an overriding duty to obtain the best price – in *Buttle v Saunders* [1950] an injunction was awarded preventing a trustee from accepting an offer to purchase property for reasons of morality when a higher offer had been received.

The self-dealing rule

The sale of trust property to a trustee is **voidable** by a beneficiary. Here the nature of the fiduciary relationship operates to prevent the *risk* of a trustee putting their own commercial interests before their fiduciary obligation to obtain the best price for the trust. This rule is strictly enforced and, in general, it does not matter if the property is purchased in good faith and for full value (*Ex p James* (1803)) or even after the trustee retires (*Wright v Morgan* [1926]), unless a significant period of time has since elapsed (*Re Boles and British Land Company's Contract* [1902]).

One interesting exception occurred in *Holder v Holder* [1968]:

Holder v Holder [1968] Ch 353

The defendant had been appointed as an executor of his father's will. He sought to renounce this position but had carried out some minor administrative tasks, which rendered this ineffective. However, he played no further part in the administration of the estate. When the other executors placed two of his father's farms for sale at auction, the defendant purchased them. However, one of the beneficiaries sought to have the purchase set aside on the basis that the defendant was a fiduciary. The Court of Appeal refused, arguing that there was no conflict of interest as the defendant had paid a fair price and had not authorized the sale.

The decision in *Holder v Holder* [1968] sits oddly with the court's generally strict approach to fiduciary duties and it is often questioned whether these rules need to be relaxed. The Court of Appeal's approach in this case might be said to be more typically *equitable* in character as it pays much closer attention to the whole circumstances of the case and broader questions of fairness than the more usual strict application of rules would allow. In this sense, *Holder v Holder* [1968] has much in common with the minority approach taken in *Boardman v Phipps* [1967], in which Lord Upjohn argued that a real conflict of duty and interest must be identified before the rule is applied.

The fair dealing rule

A trustee's purchase of a beneficiary's equitable interest in property will not be voidable, as long as the trustee acts honestly, makes full disclosure to the beneficiaries, and pays a fair price; *Coles v Trecothick* (1804).

The trustee must not compete with the trust

The fiduciary obligations of trustees towards beneficiaries entail that they should not compete with the trust; *Re Thomson* [1930].

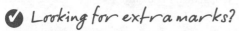 **Looking for extra marks?**

The question of how strictly fiduciary duties should be enforced raises many questions about the nature of the fiduciary relationship and the courts' attitude towards them. Impress your examiners with a good knowledge of these issues: read Jones, 'Unjust enrichment and fiduciary's loyalty' (1968) 84 LQR 472, Conaglen, 'The nature and function of fiduciary loyalty' (2005) 121 LQR 452, and Collins, 'The no-conflict rule: the acceptance of traditional equitable values?' (2008) 14 *Trusts & Trustees* 213.

The duty of investment

Whenever property is held on trust to benefit both **life tenants** and **remaindermen**, the trustees have a duty to invest the trust property in order to generate an income for the life tenant.

The previous law contained in the **Trustee Investments Act 1961** (as amended) favoured an overly protective approach to investment which was ill-suited to deal with the complexities of the modern financial world.

The **Trustee Act 2000** significantly widens the investment powers of trustees while clarifying the trustees' duties and obligations. It also protects both beneficiaries and trustees – the broader investment powers enable trustees to provide better returns for beneficiaries while the Act provides guidance to trustees on how to exercise their investment powers and the standards expected of them.

The duty to act even-handedly

Investment is about the *management of risk*. When considering their duty of investment, trustees must consider not only the need to provide an income for life tenants but also how to preserve and ideally increase the capital for remaindermen. Risky investments offer the potential for higher returns but at the same time expose the trust capital to greater risk of loss, and vice versa. *Nestle v National Westminster Bank plc* [1993] confirms that trustees have a duty to act even-handedly towards the different classes of beneficiary:

Nestle v National Westminster Bank plc [1993] 1 WLR 1260

Georgina Nestle, a remainderman of a trust, received £269,203. However, she argued that if the funds had been properly invested, the capital would have been worth £1,000,000. While the court held that the Bank had clearly misunderstood the extent of its investment powers, the policy it had undertaken had produced some savings in terms of estate duty. Even though the funds' overall growth was slow, the court was of the opinion that the trustees had not breached their duty to act even-handedly.

Staughton LJ added that the duty of even-handedness was one to be exercised in light of all the circumstances. Therefore, if a life tenant was living in poverty while the remainderman was already wealthy, the trustees could invest in such a way as to produce a greater income for the life tenant, as long as this did not unduly jeopardize the capital.

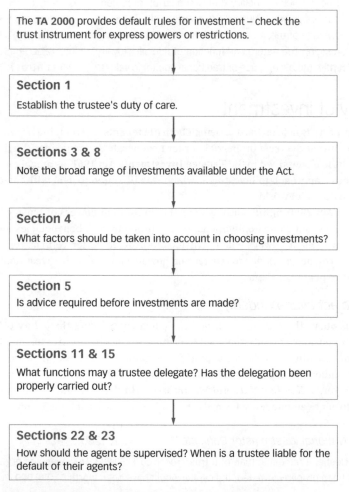

The **TA 2000** provides default rules for investment – check the trust instrument for express powers or restrictions.

Section 1

Establish the trustee's duty of care.

Sections 3 & 8

Note the broad range of investments available under the Act.

Section 4

What factors should be taken into account in choosing investments?

Section 5

Is advice required before investments are made?

Sections 11 & 15

What functions may a trustee delegate? Has the delegation been properly carried out?

Sections 22 & 23

How should the agent be supervised? When is a trustee liable for the default of their agents?

Figure 11.3 Central investment issues in the Trustee Act 2000

The Trustee Act 2000: a modern approach to investment

Consider the following issues when addressing a question on investment:

The **Trustee Act 2000** provides a set of default provisions for trustee investments. All of the provisions in relation to investment, including the **s 1** duty of care, can be expressly altered or excluded by the trust instrument.

> *Revision tip*
>
> Examiners may be most interested in assessing your knowledge of the Trustee Act 2000. Therefore, a problem question on investment will be unlikely to involve express restrictions or exclusions of the Act *except* in relation to the issue of ethical investment policies, considered below.

Section 1: the duty of care

Section 1 TA 2000 imposes a statutory duty of care upon trustees and plays a key role in controlling the greater powers the Act grants to trustees. **Section 1** states:

(1) Whenever the duty under this subsection applies to a trustee, he must exercise such care and skill as is reasonable in all the circumstances, having regard in particular–

   (a) To any special knowledge or experience that he has or holds himself out as having, and

   (b) If he acts as a trustee in the course of a business or profession, to any special knowledge or experience that is reasonable to expect of a person acting in the course of that kind of business or profession.

There are a number of things to note about this duty of care:

- Section 1 codifies the previous common law duty of care, which was to act as an 'ordinary prudent man of business'; *Speight v Gaunt* (1881). It is useful to read s 1 alongside the previous common law guidance. In *Speight v Gaunt*, the House of Lords approved Lindley LJ's description of this test in *Re Whitely* (1887) as 'such care as an ordinary prudent man would take if he were minded to make an investment for the benefit of other people for whom he felt morally obligated to provide.'

- The duty of care is an objective one – a trustee's personal view will not excuse liability unless it was reasonable in the circumstances.

- The duty of care varies according to the (actual or professed) expertise of the trustee. Therefore, a professional trustee will be expected to meet a higher standard of conduct than a lay trustee.

- Remember: the duty of care applies to all trustees' powers under the Act, unless altered by the trust instrument (**Sch 1 TA 2000**). It also applies to a number of powers under the **Trustee Act 1925**, such as the **s 19** power to insure trust property.

> *Revision tip*
>
> Students often set out the relevant provisions of the Trustee Act 2000 but then forget to apply the s 1 duty of care, eg a trustee must supervise their agents under s 22. However, just because an agent steals trust money does not mean that the trustees will be liable for the loss, unless they have failed to supervise with reasonable care and skill.

Duties on taking up the role of trustee
****

Sections 3 and 8: the scope of trustee's investment powers

Section 3(1) TA 2000 confers a 'general power of investment' upon trustees to 'make any kind of investment that he could make if he were absolutely entitled to the assets of the trust'.

Section 8(1) gives trustees the *power* to acquire freehold or leasehold land in the UK as (a) an investment, (b) for occupation by the beneficiary, or (c) any other reason.

The TA 2000 embraces a much broader definition of investment than previously operated. The previous law, contained in the Trustee Investments Act 1961, only allowed investment from a list of proscribed 'authorised investments'. In addition, the ability of trustees to invest in land was previously very restrictive. Section 8 makes it clear that 'investment' can now include capital as well as income growth.

Ethical investments

A common aspect of problems on trustee investments is whether trustees can pursue an ethical investment policy. This question was considered in *Cowan v Scargill*:

....

Cowan v Scargill [1984] 2 All ER 750

The trustees of a pension fund for coal miners were divided on how best to invest. One side, led by Arthur Scargill, argued that the pension's fund should not be invested in companies abroad and especially not with industries which competed with the coal industry. This policy would avoid helping the competition and risking miners' jobs in an increasingly competitive energies market. However, his plan was rejected by Sir Robert Megarry who said that trustees must put aside their own personal views: '[u]nder a trust for the provision of financial benefits, the paramount duty of the trustees is to provide the greatest financial benefits for the present and future beneficiaries'.

....

Despite this general rule, there are a number of ways in which an ethical investment policy may be legitimately pursued:

- Where the trust instrument expressly imposes an ethical investment policy.

- In *Cowan v Scargill*, Megarry suggested (*obiter*) that where beneficiaries held particularly strong views on the matter, these might be taken into account. For example, if the beneficiaries were devout Muslims, it might be inappropriate to invest in the alcohol industry.

- In *Harries v Church Commissioners* [1992], Sir Donald Nicholls VC considered that *charitable trusts* might be able to avoid investments which clashed with their ethical objectives, even if this caused a loss.

- Trustees should be able to pursue an ethical investment policy as long as they consider the best financial interests of the beneficiaries first, ie the wealth of investment opportunities should make it possible to invest ethically without affecting the beneficiaries' best financial interests. However, simply adopting an ethical policy without considering the best financial interests of the beneficiaries will be a breach of trust; *Martin v City of Edinburgh District Council* [1988].

Sections 4 and 5: controlling trustees' choice of investments

Sections 4 and 5 TA 2000 provide trustees with guidance on how to manage their investments choices. In choosing investments, under s 4(3), trustees must have regard to the 'standard investment criteria' of:

- suitability; and
- the need for diversification.

Suitability: the Explanatory Notes of the TA 2000 make it clear that trustees must consider the suitability of proposed investments in general and in particular. This means that they should first consider whether the type of investment (eg shares) is suitable for the trust. They must then consider whether, say, shares in a particular company are appropriate for the trust.

Diversification: this section reflects the TA 2000's adoption of the 'modern portfolio theory' set out in the first instance decision of *Nestle v National Westminster Bank plc* [1993]. Hoffmann J stated that:

> Modern trustees acting within their investment powers are entitled to be judged by the standards of current portfolio theory, which emphasises the risk level of the entire portfolio rather than the risk attaching to each investment taken in isolation.

This encourages trustees to formulate an investment strategy that balances riskier investments (which could bring greater returns) with more secure investments (which will produce lower returns but expose the trust fund to less risk). If trustees give due consideration to this, they will not be judged for the failure of individual investments.

The Act does not *require* diversification, merely that trustees consider whether there is a need. For example, it may be more sensible for a smaller trust to invest in largely low-risk investments, whereas a bigger trust fund has the scope to take more risks, as long as that risk is appropriately balanced.

Section 4(2) – trustees must review their investment strategy 'from time to time'. This encourages trustees to be diligent in monitoring and changing their investment policy to adapt to shifting circumstances. For example, if a trust largely generated its income from purchasing and renovating property for resale, a drop in property values and demand would reasonably require trustees to consider reinvesting at least part of the trust fund elsewhere.

Section 5(1) – trustees should take and consider 'proper advice' from someone 'reasonably believed to be qualified…by his ability in and practical experience of financial and other matters' (s 5(4)) whenever considering or reviewing their investments.

Section 5(3) – advice is not required if the trustee reasonably concludes that it is unnecessary or inappropriate to do so. For example, this exception might apply where the trustee is professionally experienced in investment.

Sections 11 and 15: the power of delegation

The responsibilities of trustees are often onerous, especially for the ordinary lay trustee. Allowing certain roles to be delegated allows trustees to ensure that the trust is properly managed.

Duties on taking up the role of trustee

✱✱✱✱✱✱✱✱✱✱

Section 11 outlines the roles which can be *collectively* delegated by trustees. Note: the *individual* delegation of trustees' functions is still governed by **s 25 Trustee Act 1925**.

Section 11(2) lists the functions which non-charitable trusts *cannot* delegate. These are powers fundamental to the trustee's fiduciary responsibility and include the distribution of trust assets, the discretion to decide whether payments or fees should be made out of the trust fund (eg claims for maintenance and advancement), and the power to appoint trustees. Note: this means that trustees' power of investment *can* be delegated.

Schedule 1, para 3 – the s 1 duty of care applies in selecting an agent. *Fry v Tapson* (1885) establishes that trustees should not employ agents to carry out tasks outside their ordinary course of business.

Section 15 places special requirements on the delegation of 'asset management functions'. These are functions which include the investment, acquisition, management, and disposal of trust property (**s 15(5)**). Where such a function is delegated, **s 15** requires:

- an agreement in or evidenced by writing (**s 15(1)**);
- preparation of a written policy statement for the agent to provide guidance on how to carry out their role (**s 15(2)(a)**);
- that the agreement should contain a term ensuring that the agent complies with the policy statement (**s 15(2)(b)**).

Sections 22 and 23: review of agents and liability for their default

Section 22 states that trustees must keep their agents' actions under review and, if necessary, intervene.

Section 23 states that the trustees will be liable for the defaults of their agents if they have failed to satisfy the duty of care in appointing or reviewing their agents.

The duty of provide information

While trustees are expected to act in the interests of beneficiaries, it is the beneficiaries who will hold the trustees to account. To do this, they clearly require some access to information about the trust. But what is the extent of trustees' duty to keep beneficiaries informed about the trust?

Trustees do not have to give reasons for how they use their discretion

Trustees frequently have to exercise their discretion in carrying out their duties. For example, trustees may have a duty to take advice before making an investment, but it is they who ultimately decide whether to follow the advice or not. Another common example is the trustees' discretion to choose which members of a class to benefit in a discretionary trust.

The case of *Re Beloved Wilkes' Charity* (1851) established that *trustees do not have to give reasons for the use of their discretion*. While this decision limits trustees' accountability, it also allows trustees to fulfil their role as fiduciaries:

- for trustees to act impartially, they must be free of pressure from beneficiaries;

- in the context of family trusts, protecting trustees from having to explain their decisions may prevent family conflict.

Note: Lord Truro added that the court can supervise and possibly intervene where:

- there is evidence of bad faith or dishonesty; or
- the trustees provide reasons for their actions – in these circumstances the court can consider their conclusions.

If trustees are not required to give reasons for the use of their discretion, to what information are beneficiaries entitled?

Other information about the trust

Accounts

All trustees must keep accounts and make them available to the beneficiaries for inspection; *Pearse v Green* (1819). This includes beneficiaries under a **discretionary trust**, although this right may be limited where they are part of large class; *Murphy v Murphy* [1999].

Information about the trust

In *O'Rourke v Darbishire* [1920], the House of Lords stated that the beneficiaries' right to information was based on their proprietary interest in the trust. This entitled beneficiaries to access all 'trust documents'.

In *Re Londonderry's Settlement* [1965], Salmon LJ attempted to define 'trust documents':

(1) they are documents in the possession of the trustees as trustees;
(2) they contain information about the trust, which the beneficiaries are entitled to know;
(3) the beneficiaries have a proprietary interest in the documents and, accordingly are entitled to see them. If any parts of a document contain information which the beneficiaries are not entitled to know, I doubt whether such parts can be truly said to be integral parts of a trust document.

However, this definition does little to clarify the scope of the term 'trust documents'. In addition, the court stressed that the beneficiaries' right to see 'trust documents' did not include:

- documents which might reveal how the trustees had exercised their discretion;
- confidential information, including the agendas of trustee meetings and correspondence among trustees or beneficiaries.

A different approach was taken by the Privy Council in *Schmidt v Rosewood Trust*:

. . . .

Schmidt v Rosewood Trust [2003] 3 All ER 76

The claimant sought disclosure of the accounts and information on trust assets in relation to a discretionary trust. The trustees resisted the claim on the basis that as a mere potential beneficiary under a discretionary trust, the claimant had no proprietary claim to see the requested documentation.

Lord Walker stated that while the beneficiaries' right to information *could* be described as a proprietary interest, such an interest was neither sufficient nor necessary to found the claim. Instead, the beneficiaries' right to information was better described as *an aspect of the court's inherent jurisdiction to supervise the administration of trusts.*

. . . .

Schmidt signals a significant change in direction because, in effect, beneficiaries no longer have an automatic right to demand information. This could also be said to permit trustees to be secretive, as the cost of litigation may discourage beneficiaries from complaining.

On the other hand, the Privy Council's approach means that the court could potentially order the disclosure of any documentation it deems relevant, thus enhancing the accountability of trustees.

Schmidt also offers the court the flexibility to respond to different circumstances by allowing the court to balance the interests of trustees, beneficiaries, and any third parties. See *Breakspear v Ackland* [2008], where Briggs J accepted the trustees' argument that disclosure of the settlor's **letter of wishes** would cause family conflict and refused to order disclosure. Note: Briggs J emphasized that the confidentiality issue identified in *Re Londonderry's Settlement* [1965], should be seen as an important but not decisive factor in resolving questions of disclosure.

While *Schmidt v Rosewood Trust* [2003] is a Privy Council decision and, therefore, strictly persuasive only, it is arguable that Lord Walker's reasoning provides a more workable and conceptually satisfying approach to the question of beneficiaries' rights to information.

✅ *Looking for extra marks?*

The unsettled nature of the law in this area makes it a prime area for an essay question on the accountability of trustees. Improve your marks by demonstrating knowledge of both the current law and calls for greater accountability. Kirby P argues for greater accountability in his minority judgment in the Australian case *Hartigan Nominees Property Ltd v Rydge* (1992). A good discussion of the debate can also be found in Sir Gavin Lightman's article 'The trustees' duty to provide information to beneficiaries' [2004] PCB 23.

The duty to distribute

Trustees are under a duty to distribute the trust property in accordance with the terms of the trust. The failure to distribute or distributing the trust property to the wrong person is a breach of trust; *Re Diplock* [1948]. The law provides a variety of options for trustees who are uncertain about who the beneficiaries of a trust are or the extent of their entitlement.

Applying to the court for directions

Trustees can apply to the court for directions if there is any uncertainty as to how the trust should be carried out. This is an invaluable option for a wise trustee: if the trustees follow the court's directions, they will not be liable for any losses arising from the court's advice.

What if the trustees cannot find the beneficiaries?

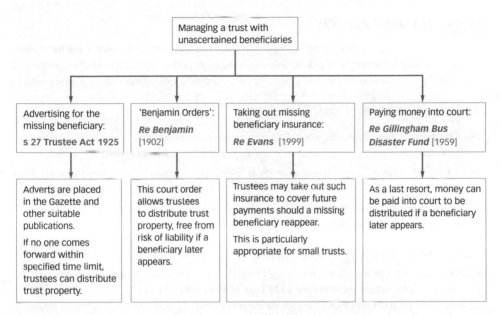

Figure 11.4 Managing a trust with missing beneficiaries

Revision tip

These different methods protect trustees should a missing beneficiary appear. Remember: while the trustees will be protected from liability for breach of trust, the beneficiary may pursue his share of the trust against the other beneficiaries.

Powers of maintenance and advancement

During the administration of a trust, trustees may be asked to assist beneficiaries financially before their interest vests. The trustees can do so, at their absolute discretion, through their powers of maintenance and **advancement**.

Maintenance

The power of maintenance allows trustees to use the **income** from their interest to provide for the maintenance of a minor beneficiary. Maintenance powers can arise from:

- Express provision in the trust instrument
- Section 53 Trustee Act 1925 (see chapter 10)
- Section 31 Trustee Act 1925

Section 31 Trustee Act 1925

- Trustees may apply *part or all* of the income for the 'maintenance, education or benefit' of a minor beneficiary as is reasonable in all the circumstances (s 31(1)(i)). Payments will typically be made to the minor's parents or guardians, unless the minor is married.

The trustees' exercise of their discretion

- The minor's best interests should be paramount but incidental benefits to a parent or guardian will not prevent trustees from acting; *Fuller v Evans* [2000].
- Trustees must consider the use of their discretion in good faith; *Bryant v Hickley* (1894).
- Trustees must consider the use of maintenance powers periodically – money should not be paid over automatically; *Wilson v Turner* (1883).

Limitations on the power of maintenance

Section 31(3) – for a power of maintenance to exist, the trust interest must carry the entitlement to the intermediate income (see s 175 Law of Property Act 1925).

There are a small number of interests which do not satisfy this section. The most common is the contingent pecuniary testamentary disposition, eg £200,000 to my daughter, Lesley, on her 21st birthday.

If the income is already subject to a prior interest, it cannot be used for maintenance, eg My shares for Laura, when she turns 25. Until that time, the income shall be appointed to Clara.

The power of maintenance can be excluded by a contrary intention on the part of the settlor (eg *Re Erskine's ST* [1971]).

Contingently entitled adults

Section 31(1)(ii) – adults with a contingent trust interest are automatically entitled to the income from that interest, subject to any contrary intention. However, they will only be entitled to the income arising from the time they reach majority (ie 18). For example, if Patrick is left 500 shares on trust for when he turns 30, he will be entitled to the dividends on the shares from the age of 18.

Advancement

The power of advancement allows trustees, at their absolute discretion, to appoint part of a beneficiaries' entitlement to the **capital** of the trust before it vests absolutely. Advancement powers can arise from:

- Express provision in the trust instrument
- Section 53 Trustee Act 1925 (see chapter 10)
- Section 32 Trustee Act 1925

Section 32 Trustee Act 1925

Trustees may apply part of the beneficiary's capital interest for the 'advancement or benefit' of a minor or adult beneficiary (s 32(1)). *Pilkington v IRC* [1964] defines 'advancement or benefit' as 'any use of money which will improve the material situation of the beneficiary'.

Figure 11.5

Case	Example of 'advancement or benefit'
Re Williams WT [1953]	To purchase a house for the beneficiary
Roper-Curzon v Roper-Curzon (1871)	To help a beneficiary in their career
Lowther v Bentlnck (1874)	To pay off debts
Pilkington v IRC [1964]	To provide tax advantages for the beneficiary

The trustees' exercise of their discretion

- Trustees must consider whether to exercise their power of advancement and not simply appoint money without thought.
- If trustees make an advancement for a specific purpose, they must check whether that purpose has been carried out; *Re Pauling's ST* [1964].

Limitations on the power of advancement

- Section 32(1)(a) – no more than *half* of the beneficiary's share in the capital can be advanced.
- Section 32(1)(b) – any advancements made will be deducted from their final entitlement.

Key cases

****

- Section 32(1)(c) – no advancements can be made where there is a *prior interest* on the capital, unless that person exists, is an adult, and consents in writing.
- The power of advancement is defeated by evidence of a contrary intention, such as a direction to accumulate; *IRC v Bernstein* [1961].

 **Key cases**

Case	Facts	Principle
Bristol and West Building Society v Mothew [1996] 4 All ER 698	A solicitor's negligence in wrongly advising the claimant was held not to be a breach of his fiduciary obligations.	The core obligation of a fiduciary is loyalty. Fiduciaries must act on good faith and avoid conflicts of interest.
Cowan v Scargill [1984] 2 All ER 750	The court refused to sanction an investment policy which put the economic interests of the mining industry ahead of the best financial interests of the beneficiaries of a pension scheme.	In general, trustees must consider the best financial interests of the beneficiaries when choosing investments.
Keech v Sandford (1726) Sel Cas Ch 61	When a landlord refused to renew a lease held on trust for an infant beneficiary, the trustee took it over. It was held that the trustee held the lease on constructive trust for the beneficiary.	Trustees cannot retain any profits deriving from their connection with the trust.
Nestle v National Westminster Bank plc [1993] 1 WLR 1260	The claimant argued unsuccessfully that the value of her interest should have been greater and that the defendant's overly cautious investment strategy constituted a breach of trust.	Trustees must treat all beneficiaries even-handedly. Trustees are to be judged on their investment policy overall rather than on individual failures – modern portfolio theory.
O'Donnell v Shanahan [2009] EWCA Civ 75	Two directors of a company entered into a personal property investment deal when the original deal brokered by the company fell through, depriving the company of its commission.	Fiduciaries must avoid conflicts of interest with their principal. Opportunities that arise through a fiduciary relationship are properly considered the property of the principal and full consent must be obtained before a fiduciary may take any advantage of them.
O'Rourke v Darbishire [1920] AC 581	A claimant alleged that he was the beneficiary of a trust and sought access to relevant documents pertaining to how the 'trust' had been managed.	Beneficiaries are entitled to see trust documents, as long as they do not reveal reasons for trustees' use of their discretion or confidential information.

Case	Facts	Principle
Schmidt v Rosewood Trust [2003] 3 All ER 76	A claimant sought access to a wide range of documents relating to two trusts under which he claimed a discretionary interest.	Beneficiaries' access to information is an aspect of the court's inherent jurisdiction to supervise the trust. The court must balance the interests of trustees, beneficiaries, and third parties in deciding whether to order disclosure.

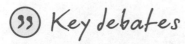

Key debates

Topic	Why are trustees' fiduciary duties so strictly enforced?
Academic/ Author	Webb and Akkouh
Viewpoint	Fiduciaries' core obligation of loyalty requires fiduciaries to be deterred from any potential conflict of interest.
Source	*Trusts Law* (2008), ch 9 provides an extremely accessible discussion of this complicated area.

Topic	What is the impact of the Trustee Act 2000?
Academic/ Author	Clements
Viewpoint	The Trustee Act 2000 was urgently needed to address problems with the previous law and to allow trustees to operate effectively in the modern financial world.
Source	[2004] 2 Web JCLI.

Topic	Should beneficiaries have greater access to information about the trust?
Academic/ Author	Lightman
Viewpoint	The beneficiaries' ability to enforce the trust requires access to information. Greater accountability is needed.
Source	[2004] PCB 23.

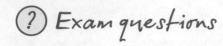

Problem question

Jan and Beth hold £500,000 on trust for Toby with the remainder for Lisa. They have little knowledge of investments. A friend recommends Paul, a computer engineer, as someone who could manage their investments. Paul recently inherited £10,000 and, after investing it, made a profit of £2,000.

Jan and Beth employ Paul, who makes the following investments in May 2007:

1. £200,000 in a range of unit trusts.
2. £100,000 in shares in Carfax, a leading UK bank.
3. £150,000 in villas to rent out on the Spanish Costa del Tan.
4. £50,000 in investment capital for IP-Ops, a computer repair company owned by Paul.

In May 2008, Paul tells the trustees that the unit trusts and villas are performing well and that IP-Ops has had an extremely profitable first year of business. However, following a drop in consumer confidence, the shares in Carfax Bank have lost 25% of their value.

They instruct Paul to move the Carfax investment to a more stable company.

Three months later, the trustees meet with Toby and Lisa and inform them of the trust's performance. On investigation, Toby discovers Paul has not yet sold the Carfax shares, which have now lost another 25% of their value.

The beneficiaries are concerned that the trust is being poorly managed. Advise the beneficiaries.

An outline answer is included at the end of the book.

Essay question

> It is an inflexible rule of a Court of Equity that a person in a fiduciary position…is not, unless otherwise expressly provided, entitled to make a profit; he is not allowed to put himself in a position where his interest and his duty conflict. (Lord Herschell in *Bray v Ford* [1896])

Critically discuss whether fiduciary duties are enforced too strictly in England and Wales.

An outline answer is available online at www.oxfordtextbooks.co.uk/orc/concentrate/

#12
Remedies for breach of trust

Key facts

- Beneficiaries will have a claim against a trustee in breach.

- Liability between trustees is joint and several.

- A remedy can be provided for breach of a trust or fiduciary obligation.

- Remedies can be against the trustee or third parties.

- The fiduciary obligation can arise in a variety of factual situations.

- The remedy can be personal or proprietary.

- The remedy can be at common law or in equity.

Introduction

When property is held on trust, arising expressly or implied by law, then any breach of the trustee/fiduciary obligation will lead to a remedy. This chapter will explain the personal and proprietary remedies available to the claimant:

- A personal claim means that the claim is made against the trustee/fiduciary personally; it is not based upon the recipient having the property in their possession.

- A proprietary claim is based upon the defendant having the property or its replacement in their possession and being required to return it, or its substitute, to the claimant.

The claimant, after identifying the breach, will often have the choice of which claim to make. There may be more than one possible remedy for the claimant.

> *Revision tip*
>
> The first step in an answer is to identify the breach, who committed the breach, and where the property is held. This will enable your answer to take the correct approach.

The table illustrates the possible routes for a claimant.

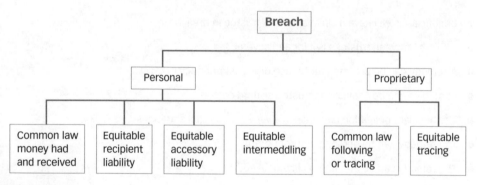

Figure 12.1

Personal actions

Against the trustee

Trustees have certain powers and duties under a trust (see chapter 11). These powers and duties can lead to a breach, where there is:

1. A failure to carry out a duty.

2. A trustee acts outside her powers.

3. A trustee acts without the required standard of care.

If there is more than one trustee, you should identify which of the trustees the claim is against. A trustee is not **vicariously** liable for the actions of other trustees. However, a failure to act with due care (that exercised by the prudent and reasonable person (*Speight v Gaunt* (1883)) or a breach of the statutory duty of care contained in s 1 Trustee Act 2000) is a breach in itself. Breaches include:

- leaving one trustee in sole control of the trust property; and
- inaction or standing by while other trustees breach their duty; *Styles v Guy* (1849).

Trustees are not responsible for breaches that occur *before* they became a trustee or for breaches which occur after they have retired. However, every trustee who participates in the breach is **jointly and severally** liable for any loss. So although there is no vicarious liability the fact that you have not exerted control over the actions of your fellow trustees, your inaction, may be a breach in itself, incurring liability.

The loss caused by the breach can include where a trustee has made a profit from a breach of trust. If there is more than one breach it is important to identify the losses which flow from each breach; *Target Holdings Ltd v Redferns* [1995]. If one breach creates a profit, eg an unauthorized investment generates a profit, this cannot be offset against losses caused by a different breach.

The claims are made directly against the trustee, a personal action, to compensate the claimant for losses caused by the breach in the same way as an action for damages for a breach of a contractual obligation.

Revision tip

In structuring your answer, having established the breach and the liability, consider if there are any defences available to the defendant.

Defences

A trustee may be granted relief or an **indemnity** from the breach. The following are situations which will provide the defendant trustee with a defence to an action for breach of trust:

Exemption clauses

The trust documents may include an exemption clause. Such clauses usually cover breaches which occur despite the trustee acting with all care, but if widely drafted it could include negligent breach. Where the trustee is a professional the courts are less likely to allow a broadly drafted exemption clause to allow a trustee to avoid liability for gross negligence; *Armitage v Nurse* [1998].

Consent and acquiescence

Consent of the *sui juris* beneficiary in the breach will provide a defence to the trustee against claims by that beneficiary but not against other beneficiaries who may have suffered a loss.

Personal actions

****

Section 62 Trustee Act 1925 provides the court with a discretion to impound the beneficial interest of a beneficiary who has encouraged or acquiesced in a breach. This will be used to pay compensation to the beneficiaries who did not participate in the breach; *Re Pauling's Settlement Trusts* [1964].

Judicial discretion

Section 61 Trustee Act 1925 grants wide discretionary power for the courts to grant relief if the trustee in breach has acted in all honesty and good faith; *Re Pauling's Settlement Trusts* [1964].

Time barred

Section 21 Limitation Act 1980 bars claims made after six years, although this does not apply if there has been fraud.

Trustee's claims

As the trustees are jointly and severally liable for their breaches, a claimant may decide to bring a claim against all of the trustees or just one, usually the richest. As the breach may also include a trustee's inaction, this could be said to be inequitable; the beneficiary may target the wealthiest rather than the most culpable. However, the trustee may have a claim against their fellow trustee which is independent of the beneficiary's claim.

The trustee who has been required to pay compensation may be able to require the other trustees to contribute to their costs. The following situations may provide some relief:

- A co-trustee may be ordered to indemnify a trustee for the compensation they have paid out where:
  - there has been a fraud by the co-trustee;
  - the co-trustee has breached for their own benefit; *Bahin v Hughes* (1886);
  - a solicitor has exercised a controlling influence on a lay trustee; *Re Partington* (1887);
- The **Civil Liabilities (Contribution) Act 1978** grants the courts powers to order co-trustees to contribute to the losses claimed if it is 'fair, just and reasonable'.

The remedies against the trustee may be adequate as long as they are solvent. However, if there are no available remedies or the trustee is unable to compensate the beneficiary, the most appropriate remedy for a claimant may be against a third party to the trust. (Refer back to Figure 12.1 at the beginning of the chapter.)

Personal actions against third parties

Actions may be brought against those who are not appointed as trustees; termed 'strangers' as they are strangers to the trust. The actions may be personal or proprietary and be available at common law or in equity.

Common law personal claims

The remedy for money had and received is based upon a remedy in the law of restitution. The law of restitution has developed immensely over the last decades and the scope of this book means that it cannot be fully developed here. The basic requirements are:

- Property is received in an unmixed form.
- Claimant must be legal title holder.

The basic principle is that the law will identify property which the recipient has or had in their possession. Property that is identified as belonging to the claimant will be followed into the possession of the recipient. The courts may require that the property is returned to the claimant (the proprietary remedy). However, for reasons explained below, the claimant may elect to take the personal remedy of requiring the recipient to account for the benefit they have received.

Revision Tip

In order to identify the person who must compensate, the claimant must prove that the defendant actually has or had their property. Students often become confused about the interplay between the following and tracing *process* and the *proprietary remedies* which may follow this process.

Tracing or following is used to locate the property, after which the claimant will usually be able to elect which remedy to pursue against the defendant.

The liability for the claim is strict, once the breach has been established then it becomes unjust for the recipient to retain that benefit.

. . . .

Lipkin Gorman v Karpnale [1991] 2 AC 548

A solicitor removed clients' money from the client account and used the money for gambling at the Playboy Club. This was a breach of the solicitor's fiduciary obligations. The Playboy Club had received that money under a void contract (gambling contracts were at the time void). As the Playboy Club had no legal claim to the money they were required to return its value to the 'real' owner.

. . . .

The Playboy Club was unaware of the breach by the solicitor. It was the fact that they had the money, or its value, in their possession that gave rise to the claim for restitution. They could not return the actual money but could return its value.

Defences to the claim

Equity's Darling

An absolute defence to any claim is that the recipient obtained the property as a **bona fide** purchaser for valuable consideration without notice, or 'Equity's Darling'.

- *Bona fide*: this is a question of fact for the courts to decide. If the party can prove that they acted 'without notice' then they are likely to be *bona fide*.

Personal actions

✳✳✳✳✳✳✳✳✳✳

- *Purchaser for valuable consideration* requires that the receipt forms part of a valid contract, which is only valid if there is consideration.

Change of position

The change of position defence is a development by the courts which has softened the impact of the strict liability of restitutionary claims; having identified the property **'in the hands'** of the recipient they may be able to retain some benefit. The extent will be measured by how much the recipient has 'changed their position' in reliance of the receipt; *Lipkin Gorman v Karpnale Ltd* [1991].

Figure 12.2 What constitutes change of position?

Change of position	Success?
Paying off a mortgage: *Scottish Equitable v Derby* [2000]	Unsuccessful as the mortgage payment was not a change of position.
Paying off a mortgage: *Boscawen v Bajwa* [1996]	Successful – The claimant can be 'subrogated' to the mortgage provider. This means that the claimant takes the place of the mortgage lender. The debt that was paid is now owed to the claimant.
Paying out winnings from gambling; *Lipkin Gorman v Karpnale Ltd* [1991]	Successful – The club had acted in good faith and paid out money in reliance of the bets placed.

Revision tip

This defence has been developed in response to a common law claim but it has been suggested as a defence for an equitable claim too.

Equitable personal claims

In addition to the common law claim there are claims which can be made in equity. The courts treat the intermeddler, recipient, or assistant *as if they were a trustee* in the following situations:

- a person who intentionally intermeddles with a trust;
- the recipient of trust property; and
- a person who assists in a breach of trust.

Intermeddling

A person who makes a deliberate decision to interfere with trust property and the duties of a trustee will be considered a '*trustee de son tort*'; *Mara v Browne* [1895]. This means that they act in relation to the trust property as if they were the trustee, the meddling is not itself a breach but they will be liable for any later breaches as if they had been a properly appointed trustee.

Recipient liability and accessory liability

Often referred to as 'stranger liability'; the 'stranger' refers to the fact that the person on whom liability is imposed in not appointed a trustee, nor does he elect to intermeddle with the trust. Although he is not appointed a trustee the courts have imposed upon him a liability as extensive as a trustee properly appointed.

✓ Looking for extra marks?

This is an area of fierce academic and judicial debate. The subjects are outlined here, but for an in-depth understanding see some of the suggestions in key debates.

The origins of stranger liability come from the statements in *Barnes v Addy* (1874), where Lord Selborne said that liability shall not arise unless the stranger 'receives and become chargeable with some part of the trust property, or unless they assist with the knowledge in a dishonest and fraudulent design on the part of the trustees'.

The 'stranger' will become liable 'as if they were' a constructive trustee. This is because their conscience is so affected that equity will not 'suffer a wrong without a remedy'.

Recipient liability

This area of law is fraught with confusion and has been labelled as 'knowing receipt' which raises issues of what knowledge is required to impose liability. *Baden, Delvaux and Lecuit v Société Générale pour Favoriser le Développement du Commerce et de l'Industrie en France* [1989] (referred to now as *Baden)* set out five categories of knowledge that may be relevant:

1. actual knowledge;
2. wilfully shutting one's eyes to the obvious;
3. wilfully and recklessly failing to make such inquiries as an honest and reasonable man would make;
4. knowledge of circumstances which would indicate the facts to an honest and reasonable man; and
5. knowledge of circumstances which would put an honest and reasonable man on inquiry.

The first three categories are often referred to as *actual knowledge* and the latter two as *constructive knowledge; Agip (Africa) Ltd v Jackson* [1990]. Whether the knowledge needs to be dishonest, which would affect the conscience of the defendant, has been problematic; however, the courts struggle with exactly what equates to knowledge and dishonesty.

In *BCCI v Akindele* [2000] the Court of Appeal relied upon the decision in *Belmont Finance Corp v Williams Furniture Ltd (No 2)* [1980] and Nourse LJ referred to the constructive

Personal actions

✳✳✳✳✳✳✳✳✳✳

trust being based upon whether it was '**unconscionable**' for the recipient of trust property to retain the benefit of receipt.

On the facts of *Akindele* [2000] it is difficult to see exactly what 'unconscionable' means. One factor may be that in a commercial context there is a need to encourage commercial flexibility. It is worth keeping in mind as you study this area that the financial markets are important to the British economy. Many of the debates and decisions are aimed at oiling the financial market.

 ✅ *Looking for extra marks?*

Read a summary of *Re Montagu's Settlement* [1987] and *Belmont Finance* [1980] on the different and conflicting interpretations of knowledge in relation to recipient liability. The decision of the Court of Appeal in *BCCI v Akindele* [2000] has been questioned by Lord Millett in the House of Lords in *Twinsectra v Yardley* [2002]. The concept of 'unconscionability' has been seen in other areas; see *Pennington v Waine* (2002). As equity acts *in personam* the issue of unconscionability is a very live issue in creating rights. It is a thread in many areas of equity.

Accessory liability

This has been called both 'dishonest assistance' and 'knowing assistance'. The change in labels reflects the problem of defining what knowledge is needed to impose liability for an accessory. It may be wrong to call such a person a constructive trustee as the property never vests in the 'stranger'. The label stems from the fact that liability is imposed upon the accessory 'as if' they were trustees.

In *Royal Brunei Airlines Sdn Bhd v Tan* [1995] Lord Nicholls in the Privy Council stated that the accessory would be liable if they acted dishonestly which: 'means simply not acting as an honest person would in the circumstances. This is an objective standard.' He admitted honesty had a strong subjective element and suggested that 'a court will look at the circumstances known to the third party at the time; having regard to the personal attributes of the third party, such as his experience and intelligence, and the reason why he acted as he did.'

This decision has been interpreted by the House of Lords in *Twinsectra v Yardley* [2002]. A majority of the House *seemed* to equate Lord Nicholls' *ratio* with that of the *Ghosh* test in criminal law. Lord Hutton's judgment suggests a person is dishonest if:

- *the objective element*; the actions be seen as dishonest by the standards of the ordinary reasonable person; and

- *the subjective element*; that the defendant *himself* realized that by those standards he was dishonest.

However, Lord Millett's strong dissenting judgment took an alternative view of Lord Nicholls' judgment in *Royal Brunei*. In *Barlow Clowes International v Eurotrust International* [2005], the Privy Council with Lord Hoffmann, a member of the majority in *Twinsectra*, on the panel, sought to 'clarify' the test in *Twinsectra*. The two-stage test is there but follows Lord Millet's explanation. The Privy Council, a persuasive authority, has been followed by the Court of Appeal in *Abou Rahma v Abacha* [2006] where they asked the same first question but then imbue the reasonable person with the 'characteristics' of the defendant.

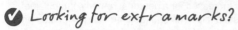
✅ Looking for extra marks?

The decision in the House of Lords in *Twinsectra* and the Privy Council in *Eurotrust* have caused much academic debate and illustrate the problems with imposing liability in this area. See an excellent discussion in Hudson, *Equity & Trusts*, 6th edn.

Proprietary claims

The issue for the courts is to identify the property that is being claimed by the beneficiary. There are a number of advantages to bringing a proprietary claim:

- if the trustee/recipient has become bankrupt the beneficiary takes **priority** over other creditors.
- any increase in value of the property taken by the trustee is recoverable; and
- there are no time limitations to bring a proprietary claim.

The first step is to identify the property in the hands of the trustee, or a third party, as being the trust property, which will then help you decide on a personal or proprietary (or combination of both) claim.

The tracing (following) process

It is important that the rules below are seen as a process. The aim for the claimant is to find who now has possession of the property which is being reclaimed. Once the property has been identified then the claim is made.

Revision tip

If the trust property has remained unchanged then the courts *follow* the asset into the hands of the trustee, or third party. If the property has changed in nature then the courts *trace* the property. These are often called the equitable remedies of following or tracing but they are in fact a process by which the property is identified; *Westdeutsche Landesbank Girozentrale v Islington LBC* [1996].

Example

In breach, a trustee spends £5,000 to buy a horse.

If the seller of the horse is a *bona fide* purchaser for valuable consideration without notice (Equity's Darling) there is no claim against them for the money. So the money has now become a horse. The property that is being claimed is the horse: its nature has changed but the property rights in it are the same.

Proprietary claims

✳✳✳✳✳✳✳✳✳✳

Common law proprietary claim

When a party receives property to which they are not legally entitled they are under an obligation to return the property to the rightful owner. They may receive this property because:

- property is received under a void contract; or
- property is received without the recipient giving valuable consideration.

The law will follow the property to the recipient, into the hands of another, by the process identified above. The liability for this claim is strict: once the property is found in the hands of the recipient then the property must be returned, subject to defences. A common law claim requires that:

- the claimant has legal title. So a beneficiary cannot use this remedy but a trustee could; and
- the property is unmixed.

Following at common law cannot be used when the property has been **mixed** with another person's property. This means that the property claimed has been combined with another person's property. The common example is for money to be taken in breach and placed in a bank account with the recipient's own money. But the principle applies to all property.

In *Agip (Africa) Ltd v Jackson* [1990] money was transferred through the electronic banking system and was found to have been mixed in the New York clearing system, losing its identity. However, the *clean* substitution of one property for another does not prevent the claim; *Taylor v Plumer* (1815). In this case the claimant's money was used to buy bonds and bullion; Lord Ellenborough said that 'the product or the substitute for the original thing still follows the nature of the thing itself'.

✅ Looking for extra marks?

Compare the tracing process with the protection of suppliers of materials to a company (creditors) offered by a (Romalpa) retention of title clause; *Aluminium Industrie Vaasen BV v Romalpa Aluminium Ltd* [1976]. In this way the supplied goods never become the property of the company and should the company be liquidated the goods are reclaimed by the seller; *Hendy Lennox Ltd v Grahame Puttick Ltd* [1984].

Problems arise when the property supplied with such a clause is used to manufacture goods. In *Re Peachdart Ltd* [1984] leather supplied was deemed to have been mixed in the production of handbags; although the leather was legally physically recognizable, it had lost its identity. See also *Borden UK Ltd v Scottish Timber Products Ltd* [1981].

> ### Revision tip
>
> The principle with the retention of title is exactly the same as the common law tracing. The seller retains the legal title. You may see in the cases that the buyer may hold a position as **bailee** or agent; but keep in mind what the purpose of the clause is, to retain a property interest.

Equitable proprietary claim

In contrast to following at common law, tracing in equity does not 'stop at the doors of the bank'; *Chief Constable of Kent v V and another* [1983]. Tracing in equity is therefore more flexible than following at common law as it can be used to trace property into mixed funds. The problem is identifying how much of the mixed property belongs to the claimant.

Essential elements for a tracing claim

From *Re Diplock* [1948] it is clear that to use equitable tracing there must be two requirements:

- a fiduciary relationship; and
- an equitable interest.

In a trust situation there will be a fiduciary relationship between the trustee and the beneficiary. In chapter 9 we identified classic relationships where a fiduciary relationship exists. However, it has become increasingly easy to establish a fiduciary relationship. Lord Browne-Wilkinson in *Westdeutsche Landesbank Girozentrale v Islington LBC* [1996] stated that a thief creates a 'fiduciary relationship' when he takes property belonging to another.

A fiduciary relationship is created from a constructive trust. The thief's conscience is affected thus giving rise to a constructive trust. This then creates an equitable interest. It is not necessary that the equitable interest pre-exist the acquisition of property by another. This leads to a 'chicken or the egg' situation of the two requirements for equitable tracing, which may be more apparent than real. This may be why Lord Millett doubted if a fiduciary relationship was even necessary; *Foskett v McKeown* [2001].

> ### Revision tip
>
> Once a constructive trust has been established then this gives the claimant a right to trace the property. Therefore if property is found in the possession of a recipient with the requisite knowledge to create recipient liability, they become a trustee and the claimant can decide to make a proprietary claim, not merely a personal one. This is the point at which the personal claim and the proprietary claim overlap. Often students are uncertain as to which claim to pursue, the answer for a claimant is usually financial. Which claim will give the best financial result?

Where there has been a breach of trust then the claimant must identify where the remedy lies. There will always be a personal remedy against the trustee but a common problem,

Proprietary claims
****

especially in exams, is that the trustee has become bankrupt or has disappeared. In this situation, then, the personal claim may be worthless.

Terminology tip

Students sometimes say in this situation that there is no personal claim. This is not true. There is a personal claim – it is just not worth pursuing. Try to avoid this terminology in exams.

Identifying who has the property

The rules in the tracing process need to be understood as falling into two categories:

- claims against the fiduciary (trustee); and
- claims between two 'innocent' claimants.

Revision tip

Always identify who has the property that is being claimed. The claim may be made against the fiduciary or trustee in breach but it may sometimes happen that the trustee has mixed two trust funds' monies in the same account or purchased property with a mixed fund.

Chapter 9 established that property which is purchased with the funds of two people is shared between them in proportion to their contribution under a resulting trust. *Sinclair v Brougham* [1914] presumes between all parties tracing their property that it is shared **rateably**: *pari passu*. The same reasoning applies to tracing claims where more than one person's money has been used to purchase property subject to a tracing claim, regardless of the claim being against the fiduciary or another innocent claimant. The courts are seeking to identify the property that is owned by the beneficiary. If the property being traced is an asset that has been purchased or exchanged for the trust property the basic principle is to identify how much of the asset belongs to the trust and how much to an innocent contributor, a recipient, or a trustee in breach.

So if a trustee takes a picture from the trust property and exchanges the picture and his own gold watch for a car, the courts would need to ascertain in what proportion the car belonged to the trust and to the trustee in breach. It is more common in exam questions to have the value represented in monetary figures. This is the process of tracing.

Claim against a trustee in breach

The rules in relation to claims against a trustee in breach will be explained by working through an example.

Revision tip

In an exam be clear where the money is coming from and where it is going to. It may be useful in your answer plan to draw an accounting table of the sums you are dealing with. This is one suggested layout but any method that can help you identify who owns what share of property is helpful. Carefully planning the answer in this way will pay dividends.

Payments into an overdrawn account

Trustee in breach takes £2,000 from Trust Fund A and places it into his current account which has an overdraft of £1,000.

Figure 12.3

Balance in the current account after transfer	Trustee's interest	Trust A's interest
1,000	−1,000	2,000

The money to pay the overdraft has been dissipated; there is no asset into which to trace the property.

✅ *Looking for extra marks?*

It has been suggested that 'backwards tracing' may provide an answer (see some comments in *Foskett v McKoown*. This means that if the overdraft was caused by purchasing an asset for the trustee then the claimant should have a claim on that asset. This has not found favour with the courts.

The presumptions of honesty

(a) Trustee in breach takes £2,000 from Trust Fund A and places it into his current account which has an existing balance of £1,000.

At this point the money in the account would be shared 1/3 for trustee and 2/3 for Trust A because this is the proportion in which they made the contributions.

Revision tip

In an exam question, commonly the trustee will spend the money in the account, because otherwise, although the trustee may be imprudent with the trust money, there is no difficulty in reclaiming the money.

Re Hallet's (1880) deals with the situation where money is taken from the trustee's account. The court uses a presumption of honesty, meaning that the trustee is deemed to spend his *own money first*. So when the trustee then buys a picture for £1,500 the picture would be purchased in the same proportion as the contribution: 2/3 by trustee and 1/3 by Trust A. This rule will be applied even if the value of the picture increases; *Re Tilley's WT* [1967]. The beneficiary is protected as the fund is safe and identifiable and the share of the picture is identifiable. The remedy is not to punish the trustee but to protect the property of the trust fund.

Proprietary claims
****

Figure 12.4

Balance in the current account	Trustee's interest	Trust A's interest
3,000 (after transfer)	1,000	2,000
–1,500 (purchase of picture)	*1,000*	*–500*
1,500 (after purchase)	0	1,500

(b) If the balance in the bank (above) was then dissipated by the trustee the courts may reverse the application of *Re Hallet's* (1880) by using *Re Oatway* [1903].

> *Revision tip*
>
> A common mistake for students in exams is to apply *Re Oatway* immediately. More marks will be gained for explaining the presumption in *Re Hallet's*, and how that would affect distribution of property rights, then explaining how *Re Oatway* modifies that.

Applying Re Oatway (1903) – Trustee in breach takes £2,000 from Trust Fund A and places it in his current account, which already has £1,000 in it. Then he purchases a picture worth £1,500. He then spends the balance of the bank account on a world cruise.

Figure 12.5

Balance in the current account	Trustee's interest	Trust A's interest
3,000 (after transfer)	1,000	2,000
–1,500 (purchase of picture)		*–1,500*
1,500 (after purchase of picture)	1,000	500
–1,500 (purchase of cruise)	*–1,000*	*–500*

This means that the money used to buy the picture, which remains an identifiable asset, was in fact that of the trust. So the picture is owned by Trust A and the money dissipated is only £500 of Trust A's and the bulk is the trustees'. This preserves the property of the trust fund as much as possible. If the picture has increased in value then there will be a proprietary claim. If the picture has reduced in value the claimant can place an equitable lien over the property to the value of the money taken (not the money spent on the picture) to protect any personal claims they may make.

The aim is to protect the interest of the (innocent) beneficiary and ensure that the wrongdoer risks the loss. The presumption would be that (still trying to be honest) the trustee in fact spent the trust fund money and dissipated his own. This then secures the trust funds against the asset. It is unclear from *Re Oatway* if all the money from the account needs to be dissipated.

Terminology tip

'Dissipated' means that there is no asset to attach a property right to, not that the property is worthless. For example, the money has been spent on a holiday or a meal. Not that shares or other property purchased with the trust money now has no value.

The seller of the picture cannot be made to return the money as they are *Equity's Darling*. This is an absolute defence for the seller. However, if the money had been donated to a charity or given as a gift, then the *Equity's Darling* defence would not apply. The trust can trace 'into the hands' of the innocent volunteer.

Later payments into the account by the trustee in breach

The rule in *Roscoe v Winder* [1915] is that should the trustee in breach mix his own, later acquired, money in the same bank account with trust money the presumption is that this is *not* a repayment of the money used in breach. The presumption will only be rebutted if there is clear evidence that the intention of the trustee was to repay the money taken in breach.

The trustee takes £500 he won on the lottery and places it into the account that has £1,000 of Trust A money remaining in it after the trustee spent £1,000 on a holiday.

Figure 12.6

Balance in the account	Trustee's interest	Trust A's interest
2,000		2,000
–1,000 *(spent on a holiday)*	0	1,000
+500 *(lottery winnings)*	+500	
1,500	500	1,000

The trustee has the property right in this money and is not deemed to repay the beneficiary unless there is evidence of that intention; *Roscoe v Winder* [1915]. This may seem an anomaly to the 'presumption of honesty' but the claim is proprietary and as such the £500 was never the property of the trust. On this basis it makes sense that Trust A cannot claim that the £500 represent their property. They have no pre-existing property right in the £500 that the court will protect. Their personal claim remains intact.

Proprietary claims

✱✱✱✱✱✱✱✱✱✱

Two innocent volunteers mixed funds in a bank account

The rules that operate between two innocent parties are different in some aspects. If the trust property remains identifiable then the property is shared rateably as between the trustee and the trust fund; *Sinclair v Brougham* [1914].

The trustee takes £1,000 from Trust B and places that in the account which already has £750 of Trust A funds in it.

Figure 12.7

Balance in the account	Trustee's interest	Trust A's interest	Trust B's interest
1,750 (after transfer)	0	750	1,000

The position is now that there is a mixed fund between two innocent parties. Different rules apply in relation to how they are dealt with between each other compared with how the trustee is dealt with in relation to them. If the trustee now spends the money in the bank the rule in *Clayton's Case* (1817) will apply. This states that, in a current account, money is assumed to be taken on a first in, first out basis. This means that between the two innocent parties the money that was in the account first will be the first to be spent. This is a simple accounting issue.

Following on from above, the trustee spends £1,500 on shares, which, since purchase, have reduced in value and are now worth £500. Trust A had their money in the account for several months before Trust B had their money placed in the account.

Figure 12.8

Balance in the account	Trustee's interest	Trust A's interest	Trust B's interest
–1,500 (purchase of shares)	0	–750	–750
250	0	0	250

As Trust A was the first to have money in the account the 'first in, first out' rule from *Clayton's Case* (1817) will take that money first then the balance will come from Trust B.

The remaining money in the bank belongs to Trust B. This rule can work harshly, for example if Trust A will be exhausted on this interpretation but Trust B still has a significant amount left. If this does cause an inequitable result then the rule in *Clayton's* can be set aside; *Barlow Clowes v Vaughan* [1992]. This is increasingly the position of the courts.

Innocent volunteers who receive trust property

'Innocent volunteer' also applies to situations where a person receives property under an invalid contract such the Playboy Club in *Lipkin Gorman* [1991]. Tracing will identify the property in the possession of the innocent recipient. Once it has been found in the possession of the recipient liability is strict.

Defences available to the innocent volunteer

Re Diplock [1948] suggested that in this position the innocent volunteer may claim that it would be unconscionable to return the property. The personal claim against the trustee in breach remains (*Ministry of Health v Simpson* [1951]), but the proprietary claim may fail. This is the same principle as the change of position defence in common law claims. In *Boscawen v Bajwa* [1996] it was stated that the common law defence of change of position could apply to the equitable claims.

 Conclusion

The remedies for breach of trust can be personal against the trustee as with any breach of obligation. In addition to these claims a proprietary process can be used to help identify property taken in breach of trust. Once the property has been identified in the possession of another, this can be in its original form or in replacement property (substitutes), then the claimant can elect to make a personal claim or a proprietary one.

Claims can be brought not only against the trustee in breach but also against innocent recipients, dishonest recipients, and people who assist in a breach of trust. The key step is to identify where the property taken in breach is, then decide what type of claim would be most beneficial.

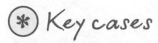 Key cases

Case	Facts	Principle
Agip (Africa) Ltd v Jackson [1990] Ch 26	A senior officer innocently signed a forged payment order. The forger, an accountant, was employed by the company. Payment was made by innocent banks. The forgery was discovered too late to stop payment.	Where there had been no mixing the property could be traced at common law. Money transferred by electronic transfer as there was no physical asset which could be traced. The fraudulent accountant owed a fiduciary duty to the company. He would be liable to account as constructive trustee as he knowingly assisted in the fraud.
BCCI v Akindele [2000] 4 All ER 221	Money was loaned on very favourable terms. BCCI collapsed and the creditors tried to claim against the money paid to Chief Akindele for his assistance in fraud.	The level of dishonesty needed to create liability as constructive trustee was 'such that it would make it unconscionable for them to retain the receipt'.

Key debates

****

Case	Facts	Principle
Foskett v McKeown [2001] 1 AC 102	Deposits paid for property were used to pay for insurance premiums by M. M committed suicide and over £1 million was paid on the insurance policy. Claimant traced the money into the insurance payment.	Claimant entitled to a charge over the payment, with interest paid on that amount but their claim was not restricted to this (as the CA had found). They could claim a proportion of the payment equivalent to their contribution.
Lipkin Gorman v Karpnale Ltd [1991] 2 AC 548	Mr Cass, a solicitor, removed clients' money from the client account and used the money for gambling at the Playboy Club. This was a breach of the solicitor's fiduciary obligations. The Playboy Club had received that money under a void contract (gambling contracts were at the time void). As the Playboy Club had no legal claim to the money they were required to return its value to the 'real' owner.	The liability to repay the solicitor was strict but subject to a defence of change of position. The argument by the Playboy Club that they were *Equity's Darling* failed as their contract was void under the existing gambling laws of the time.
Twinsectra v Yardley [2002] 2 AC 164	Money was lent to Sim, acting for Yardley, for the sole purpose of buying property. In breach, Sim paid the money to Yardley's solicitor, Leach. He released it to Yardley. On default Leach was sued for dishonest assistance.	Loan was made as a *Quistclose trust*. Case decided on the 'combined test'. Has D transgressed the standards of conduct? Does D realize the transgression? Note: the test has been 'reviewed' by the Privy Council in *Eurotrust v Barlow Clowes* [2006] 1 All ER 333.

🟢 Key debates

Topic	Meaning of dishonesty in accessory liability
Academic/ Author	Lord Millet
Viewpoint	The liability should be objective and not have a subjective element.
Source	Lord Millet's dissenting judgment in *Twinsectra v Yardley* [2002]. For overview of the issues see Pearce and Stevens, *Law of Trusts and Equitable Obligations*, 4th edn (2006), pp 826–37.

Topic	Strict liability for recipient liability
Academic/ Author	Birks
Viewpoint	Liability should be strict subject to defences as with common law money had and received.
Source	[1989] LMCLQ 296.For overview of the issues, Pearce and Stevens, *Law of Trusts and Equitable Obligations*, 4th edn (2006), pp 841–62.

Topic	Causation of Loss
Academic/ Author	Pearce and Stevens
Viewpoint	The problems with multiple causes of loss.
Source	Pearce and Stevens, *Law of Trusts and Equitable Obligations*, 4th edn (2006), pp 744–55.

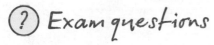

(?) Exam questions

Problem question

Jack, a solicitor for Badger & Co, takes £3,000 out of the customer account. He spends £2,000 at the local casino, Fungirls & Co. He places the remaining £1,000 in his bank which already has a balance of £500 in it. He takes £1,000 and buys a picture from his friend Augustus, which is now worth £2,000. The remaining £500 in his account, he spends on a holiday weekend in France.

Advise Badger & Co as to their remedies.

An outline answer is included at the end of the book.

Essay question

The rules on common law and equitable tracing should be united into a coherent system of rules. Discuss.

An outline answer is available online at www.oxfordtextbooks.co.uk/orc/concentrate/

#13
Equitable remedies

- Equitable remedies are discretionary.
- Equitable remedies are granted where common law remedies would be inadequate.
- Equitable remedies can be granted at full trial or at an interim stage before a full trial.
- They operate *in personam*, against the defendant personally.

Introduction

The common law provides the remedy of **damages** as of right for any breach. However, damages may not always provide a suitable or adequate remedy. For example, if a person was trespassing on your land then money would not be the suitable remedy as the trespass itself has caused no financial loss. One of the key equitable maxims states that 'equity will not suffer a wrong without a remedy'. Therefore, over the years the courts have developed a number of equitable remedies to address the limitations of the common law response. As these remedies have been developed to ensure fairness, they are not available as of right, but are always granted at the discretion of the court. This chapter will consider the range of equitable remedies which have been developed by the courts:

1. specific performance;
2. injunctions;
3. rescission;
4. rectification; and
5. account.

Specific performance

In most situations where there is a breach of contract, the loss suffered will be capable of being compensated by a common law award of damages. However, in some cases, the court may choose to compel the defendant to perform their original obligation under the contract by making an order for specific performance. Typically, such an order will be made where monetary damages would not provide an appropriate remedy or compensate for the loss suffered. As this equitable remedy compels the completion of an obligation, it would be inappropriate to grant an order of specific performance without a full hearing. Therefore, specific performance is only available at full trial and cannot be awarded at an **interim** stage.

Unique

Damages will be considered inadequate when the obligation which the claimant seeks to enforce is unique. A simple illustration of this can be found in contracts for the sale of land. Although, an award of monetary damages may allow you to purchase *similar* land, you will never be able to replace the land that you were originally promised.

The courts have interpreted what is 'unique' broadly. It does not mean that the goods are literally unique but that they are effectively unique in the context of the contract.

- *Sky Petroleum v VIP Petroleum* [1974]: a contract to supply petrol could be specifically enforced. The issue had arisen during a national petrol shortage, making it impossible to find an alternative supplier. The risk from the refusal to deliver, that they may inevitably go out of business, meant that the remedy was necessary.

Specific performance
✳✳✳✳✳✳✳✳✳✳✳

- *Behnke v Bede Shipping Co Ltd* [1927]: delivery of a ship was granted specific performance because the ship was of 'peculiar and practically unique value to the plaintiff'. They could not easily seek an alternative supplier of that kind of vessel.

Revision tip

It is very important in a problem exam question that you apply the law to the facts. For example, a contract for a car will not usually be unique, but if the purchaser needs to buy a specific car, perhaps one that was a prop in a James Bond film, then that car may be said to have a unique quality.

A common problem for good students who know the law is a failure to *advise* the client – that is, not just stating what the law is but also applying it to the facts of the case before you.

Considerations in granting an order

It is important to remember that equitable remedies are discretionary. So even if the situation appears to warrant specific performance, there are certain circumstances in which the court will refuse to make such an order.

Supervision

Even if the court believes that there is a unique quality to the obligation sought to be enforced, it will not award specific performance if the performance of that obligation would require the constant supervision of the court. This means that if the claimant would have to continually return to the court for successive orders, the remedy would essentially be ineffective. In *Co-operative Insurance Society Ltd v Argyll Stores Ltd* [1988] Argyll Stores decided to close their store in a shopping centre owned by the claimant as it was losing money. The lease agreement required them to remain open during normal business hours. The House of Lords reversed the Court of Appeal decision to grant specific performance, as to enforce the contract would require the constant supervision of the courts.

Personal services

The courts are reluctant to enforce a contract for a personal service for many reasons. It is reluctant as it may turn a contract for service into a contract of slavery; *De Francesco v Barnum* (1890). This reluctance is now statutory based in **s 236 Trade Union and Labour Relations (Consolidation) Act 1992**:

> no court shall…by way of an order for specific performance…compel an employee to do any work.

However, this only applies to employee contracts. The courts distinguish between contracts '*of service*' and '*for service*'. An example may help to illustrate the difference.

Example 1

Mark is hired by Lois to build her a conservatory. This is a contract *for* service. The task is discrete and clearly defined (see *Posner v Scott-Lewis* [1987] below). It would be relatively easy to require the promised performance to be completed by an order for specific performance.

Example 2

Mark is hired to work in Lois' factory which produces window frames. This is a contract *of* service. There is an ongoing employer – employee relationship and unlikely to be enforced.

Revision tip

Do not leap to the conclusion that a person is an employee. Apply the facts. Consider what the person is being required to do.

In *Posner v Scott-Lewis* [1987] a leasehold covenant required the landlord to employ a resident porter to carry out clearly specified duties at a block of flats. The court felt the terms were sufficiently clear and ascertainable.

Compare this to *Warner Bros Pictures Inc v Nelson* [1937] where the actress Bette Davis was contracted to work exclusively for Warner Bros Pictures. The courts would not compel her to work, by an order of specific performance, as it was akin to 'slavery'.

However, even if it is a contract for service the courts may still decide not to give specific performance. It may be that the service can easily be performed by another. In Example 1, it is likely that damages would be adequate to pay for a replacement supplier of conservatories. This stance can be explained by the equitable maxim, 'equity will not act in vain'. If a defendant is forced to perform a task, she may not perform the task to a high standard. If being forced to complete the obligation would lead the defendant to deliberately perform badly, an order of specific performance is unlikely to be an effective or appropriate remedy and the court may decide it is easier to award damages from the outset.

Defences

Hardship

If the grant of specific performance would cause hardship, to either party, then the court may not grant specific performance; *Patel v Ali* [1984].

Mistake and misrepresentation

The courts may refuse to rescind a contract for misrepresentation and leave the claimant to a remedy of damages. The courts will generally hold the defendant to the performance of his contract unless it causes real hardship; *Tamplin v James* (1880).

Conduct of claimant

In line with the equitable maxim that those who seek equity must come with clean hands, the conduct of the claimant may bar an order for specific performance. The claimant must prove that they have either performed, or are willing and able to perform, their obligations; *Cornish v Brook Green Laundry* [1959].

Delay or laches

Although generally in equity time is not of the essence, in balancing the equity between the parties unreasonable delay may defeat equity. What is unreasonable will depend on the facts, particularly the object matter of the contract; *Lazard Bros v Fairfield Property Ltd* (1977). Where time is of the essence then specific performance will not usually be granted after the date of performance; *Union Eagle Ltd v Golden Achievements Ltd* [1997].

Injunctions

Injunctions can be awarded at two stages of the trial process. It is more common for injunctions to be granted at the conclusion of the full trial hearing. These injunctions are known as **perpetual** and act as the final conclusion to the legal dispute. However, in certain circumstances, the urgency of the matter requires swifter action. For example, where the claimant alleges that the defendant is planning to release documents containing trade secrets to a competitor in breach of confidence, by the time the full trial takes place the damage may already have been done and the claimant will have been deprived of an effective remedy. In this situation, the claimant would seek an *interim* injunction to stop the defendant from acting before the full trial.

Interim injunctions are temporary in nature and will typically last until the conclusion of a full trial hearing. It is vital that such orders are temporary as they are often granted before the court has had the opportunity to hear all the arguments and evidence relating to the claim.

Terminology tip

Do not be confused if you come across references to 'interlocutory' injunctions in textbooks, articles, and cases. Until recently, interim injunctions were known as 'interlocutory' injunctions.

Injunctions are a more flexible type of equitable remedy than specific performance because they can perform different roles. There are three broad types of injunctions:

1. Prohibitive injunctions – these prevent a defendant from doing something and therefore stop a breach of an obligation.

2. Mandatory injunctions – these compel a defendant to do something (and therefore work in a similar way to specific performance).

3. *Quia timet* injunctions – these injunctions may be either prohibitory or mandatory and are made where the harm alleged has not yet happened but is feared by the claimant or threatened by the defendant.

Perpetual injunctions

Prohibitive injunctions

Prohibitive injunctions prevent a breach of an obligation. This can include a breach of confidence, such as information obtained during employment. It can include very wide powers to prevent disclosure of information on a worldwide basis, where the release of such information would create serious risk of personal injury. This can be seen in the case of *Venables v News Group Newspapers* [2001], where the identity and whereabouts of one of the killers of the toddler Jamie Bulger were not to be published. This was the only way to protect the claimant's rights under the **Human Rights Act 1998**.

Revision Tip

In an exam consider if one remedy does not achieve your purpose another one would. In *Warner Bros Pictures Inc v Nelson* [1937] an injunction was ordered against an actress to prevent her from working for any other film company for the duration of her contract with Warner Bros. The claim for specific performance was denied but they achieved their aim with an injunction.

Mandatory injunctions

Mandatory injunctions at full trial require the performance of an obligation in the same way as specific performance does. If the obligation is contractual then specific performance is the more common remedy. There may also be a 'restorative' mandatory injunction. This will be given where a wrong has been done which may have been prevented by a prohibitive injunction. A mandatory injunction may be ordered to undo the wrong; *Jones v Stones* [1999].

Interim injunctions

Prohibitive injunctions

For a grant of an interim injunction the courts are making a decision without the benefit of a full trial. To make sure that they have considered the grant carefully they follow the guidelines set out by Lord Diplock in *American Cyanamid Co v Ethicon Ltd* [1975]:

- There is a serious question to be tried.
- Damages are inadequate.
- The balance of convenience requires the grant of an injunction.

✅ Looking for extra marks?

To fully understand the importance of Lord Diplock's test it is worth understanding what the test was prior to *American Cyanamid*. The claimant was required to show a strong *prima facie* case that rights had been infringed, that damages were inadequate, and that justice required the grant. This was a heavy burden on the claimant to prove it more than likely that they would obtain a full injunction at trial.

Injunctions

✳✳✳✳✳✳✳✳✳✳✳

Serious question to be tried

The courts will only consider such an order if there are serious issues at stake. In *Morning Star v Express Newspapers* [1979] the *Morning Star* newspaper objected to the publication of the *Daily Star*, claiming that people would confuse the two. The judge felt that 'only a moron in a hurry' would make the mistake and that there was no case to answer.

Adequacy of damages

Essentially, the test for all equitable remedies is, 'Would money compensate?' There are two stages to the test.

1. Would money be able to compensate and would D be in a position to pay?
2. If it later appears that the injunction has been given incorrectly then the undertaking by the claimant in damages will be an adequate protection.

One consideration would be if the type of damage is irreparable; such as the loss of a right to vote or the loss in non-pecuniary, such as libel or nuisance, also if damages would be hard to assess, such as the value of goodwill or serious disruption to business. Should damages be adequate the courts will then consider if the defendant would be unable to pay should the claimant win. If the claimant fails to prove damages are inadequate then the claim will end there.

The claimant will make an undertaking in damages. This means that if it later appears that the injunction was wrongly granted the claimant can compensate the defendant with money. The inability of the claimant to be able to compensate with money will not be determinative of the decision of the grant of an injunction; *Allen v Jambo Holdings Ltd* [1980]. If the claimant cannot make an undertaking the courts will go on to consider the balance of convenience.

Balance of convenience

Lord Diplock said that it would be impossible to list the considerations but in *Cayne v Global Natural Resources plc* [1984] it was said that it is not the mere convenience that needs to be weighed but the risk of doing an injustice to one side or the other. Each case turns on its own facts so should be carefully considered in any problem question.

Factors which have been considered

Figure 13.1

Factor considered	Case
Loss of employment	*Fellowes & Son v Fisher* [1976]
Damage to business by picketing	*Hubbard v Pitt* [1976]
Closing a business	*Potters – Ballotini Ltd v Weston-Baker* [1977]

Factor considered	Case
Protecting confidential material	*X AG v A Bank* [1983]
Keeping a life-saving drug on the market	*Roussel-Uclaf v GD Searle & Co Ltd* [1977]

If the balance of convenience is equal then the court will maintain the *status quo*. In *Garden Cottage Foods Ltd v Milk Marketing Board* [1984] it appears that it is the *status quo ante* (before D began the conduct complained of) which is maintained, which tends to favour the claimant.

As with all equitable remedies delay may defeat equity. If the claim has been delayed then the *status quo ante* will not be maintained but the *status quo* as it is at the time of claim. What is an undue delay varies on the facts; *Shepherd Homes v Sandham* [1970].

✅ Looking for extra marks?

In *Series 5 Software Ltd v Clarke* [1996], a first instance decision, it was felt that despite the guidelines above what was required was a review of all the evidence disclosed. This, however, does appear to be a return to the finding of a *prima facie* case to be answered which Lord Diplock in *American Cyanamid Co v Ethicon Ltd* [1975] had wanted to avoid. If asked to comment on the test it may be worth noting the High Court's decision in this case.

Revision tip

The question over delay must be applied to the facts. In *Shepherd Homes* [1970] an unexplained delay of five months prevented the grant. However, in *Bulmer v Bollinger* [1977] the word 'champagne' had been used since 1906 by the firm in marketing 'BabyCham', well known to the claimant. However, the delay in the claim did not defeat the order.

Mandatory injunctions

Unlike specific performance, mandatory injunctions can be awarded at an interim stage. The test set out for interim injunctions in *American Cyanamid Co v Ethicon Ltd* [1975] will apply but in balancing the justice of the case the Court of Appeal in *Locabail International Finance v Agroexport* [1986] approved the guidance of Megarry J in *Shepherd Homes v Sandham* [1970], that the courts required a 'high degree of assurance' that the grant of an injunction would be found to be the correct decision when the case finally came to court.

The courts take serious note of the balance of convenience between the claimant and the defendant; *Evans v BBC and IBA* (1974) regarding the transmission of party political broadcasts.

Revision tip

Always consider the higher burden on the claimant to prove that they should be granted an interim mandatory injunction.

Injunctions

****

In addition to the remedies above, there are remedies which can be sought in the absence of the defendant; these are **ex parte** orders. In considering these orders it is important to consider the **Human Rights Act 1998** as the defendant is not there to present their case, raising issues of a fair trial. The courts still feel that in some circumstances the interests of the parties call for such an *ex parte* application to be allowed. There are more stringent tests for such orders.

Search orders (formerly Anton Pillar orders)

During the trial process all parties are required to disclose documents that will be relevant to the trial. If the claimant feels that the other party to the litigation will not do so, they may ask for a search order. This order is granted without notice; because to give notice would possibly defeat the purpose of the order. These mandatory orders require D to permit the search of their premises to find documents. Such an order was first used in *EMI Ltd v Pandit* [1975] but the leading case on these orders is *Anton Piller KG v Manufacturing Processes* [1976]. In this case Ormrod LJ said that the remedy was one of 'last resort' because of the impact it could have on D's business. In deciding to grant an order there must be:

- an extremely strong **prima facie** case;
- extremely serious potential (or actual) harm to claimant;
- clear evidence that the information or items, which are the subject matter of the order, are in D's possession;
- a real possibility that they will be destroyed or removed without such an order; and
- a full and frank disclosure by the claimant of all material matters in the case.

There are procedural safeguards for the defendant set out in the Practice Direction of the Civil Procedure Rules, granting the jurisdiction for these order in s 7 Civil Procedure Act 1997. These include the presence of a supervising solicitor, that the search take place in office hours, that D or a responsible employee is present, it must not be a fishing exercise, and only the subject matter listed in the order can be taken. The defendant is also protected in that she can make an application at short notice to have the order removed or varied; *Lock International plc v Beswick* [1989]. These procedural safeguards indicate the balance the court has to make between protecting the interests of both parties and the possible abuse of the order by a claimant.

Revision tip

A common mistake is for students to explain, in detail, the procedure for the grant of the order rather than the legal tests for its grant. Ensure that the legal requirements are fully applied.

Freezing orders (formerly Mareva Injunctions)

These are mandatory orders which will freeze the assets of the defendant. Equity will not act in vain and should a claimant win at trial they want to ensure that the award of damages will be paid. If there is a danger that the defendant may seek to remove or destroy assets to avoid paying damages then a freezing order may be sought. The order will freeze the assets of the defendant, up to the value of the claim, which will be held by the order of the court. This will prevent a defendant removing their assets from the court's jurisdiction before trial; *Mareva Compagnia Naviera SA v International Bulkcarriers SA* [1975].

The freezing order is a clear example of the personal nature of the equitable remedy. The claimant gains no property rights over the assets frozen. Additionally, anyone dealing with the property contrary to the order will be personally liable for contempt of court. Thus, if bank assets are frozen then the bank manager cannot allow the client access to the money; *Attorney-General v Times Newspapers Ltd* [1992].

✅ Looking for extra marks?

Lord Denning had said *per incurium* that the remedy was proprietary; *Z Ltd v A-Z and AA-LL* [1982]. The nature of freezing an asset, perhaps a ship or house, may have the effect of a proprietary remedy. So is the claim that it is personal, illusory?

Section 37 Supreme Court Act 1981, which gives the courts jurisdiction to grant all injunctions, now provides for these orders to be made where it is 'just and convenient to do so'. Such an order often accompanies a search order and again is made without notice.

The test set out in *Derby & Co Ltd v Weldon* [1990] is that in addition to the *American Cyanamid* test it must also be proven that:

- there is a 'good arguable' case;
- the defendant has assets in the jurisdiction; and
- there is a real risk that without the order the assets will be removed or dissipated.

The defendant can keep assets to provide for reasonable living and business costs. It may also be possible to freeze assets outside the UK; *Re BCCI SA (No 9)* [1994].

Other injunctive orders

Quia timet (because the claimant fears) orders are made at an interim stage and do not require proof of actual harm. Their purpose is to prevent a possible harm from occurring. This may be preventing publication of a story that may harm a reputation or interest. The case of *Venables v News Group Newspapers* [2001] illustrates an injunction granted when there was no actual harm but the fear of future harm.

Rescission

Rescission is aimed at restoring *both* parties to their original positions, before the wrong occurred. Where a contract is set aside then the innocent party can ask for the equitable remedy of rescission. However, sometimes the right to rescission may be barred:

- Third party rights – if an innocent third party will be adversely affected by the rescission; *Phillips v Brooks* [1919].
- Delay – based upon the maxims that delay defeats equity and is a practical point; *Leaf v International Galleries* [1950].
- Affirmation – when a claimant can rescind a contract but instead decides to continue with the contract; *Long v Lloyd* [1958].
- Impossibility – if it is impossible to return *both* parties to their pre-contractual position. However, equity does provide that substantial not precise restoration will suffice; *Erlanger v New Sombrero Phosphate Co* (1873).

The important point that will be noted with a claim for rescission of contracts is that there must be justice between both parties.

Rectification

Rectification is an equitable remedy which allows a legal document that does not reflect the true agreement of the parties to be appropriately amended. In *Craddock Bros v Hunt* [1932] a conveyance of property indicated that it included an area that actually belonged to another house. The court rectified the conveyance. However, it must be noted that the courts are reluctant to vary written documents without good evidence that it is needed; *City of Westminster Properties Ltd v Mudd* [1959].

Account

The remedy of account will be used to require a fiduciary or agent to repay unauthorized profit, bribes, or profit from a breach of confidence; *Attorney General v Blake* [2000]. See chapter 12.

 Conclusion

Equitable remedies recognize that not all contracts are for monetary gain, such as holidays or services. Torts are not always easy to compensate with mere money. Where the claimant can prove that this is the situation then equity 'will not suffer a wrong without a remedy'. The evolution of the search order and freezing order indicates that this is an area of development. A common claim by students, and some academics, is that equity is staid and stagnant. It is anything but as can be seen by the remedies available.

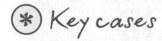 Key cases

Case	Facts	Principle
American Cyanamid Co v Ethicon Ltd [1975] AC 396	There was a potential infringement of a patent.	Court established the principles to grant an interim injunction: • A serious question to be tried • The adequacy of damages • The balance of convenience • Special factors to consider
Anton Piller KG v Manufacturing Processes Ltd [1976] Ch 55	The claimant believed that the defendant had confidential papers belonging to them. They wanted to search D's premises to find them.	'Equity will not suffer a wrong without a remedy' and a search order was granted.
Co-operative Insurance Society v Argyll Stores [1988] AC 1	Lease stipulated that a store should be open during usual business hours. The store was losing money and wanted to close.	If specific performance was ordered the court would be required to supervise compliance with the order. So the order was not given.
Lock International plc v Beswick [1989] 1 WLR 1268	Claimant said that defendant had confidential information taken from them and being used in competition. They wanted a search order to confiscate the property.	Defendant successfully had a search order discharged as they were not 'fly by night video pirates' but respectable business people and likely to comply with disclosure orders.

⟨𝟿⟩ Key debates

Topic	Search orders
Academic/ Author	Dockray and Laddie
Viewpoint	The nature of the order can be oppressive and have devastating impact on business or persons who have not had a full trial.
Source	'Piller problems' (1990) 106 LQR 601–20.

Topic	Interim orders
Academic/ Author	
Viewpoint	There may be a risk that orders made without the benefit of a full trial, especially when made without notice, could breach our obligations under the Convention on Human Rights.
Source	*Chappell v UK* (1990) 12 EHRR 1.

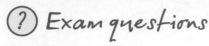
(?) Exam questions

Problem question

Hannah contracts with Ahmed to paint a portrait of her mother Joyce, for £5,000 contract price. Ahmed is Joyce's favourite artist. It will be a present for Joyce's birthday on 2 June. He begins the portrait but is then approached by Lars who offers Ahmed £10,000, if Ahmed will stop the portrait of Joyce and paint Lars in his graduation gown by 1 June. Ahmed informs Hannah that he cannot complete Joyce's portrait.

Hannah had given Ahmed Joyce's diary, containing intimate details of her mother's life, so he could get a 'feel' for her character. Joyce is a politician who is about to stand for re-election. The diaries contain details of several affairs that Joyce had during her life and some details of political indiscretions.

Hannah has been told by her friend that Ahmed has approached a national newspaper to sell some of these details. Ahmed has a bank account in this country and owns homes in Los Angeles and Switzerland.

Advise Hannah on any equitable remedies she may have.

An outline answer is included at the end of the book.

Essay question

The grant of *ex parte* equitable remedies is a breach of fundamental human rights. Discuss.

An outline answer is available online at www.oxfordtextbooks.co.uk/orc/concentrate/

Outline answers

Chapter 1

Essay answer

- Always read essay questions carefully to identify the relevant issues.

- *Illustrate* the law's adaptation to changing social conditions and *discuss* whether these changes promote certainty or some other goal.

- You cannot cover every possible example in an examination, so pick out key areas for discussion. For example:

- *Trusts of the family home*: as levels of cohabitation have increased, there has been an increasing need for the law to adapt, particularly in relation to the family home. This has revealed tensions between certainty and more welfarist concerns, such as:

– Lord Denning and the 'New Model Constructive Trust' (*Hussey v Palmer* [1972]).

– Questions over what contributions are relevant to the establishment of a constructive trust (contrast *Lloyds Bank v Rosset* [1991] and *Stack v Dowden* [2007]).

– *Oxley v Hiscock* [2004] argued that the court could quantify the beneficial interest as what was 'fair having regard to the whole course of dealings in relation to the property'. However, the House of Lords in *Stack v Dowden* [2007] rejected the 'fairness' aspect of this test as too subjective.

– The degree of uncertainty in this area is illustrated by the increasing calls for legislative reform.

- *Quistclose-type trusts*: the precise conceptual foundations of this trust remain unclear (*Twinsectra v Yardley* [2002]). While the 'Quistclose' trust clearly attempts to do justice in specific cases, its uncertain foundations lay the ground for further disputes.

- *Formalities cases*: in aiming to prevent fraud, the strict application of the formality requirements often created injustice, leading the court to uphold certain transfers in equity (eg *Re Rose* [1952]). However, such cases sit uneasily with the long-established principles of *Milroy v Lord* (1862). While

problematic recent decisions like *Choithram (T) International SA v Pagarani* [2001]) and *Pennington v Waine* [2002] attempt to adopt a positive approach to transactions where there is no risk of fraud, the underlying problem of how these approaches will be used creates uncertainty, particularly in the commercial world.

- *Injunctions*: the development of search and freezing orders helps to ensure that claimants will not be deprived of an effective remedy. However, the extensive nature of such orders required the courts to act to ensure that these remedies were not abused.

- Equity has to strike an appropriate balance between certainty and more individualized justice. Innovation is required to adapt to changing social conditions, but without a proper consideration of fundamental principles, the courts risk creating further litigation and confusion.

Chapter 3

Problem answer

Trust 1 – Certainty of intention

- Anna's bequest uses the word 'trust' but *not* in the legal sense. The bequest is more precatory than imperative (eg *Re Adams and Kensington Vestry* (1884) 'in full confidence').

- There will be no trust but Ruth will still receive the money as a gift.

Trust 2 – Certainty of objects

- This is a discretionary trust as the trustees have the power to decide who and how many to appoint.

- The test for certainty of objects – can it be said with certainty that any given individual is or is not a member of the class (*McPhail v Doulton* [1971])?

- The class to benefit must be 'conceptually certain' *Re Baden's Trusts (No 2)* [1973]. Discuss whether 'trusted work colleagues' would be conceptually certain under the different approaches taken in the Court of Appeal.

Outline answers

✸✸✸✸✸✸✸✸✸✸✸

- Even if the strict approach of Stamp LJ is used, 'work colleagues' could be interpreted to mean all the employees of the company, a group whose membership could be defined.
- Note: if this approach was adopted, the trust might be *administratively unworkable* if the employees of the multinational company are vast in number (*R v District Auditor, ex p West Yorkshire MCC* (1986)).
- However, 'work colleagues' might mean those with whom Anna worked directly. While this might satisfy the more liberal approaches of Sachs and Megaw LLJ, it is less likely to meet Stamp LJ's strict requirement that it must be possible to say of anyone whether they do or do not fall within the class.
- The greater problem is the inclusion of the word 'trusted', which could have several interpretations: it could relate to work performance or those Anna could trust with a secret. As the bequest does not allow the membership to be defined by someone else, the trust will fail as neither the trustees nor the court would know how to define this group (*Re Tuck's ST* (1978)).
- The money will be held on resulting trust for the estate.

Trust 3 – Certainty of subject matter

- Anna's mention of her 'favourite' jewels suggests that she intends to create a trust of *part* of her jewel collection.
- Unless Anna has physically separated or identified her favourite jewels, this trust will fail for lack of certainty of subject matter and fall into the residue of Anna's estate (*Re London Wine Co* [1986]).

Chapter 4

Problem answer

- Explain how title to shares are transferred at law, needing to comply with the **Stock Transfer Act** or the **Companies Act**, assuming they are outside the CREST system. This has not been complied with.
- Equity may perfect title. Apply to the facts:
- Evidence of intention to transfer interest in the words 'you can have'.
- Is it an intention to give in the future, such

as 'you can have…' Explain what is meant by present giving; *Re Freeland* [1952].
- If it was an intention to give in the present tense there is no evidence of a change of intention; *Re Gonin* [1977].
- James has been appointed executor.
- Reasoned conclusion on outcome.
- Explain that to transfer the legal title Sumita should deliver the goods, which are chattels, with the intention to give legal title (*Re Cole* (1964)) and she has failed to do this.
- The general rule would be that 'equity will not perfect an imperfect gift'.
- However, equity may look upon as done that which ought to be done on the basis of a DMC if the requirements of *Cain v Moon* [1896] are satisfied:
- Sumita considers that she is going to die soon and in contemplation of that death she has decided to give Ellie her car as in *Wilkes v Allington* (1931).
- It seems there is no express declaration that it is conditional on death. The courts have implied such an intention when the transferor is unlikely to survive; *Sen v Headly* [1991]. It may be that the courts will imply such an contingent intention on the fact that Sumita considers that she is going to die.
- There appears to be constructive (symbolic) delivery. In *Woodard v Woodard* [1995] it was held that delivery of keys to the car could be enough to transfer the dominion of the property. In addition Ellie also has the registration documents.
- A car can form the subject matter of a DMC.
- It is suggested that on these facts equity may perfect the transfer to Ellie.
- Reasoned conclusion.

Chapter 5

Problem answer

Planning your answer

- Identify the property being dealt with; is it land or personalty.
- Identify the interests Kirsty has; legal title or merely the equitable title.

Writing your answer

Blackacre:

• Oral declaration of trust in land is valid but unenforceable, **s 53(1)(b) LPA 1925**. George has an unenforceable beneficial interest on 1 March.

• On 31 March the formalities are complied with and the trust becomes enforceable.

Whiteflower

• Legal title needs to be transferred to Sanjeev in compliance with **s 52 LPA 1925** and **s 27 Land Registration Act 2002**.

• Clear intention to create a trust but as it is a trust in land it must comply with **s 53(1)(b)** as above.

Shares

• Kirsty wants to dispose of her beneficial interest in shares. She must comply with **s 53(1)(c) LPA 1925**. Failure to do so makes the transaction void; *Grey v IRC* [1960].

• Kirsty is absolutely entitled and *sui juris*. She intends that Charlie is to get legal and beneficial interest then the *Vandervell* exception may apply.

• A brief conclusion (not a repetition of your answer).

Chapter 6

Problem answer

• Identify the relevant issues:

1. The **Recreational Charities Act 1958**: the trust aims to provide recreational and leisure facilities for the elderly.

• Such trusts must be in the interests of social welfare (**s 1(1)**).

• To do so, it must satisfy the two basic conditions (**s 1(2)**):

(1) The trust must benefit a recognized group under the Act – the centre is for the elderly, a group in need by virtue of their age (**s 1(2A) (b)(i)**).

(2) The centre must be aimed at improving the conditions of the group's lives (**s 1(2A)(*a*)**) – the centre addresses something many elderly people lack – facilities allowing them to socialize and get involved in different activities.

• The centre is also for the public benefit, as the elderly in Lincoln would constitute a sufficient section of the community. The trust should be valid.

2. **Section 2(2)(b)** advancement of education

• Public benefit? Yes – there is no personal nexus between the settlor and the beneficiaries (*Oppenheim v Tobacco Securities Trust Co* [1951]).

• Political trust? A political trust cannot be valid (*McGovern v Attorney-General* [1982]). However, Oliver's wish to help train lawyers who will challenge the government on civil liberties issues has arguably not been stated as a purpose, but merely as a hope. The main purpose is to help fund the education of law students, perhaps particularly those with an interest in civil liberties. Therefore, this should still be valid.

3. **Section 2(2)(d)** advancement of health – this head includes the provision of palliative care, such as that provided by hospices.

• Public benefit? Is the hospice a private fee-charging facility? As long as it is not profit-making and does not entirely exclude the poor, it will be considered in the public benefit (*Re Resch* [1969]).

• Cy-près? As the hospice has closed, can the money be applied to another related purpose?

• This is a case of initial failure, as the hospice closed before Oliver's will came into effect.

• Is there a general charitable intention? As the purposes of the gift are not too specific (*Re Rymer* [1895]), it is probable the court will allow the money to be applied to the work of another cancer hospice.

Chapter 7

Problem answer

• Could the bequest be charitable? In this explanation briefly explain the advantages.

• Not within any of the anomalous exceptions, with brief explanation only. Do not dwell on what is impossible.

• Gardening club may be an unincorporated association.

• Explain the categories; the ones that are unlikely to be successful should be dealt with in outline only.

Outline answers

✽✽✽✽✽✽✽✽✽✽✽

• Explain the contractual analysis and what you would want to know about the club: Can it dissolve and share assets? Is it part of a larger organization? The contractual analysis would mean that the money could be used for any purpose that the club wishes.

• Explain that if the purpose is important to Johan then the **Re Denley** [1969] may be preferable. Explain how **Re Denley** works, the ascertainable individuals who will enforce, and so no problem with the beneficiary principle. There is no perpetuity period so would seem to fail on this.

• Conclude as to the preferable interpretation.

Chapter 8

Problem answer

Planning your answer – look for the clues. There are issues of certainty but focus on the secret trust issues. Clues are dates of conversations about trusts which are not in the will. Obvious clues – a trust described as being 'on terms they are aware of', 'for purposes known to them', or other similar phrases. Deal with each bequest separately.

Bushmills
• Explain it appears to be a fully secret trust; set out the basic requirements.

• Explain the *intention* to create the trust and the three certainties. These are quite clear here.

• *Communication*: explain that it can be at any time before death. Explain that this will be acceptable, relating the facts to the relevant law.

• *Acceptance*: Kamjit has been silent; acquiescence.

• Explain problems with formalities and fully secret trusts of land.

Badger Bridges Shares
• Half-secret trust as mentioned in the will.

• Deal with the *intention* issues.

• *Communication*: it was before the will so there is no problem with the timing, but explain problems with only informing one secret trustee. There is not a problem with the letter being in the safe. Pay close attention that the

wording of the will and the communications made are consistent; any inconsistency would mean failure.

• If it fails the legatees cannot take the property for themselves. Explain why. There will be resulting trust back to the estate.

• *Acceptance*: agreement by one secret trustee as joint tenant or tenant in common explained.

Chapter 9

Problem answer

• Anne is legal owner so assumed to be beneficial owner. The burden is on Iain to prove otherwise. No express trust under **s 53(1)(b) LPA 1925** so must rely on implied trust **s 53(2) LPA 1925**.

• Resulting trust; Iain contributed 2% of purchase. The money Iain gave to Anne will not give him any interest in the home. While the car may be held by Anne on resulting trust for Iain (a voluntary conveyance of money), it does not gain an interest in the home. Iain may prefer to have 2% of the home rather than 100% of the car which may devalue.

• Constructive trust may give Iain a larger interest in the home. Deal with each possibility.

• Express common intention. Iain makes an express statement but Iain is making a statement about how people should share property; Anne has merely stated that she agrees with the idea, not that it is her intention in relation to her own property.

Additionally, is the statement by Iain about the family home or about property in general?

• If the statement is about the home, apply to facts, then Iain's detrimental reliance would seem to create an interest. If the statement is not about the home then consider an *inferred constructive trust*.

• Inferred constructive trust. There has been a financial contribution, both at the outset and additionally with the later mortgage payments.

• Quantifying the interest under the constructive trust. All the work performed by Iain may be considered. Following **Stack v Dowden**

[2007] the courts will try to find the intention of the parties from their respective actions.

• Just to finish off explain if an estoppel would arise from Anne's actions.

Chapter 10

Problem answer

• Identify the relevant issues:

• *Wider investment powers*: **s 8 Trustee Act 2000** only allows investment to land in the UK so the court's permission will be needed.

• Identify the appropriate route: **s 57 Trustee Act 1925** allows the court to approve changes to the administration or management of the trust which are 'expedient'.

• Apply: as long as the court does not believe that this enlargement will be to the detriment of the trust, it is likely to consent. The court may also impose any restrictions it deems necessary.

• *Varying the beneficial interests of the trust:*

• Identify the appropriate route: changes to the beneficial interests can only be approved under the **VTA 1958**.

• Apply: will the court give consent for the children?

• The court may consent for Connor, Deborah, and Eve under **s 1(1)(b)**. Note, although Deborah and Eve are minors, the relevant section is *not* **s 1(1)(a)** – the entitlement of all three depends on them holding a particular *status* (ie married) in the future.

• Ben: the **s 1(1)(b)** proviso will apply to Ben, so that at the time his parents apply, it will be assumed that they have died. As Ben is currently married, he will be considered to satisfy the marriage condition and, therefore, the court will not consent for him.

• Benefit? The children's accelerated entitlement provides a financial benefit. However, if Connor or Eve does not marry, Deborah would receive a larger share. **Re Remnant's ST** [1970] suggests this will not be a problem if there are other broader benefits.

• Deborah's religious objections will likely be outweighed by the benefits to the rest of the family. Approving the variation will create greater family harmony than refusing it.

Chapter 11

Problem answer

• Identify the relevant issues:

• *Trustees' duty of care*: as lay trustees, Jan and Beth will not be judged against the standards of professionals. They must exercise reasonable care and skill in the circumstances (**s 1 TA 2000**).

• *Delegation*: the trustees are permitted to delegate investment powers to Paul under **s 11**.

• However, there is no evidence that they have satisfied the special requirements for the delegation of asset management functions (**s 15**). The **s 1** duty of care applies to the choice of agent – agents should not be employed outside their area of expertise (**Fry v Tapson** (1885)). As a computer engineer with only casual experience of investing small amounts of money, it is unlikely that the trustees have acted reasonably.

• *Choice of investment*: **s 8** prohibits investment in land outside the UK. The Spanish villas are unauthorized investments and the trustees must disinvest.

• Standard investment criteria: **s 13(2)** states Paul must address the SIC set out in **s 4(3)**:

• Diversification (**s 4(3)(b)**): the investments appear appropriately diverse. Modern portfolio theory states that trustees will not be judged on individual failures (ie the loss on Carfax) if it can be shown that the investment choices sufficiently balance risk with security (**Nestle v National Westminster Bank** [1993]).

• Suitability (**s 4(3)(a)**): unit trusts and Carfax Bank would appear suitable. While IP-Ops might be suitable *in general*, the fact that Paul owns the company raises a potential conflict of interest.

• *Fiduciary duties*: as an agent, Paul stands in a fiduciary relationship to the trust. Fiduciaries cannot retain profits generated from their connection to the trust (**Boardman v Phipps** [1967]). Paul will hold the personal profits generated from this investment on constructive trust for the beneficiaries.

• *Retention of Carfax shares*: Paul's failure to move the shares will make him liable to the trust for the further loss in value. However, this also raises the question of whether the trustees have sufficiently supervised Paul with reasonable care and skill (**s 22**). If the courts decide that they have not, the trustees will also be liable for the further loss.

• *Replacement of trustees*: if the beneficiaries have lost faith in their trustees, they may replace them under **s 19 TOLATA 1996**, as long as they are both *sui juris* and collectively absolutely entitled to the trust property.

Chapter 12

Problem answer

• Identify who has the relevant property. Deal with each potential claim separately.

£2,000 with Fungirls

• This can be done by common law rules as direct receipt of property; no need to complicate.

• Personal claim, which is strict. Subject to defences; not *Equity's Darling* as not a valid contract; change of position can be applied.

£500 picture from Augustus

• The money has been changed into a picture. The money could not be reclaimed from Augustus as he has a defence of *Equity's Darling*. No evidence of any knowledge to make him liable as a 'stranger'.

• The picture is in the hands of Jack, purchased with the money belonging to the customers (held on trust). The presumption of honesty, *Re Hallet's* (1880), would mean that £500 of Jack's money was spent first, then the remaining £500 from the customer's account money. They can claim 50% of the picture which is now worth £2,000.

• However, Jack goes on to dissipate the remaining balance. *Re Oatway* [1903] would allow the principle of *Re Hallet's* to be reversed. The presumption would be that the £1,000 spent on the picture was actually all the customer account money. They can place an equitable lien over the property to claim the £1,000 and any increase in value.

• The customer account can reimbursed with the money repaid by Fungirls and possession of a picture.

Chapter 13

Problem answer

• Identify, briefly, the wrong(s) which need a remedy. A breach of contract and a potential breach of confidence. Deal with each issue separately.

Breach of contract

• Explain why damages may not be adequate. Ahmed is Joyce's favourite so no other will do, which will mean it is unique.

• May be a contract for personal services; explain and apply.

• May need the supervision of the courts; explain and apply.

• Consider if any defences apply.

• No date given but explain that Hannah may prefer an interim remedy.

Specific performance is not available at an interim stage so may seek a mandatory injunction. Explain the test for a mandatory injunction and apply.

Breach of confidence

• Explain perpetual and interim injunctions. Interim may be better as there seems a risk of imminent harm.

• Set out each part of the *American Cyanamid* [1975] test:

– Serious question to be tried, it would seem so.

– Damages would not be adequate for the apparent risks.

– Discuss the balance of probabilities – apply to the facts.

• To protect any potential award a freezing order may be sought. Set out the test for a grant; do not focus on the procedure but on the legal issues.

Glossary

Abhors a vacuum Equity requires that all property is owned by an identifiable object, person, or legal entity.

Acquiescence By agreement, not express but by failure to object.

Advancement (power of) Where beneficiaries have an interest in the capital of a trust, trustees have a power to advance part of the capital for the advancement or benefit of the beneficiary.

Anomalous exception See chapter 7 for non-charitable purpose trusts which have been declared valid.

Assign To transfer an interest, either legal or equitable, in property.

Attorney-General The principal representative of the Crown in legal matters.

Bailee Person who takes possession of property belonging to another.

Bona fide A person who has acted in good faith, with no evidence of knowledge of any wrongdoing.

Capital The trust property itself. Beneficiaries who hold a remainder interest are entitled to the capital of the trust, eg if Phoebe leaves 1,000 shares on trust to Urfan for life, remainder to Mohmin, Urfan will be entitled to the income from the shares for his lifetime. When Urfan dies, Mohmin will be entitled to the shares themselves (ie the capital).

Charity Commission The body responsible for the administration of charities in England and Wales.

Chose in action An intangible property right that is not enforceable by possession. Such as a debt under a contract.

Codicil An addition to a will which can change the original terms of the will. The codicil must also comply with the requirements of the **Wills Act 1837**.

Contempt of court The offence of interfering with or impeding the administration of justice, punishable by fine or up to two years' imprisonment.

Contingency A contingency is a condition placed on a trust, such as 'to Iain should he pass his exams'.

Damages Monetary compensation given as a remedy as of right on breach of a legal obligation.

Deed A formal contract which can create or transfer an interest or obligation without the need for consideration. The requirements of a deed are set out in **s 1 Law of Property (Miscellaneous Provisions) Act 1989**.

Dehors Outside. Not within the will itself.

Determinable An interest which may be terminated on the occurrence of certain events.

Discretionary trust A type of trust in which the trustees have a duty to apply the trust property among a class of beneficiaries. While the trustees have a duty to distribute, they have the discretion to decide which members of the class to appoint as beneficiaries and in what amounts. This can be compared with a fixed trust, where the beneficiaries and their interests are fixed from the start.

Disposition To dispose of an interest. In this text, to give away or assign.

Dominion Clear evidence of ownership or control.

Donee A person or legal entity who receives a gift. The donor is the person who gives the gift.

Economic duress A common law doctrine which renders agreements entered into as a result of illegitimate economic pressure coercing another's will, voidable.

Ex parte In the absence of one of the parties. In this context usually the defendant.

Executed Legal language used to describe the point at which a will is written and properly formalized. Do not confuse this with the point at which the will becomes effective – ie when the testator dies.

Executor/executrix (masculine/feminine) A person chosen by a testator to administer their estate. See also **personal representative**.

Glossary

****

Fiduciary A person in a relationship of trust and confidence towards another. While there are established categories of fiduciary, e.g. trustee/beneficiary and solicitor/client, the categories are not closed.

Imperfect An attempt to transfer property legally has failed. The transfer is then said to be imperfect.

'In the hands' In the possession of.

Income The profits derived from property, eg the dividends from shares. Beneficiaries who hold a life interest are entitled to the income from the trust property. Compare with **capital**.

Indemnity Payment from one party to another guaranteed to be paid if there is a breach of duty.

Intangible property Property which is not physical in nature but which can still be owned, eg stocks and shares. See, also, **chose in action**.

Inter vivos Literally 'in life'. Usually used in relation to this text when a person creates a trust or gives a gift during their lifetime.

Interim Period before full trial has been heard.

Joint tenants All property can be co-owned by more than one person. If this is the case they can own the property as a joint tenant or a tenant in common (see below). A joint tenancy in property (any property, not just land) means that all the co-owners have an identical interest in property; it is not divided into individual shares. A joint tenant can sever (see below) their joint tenancy at any time, and become a tenant in common.

Jointly and severally All trustees are equally liable (jointly) but also can be individually liable for the whole loss (severally).

Letters of wishes A settlor will often include a letter of wishes with a trust instrument, expressing their preferences regarding how trustees should exercise their discretion, eg to favour his children over members of his wider family when making appointments to a discretionary trust. Trustees should take these wishes into account but they are not binding.

Lien A legal charge or hold on particular property to secure the repayment of money owed.

Life in being This can be any person alive at the time the trust is created. Often people would attach it to the youngest member of the Royal Family but it can be anyone who is alive.

Life interest An interest in trust property which lasts for the life of the beneficiary, eg if Abigail leaves her shares in Arrowtech to Fraser for life, remainder to Colin, Fraser will hold the life interest and Colin, the remainder interest.

Life tenant A person who holds a life interest in a trust. See **life interest**.

Maintenance (power of) A power of trustees to apply any part of the income of a minor's interest towards their maintenance, education, or benefit.

Manifested An evidential matter. There should be clear evidence on which to base a legal process; usually in writing is the best evidence.

Mixed Where property does not remain in its unique identifiable form.

Next-of-kin A person's nearest relations.

Perpetual In this context it means granted at full trial. It does not mean that it lasts for ever. An injunction may be granted for a specific period or for certain timescales.

Perpetuity Means for ever. The law prevents people tying up property interests which can not be disposed of. One of the features of a property right is that it should be capable of disposal by its owner.

Personal representative The generic word for a person who administers a will.

Personalty Property other than real property, such as pictures, jewellery, or cars (but not exclusively).

Power of appointment In this text it is the power under a trust to whom to distribute the trust property.

Prima facie At first glance. On the present facts without a full investigation.

Priority Bankruptcy payment will be made to a person with priority before payments are made to other creditors.

Protective trust A trust which is determinable upon the beneficiary's bankruptcy or other identified event, at which point a discretionary trust arises for the beneficiary and their family – see **s 33 Trustee Act 1925**.

Provocation In criminal law the questions asked are:

Did the defendant lose control?

Would the reasonable person react in the same way?

The reasonable person is given certain, but not all, the characteristics of the defendant (ie age and sex).

Quantum meruit A Latin phrase meaning 'as much as he has earned'.

Rateably In proportion to their contribution, sometimes referred to as *pari passu*. Note that it does *not* mean equally. If a person contributes 10% to the purchase they get a 10% interest.

Realty Land.

Remainder interest An interest which takes effect after a life interest.

Remainderman A person who holds the remainder interest in a trust. See **remainder interest**.

Remuneration Payment for services rendered.

Resettlement Describes when a trust is ended and its property applied to a new trust. See **settlement**.

Settlement A term used to describe a trust or trust instrument.

Settlor Person who gives (settles) property under a trust.

Severance When co-owners end their joint tenancy and become tenants in common.

Subsisting An interest which exists. In this text it will differentiate between the creation of a beneficial interest and the transfer (disposition) of an existing interest.

Sui juris A Latin term used to describe beneficiaries who are adults (over 18) of sound mind. You will typically come across this phrase in connection with issues which require the consent of beneficiaries.

Tangible property Physical property, eg a house or a painting. See **intangible property**.

Tenants in common Are co-owners of property who have a separate and identifiable interest in property. Unlike a joint tenant who has an identical interest to all other joint tenants, a tenant in common has their own share of property.

Testamentary A gift or trust made by will (testament).

Testator/testatrix (masculine/feminine) A person who executes a will.

Transferee The person who is intended to receive the property.

Ultra vires Outside their powers. Eg, the authorities were found not to be legally allowed to enter into these rate swap arrangements.

Unconscionable It is impossible to give a definitive answer to what this word means. It is a question of fact which equity can apply when the courts exercise their discretion to do justice.

Undue influence An equitable doctrine which renders agreements entered into as a result of another's influence, voidable.

Unincorporated association When a group of people form a company, they become incorporated. The company has its own legal identity and can own property in the same way as any individual. An unincorporated association is a group of people who do not have the same legal personality as a company. It is merely a group of people who come together for a purpose. As they have no corporate identity any property owned by the association is owned by all the members of the association.

Valuable consideration Consideration has the same meaning as in contract law. There must be some exchange. Note also that a deed will be sufficient consideration.

Vest When a person, or entity, gains a present legal right.

Vested A present property right either to use and enjoy the property now or to use in the future. It is not conditional on any event as a contingent interest. An existing property right which can be enforced at law.

Glossary

****

Vicariously Liability which arises for the actions of another.

Voidable If a trust or contract is *voidable*, it is capable of being set aside. However, until that occurs, it remains enforceable. In contrast, if a trust were *void*, it would never have any legal effect.

Volunteer A person who has not given valid consideration for the transfer. This may be because it was a gift or because the contract was void or illegal.

Table of cases

ST and WT refer to Settlement and Will Trusts

Table of cases

****

Table of cases

✳✳✳✳✳✳✳✳✳✳✳

Table of cases
****

Table of statutes

Index

Index

****

Index

Index

✱✱✱✱✱✱✱✱✱✱✱

Index

✳✳✳✳✳✳✳✳✳✳

Questions & Answers

keeping you afloat through your exams

'What a brilliant revision aid! With summaries, tips, and easy-to-understand sample answers, Q&As really help with exam technique and how to structure answers. A great help not only during the revision process, but also throughout the course.'

Kim Sutton, Law student, Oxford Brookes University

Ask anyone for exam advice and they'll tell you to *answer the question*. It's good advice but the Q&As go further by telling you *how* to answer the questions you'll face in your law exams.

Q&As will help you succeed by:

- ✓ identifying typical law exam questions
- ✓ demonstrating how to structure a good answer
- ✓ teaching you how best to convey what the examiner is looking for
- ✓ giving you model answers to up to 50 essay and problem-based questions

Every Q&A follows a trusted formula of question, commentary, answer plan, and suggested answer. They're written by experienced law lecturers and experienced examiners to help you succeed in exams.

Additional online resources accompany the Q&A series.
Visit **www.oxfordtextbooks.co.uk/orc/qanda/**